SOLVING THE RIDDLES OF RIDING

Building Body Mechanics and Balance

Solving the Puzzles of Riding Piece by Piece

Tara Jones

Pieceful Solutions Riding and Training

Written by Tara Jones

Acknowledgements

Throughout your life you will have friends and meet new people that will drift in and out of it. My mother always told me that family will always be there no matter what. I would like to thank my family for their endless support and dedication. They raised me by instilling good values, a strong work ethic, and a powerful drive to succeed.

Mom, I love you. You will always be my best friend. You have always been there for me, and I thank you for allowing me to grow, and become stronger and wiser. Your constant empowerment and encouragement pushes me to reach for the impossible.

Dad, without you I wouldn't be where I am today. I love you with all my heart, and will always be your little girl. You have given me the start to this incredible journey, and have looked out for my best interest since day one. I hope to always make you proud and to ride with pride,.

My only sister, as we grow older the gap between us becomes smaller. I love you and look up to your underlying strength and willingness to help me succeed. Not everyone is blessed with such a special sister. I am truly thankful for all you have done for me.

As I continued through life I have met some very monumental people. Kenny Harlow, you have been a teacher and a guide to help me make responsible decisions about my career. Thank you for your teaching style, and for sharing your gift of horsemanship.

To Jose and Fay Mendez, you have showed me the finer points of riding, and taught me to seek goodness in all parts of training. I thank you for opening your home to me which allowed me to visit Australia and discover the wonderful possibilities that lie ahead. Most of all you showed me the "beautiful" aspects of dressage and enlightened my path to keep the drive to be the best at the highest level possible. Your guidance taught me to look for the intricacy in the movement and to always strive to be better.

To the other friends who have always been there, you know who you are. You are people I cherish, honor and value. You share my love for what I do and understand who I truly am. You commit to making me a better person and helping me through the struggles of daily ups and downs. It is wonderful to know I always have true friends to confide in and count on when I need them the most.

Finally, you can never be a great rider without the help of a great horse. I have ridden and taught many horses how to trust and to give their rider their heart and soul. Their beauty and majesty is something to be cherished and they are, in fact, our greatest teachers. "Phantom" you are the horse who has taught me so much and kept me reaching for new heights with my training and riding knowledge.

A special thank you

To those of you who have always believed in my ability, encouraged me to work hard, and set standards for myself that kept me reaching for new heights with my professional career, I dedicate this book to you. I also dedicate it the dreamers, the achievers, the hard workers, and the constant education junkies that have a deep hunger to reach their ultimate potential. Dig deep, you can, and you will, accomplish what seems impossible.

This journey is only the beginning for me, and I hope to keep going, keep teaching, and to keep learning. Horses are not just a hobby for me, but a way of life. Riding has become a study course at which I hope to graduate with honors someday. The road I'm traveling may be windy, may have a few bumps along the way, and may have some road blocks, but with the help and support of those who believe in my ability, and my drive to become the best, anything is possible if I dare to dream.

"In life you cannot direct the wind but you can adjust the sails"

Foreword from the Author

As a rider and professional horse trainer, I have been blessed to travel to different places both in the U.S and internationally, working with the everyday trials of riders, trainers and their horses. Throughout the course of my time spent meeting different riders of all levels and areas of experience, I have discovered one thing-We all want to learn how to become better riders and better communicators for our horses. We all have different goals and different dreams, but they are all one and the same.

I remember watching elite riders at the top of their game, and envying and admiring their riding ability and horsemanship skills. I would wonder in astonishment. Could I ever be that good? I felt sure they had spent countless hours in the saddle, as well as endless amounts of money and time on something that is just a hobby to an everyday rider like me. But who's to say that any of us is an everyday rider? Who's to say you can't also ride at their level?

I have been one of those riders, just like you, who wished that I could someday be that spectacular rider who takes your breath away; that I would have confidence, timing, athletic ability, strength, balance, tone, elegance and talent they all seemed to have. My ultimate goal as a rider is to be invisible. Onlookers would say," I don't even see her aids. She looks as though she is part of the horse."

I saw riders of that caliber, but I just didn't know how they got to that level I, like you, shed many tears, worked through the sweat, spent countless hours and lots of money to learn from all different types of trainers and instructors. I thought someone would have the magic potion that would automatically make me great. What I found were a lot of things that I did NOT want to do. I left frustrated, defeated, and feeling as though I would never be as good as the riders I envied. I didn't have what it took. I wasn't a natural. It was then that I began my journey.

Have you ever felt this way as a rider? If you have then you are no different from a lot of riders out there left wondering, how do I get better? How do I gain confidence? How do I reach that desirable level I dream of?

I decided to write this book not only because all my students said I needed to get my voice out there in the world of riding instruction, but also because I want to see you succeed both for yourself, and for your horse. You can be the top level rider you dream of becoming, or you can gain confidence back under saddle and feel like you don't need to be frightened every time your horse takes a wrong step. But most of all, you too will feel the wind blowing through your hair at a canter, have a smile that is hard to wipe off your face, and a feeling of total oneness with your horse.

What I have learned over the years is, if you are not learning then your instructor may be failing you. There is always a way to teach you to become a better rider. I am going to teach you how to think as a rider, and use your body in ways you can understand.

This book is meant to show you how to condition your body and get you ready to become the most effective rider you have dreamed of becoming. You will also learn to influence your horse, not just to become a pretty rider, but an immovable rider. Learning proper biomechanics and how the human body works when properly aligned, will help your confidence grow along with your ability. You will learn how to teach your horse to conform to your body, instead of your body conforming to your horses.

It's time for the commitment. Your goals, your dreams, your aspirations of becoming great must start right now. Don't keep wondering if you can do it; start taking the necessary steps to get there.

There are no naturals in my book. There are hard workers, and harder workers. The passion, drive, and determination are your choice. I can teach anyone who is willing to learn and become part of making their dream become a reality. You just need to want it bad enough.

There is nothing wrong with me dreaming of wearing an American flag across my jacket, representing my country in the biggest most prestigious competition of my life. One can dare to dream, it keeps you honest about your path in life. Good luck, and always...

"Allow your heart and desire... to inspire"

I have discovered the heart that lies within competitive horses bred to run. Many look for a second chance, and are eager to share their desire to be better at their next career with a new jockey to show them the way. They share their generosity with me, along with a piece of their soul. They choose me to protect and honor what lies inside them as they all become winners once again. They are the ones who share their lessons in both life, and with all their love to trust me with their inner beauty that is a bit tarnished, but ready to be polished in order to shine brightly once again. Enjoy the pictures of my two grey off the track thoroughbred mares "Jiggy" and" Loops". They have brought so much joy to my career. They have also taught me the value of what it means to have a second shot at becoming something wonderful.

"I have now earned my wings to fly & the courage to soar"

Table of contents

HOW TO USE THIS BOOK

I am a firm believer in constant education. As you discover new ways to become a more effective rider you will learn why this is true. The more you learn as you continue to ride, the more you will hear differing opinions. I am sharing my opinion of what I have learned through my personal experiences, and the time that I have spent developing my skill. This book is my personal insight to becoming an effective rider who is in constant communication with the horse's mind and body.

I have handled and ridden countless horses who all have taught me something, whether it is something very small, or something monumental. I struggled through years and years of mistakes, hard work, and learning how to make a movement better. It has become my mission to help those who want a better understanding of how to communicate with their equine partner.

As you read through this book, integrate what you like and use it in your system. If I can help you improve 40% then I helped to impact the way you ride and train. Understand that I am not trying to re-invent riding as a whole. This book is not meant to teach you a different riding style; it's meant to show you how to obtain what the top level riders do. Its in-depth detail will help you understand the intricacies of your body and how it works aboard a horse.

Read, and re-read this book. Take notes. Have someone read it to you as you ride. Do whatever it takes to help you learn, and by all means, take it one step at a time. As you progress in your riding you will gain a different perspective each time you read it. As your education grows, so will your relationship with your horse. We can all learn from each other. The only thing I ask of you is to keep an open mind as you work. Open your heart and listen to your horse. The horse is the best teacher you will ever have. They talk to you every minute of every day and every moment of a riding session. Sometimes we tune them out while in the learning process, but be sure to check in with them and allow them to shed light on your accomplishments as well. Horses are honest. They don't lie, they don't sugar coat the truth. They will be truthful about your progress. Listen and learn. They are the professors, and the masters of their progress and yours.

"Education is for those seeking a higher standard of ideas. Ideas happen at various moments everyday , therefore education may never end."

FIND INSPIRATION IN THE WORDS

Someone once asked me if my life and career did not involve horses, what would I choose instead to spend my life achieving? I sat back and thought for a moment, and to my surprise I blurted out"I would become an inspirational speaker." After I said that, I wondered why I chose that avenue. That does not fit me at all. It goes against everything I am comfortable doing. I am scared to talk in front of a crowd, I find myself getting tense and nervous at the thought of confrontation, and I have butterflies thinking about the fact that people will be judging me. Why on earth did I choose that career? After a few years I discovered exactly why I chose that path.

When you find something you truly enjoy, and something you are passionate about, it is only natural to want to shout it to the masses. I helped people unite with their horses, and watched them grow and prosper with confidence and poise. I have helped people improve. But the biggest compliment I ever received was that I was an inspiration. I paused and pondered that comment for a moment, and I realized that comment provided that wonderful drive which was to keep me going.

I ask you to find inspiration in this book. Read the words, and allow your horses to inspire you as well. What a gift when you find it. There is nothing greater than knowing that you accomplished a goal in life that has been hard to achieve.

As you choose a path for yourself I have found that life leads you to where you need to be, regardless of what we think our path should be. Most times the road is already ahead of us. We decide to exit, or take the road less traveled. We may even detour every once in awhile, but all in all, it is about what you find joy in, and what you feel you are good at. When you are confident, you are bold. When you are bold, you are less fearful, and when you are fearless, you are unstoppable.

I have been too many places, and have had the great honor to travel to many different areas of the states. I never thought that this would lead me to the road I am traveling upon now. In life, I believe you choose, through no certain terms, how ideas will mesh together and blend to become more complete. I have always said that my true goal was to inspire people. I want riders to look at me and become inspired by my determination, my work ethic, and my strong will. Being a woman in this industry is more challenging than ever. We are few and far between. That is the motivation that keeps me going. I want us all to be better at every idea, every wish, every hope and every prayer. I designed my business to reach out to those of you who want to seek an understanding with their horses. Who want to reach goals.

My very good friend said to me recently that I had earned my wings. My wings to fly, and my wings to grow. We all grow in our lives, and we all dream the impossible dreams. During the course of life we have our roots where we feel comfortable and safe, but we also get wings. It is up to you to fly. To fly to the uncertain destinations you fear, and grant yourself the determination to travel into unknown territory.

Throughout this book you will find inspiration in my teachings. I want you to think more than you have ever thought before about what you truly want to accomplish in life whether it's on a horse, or with your daily living routine. Seek truth, discover wisdom, and put your heart and soul in all you do. If you go at anything whole hearted, you will never skip a beat.

If it is competition that you are seeking, or becoming an instructor, or even just improving your relationship with your horse, don't wish for it to happen. Make it happen.

"Motivation is the drive to pure determination; those moments are what make up unforgettable instances that become inspirational."

The Missing Pieces Before we Get Started

CONSTRUCTIVE ADVICE TO BUILD TOWARD YOUR GOALS PIECE BY PIECE

HOW DO I FIND THE CORRECT INSTRUCTOR?

Choosing an instructor is no easy task. They will not only become the person you trust and confide in, but they will become your mentor and your guide to help you choose what is going to be the destiny of your prized possession. Every instructor I have ever worked with had a different technique, and a different way of explaining things. That is what made each instructor unique. Some instructors choose to specialize in certain disciplines, while others choose to teach only a certain level of riders. The point is that these individual instructors were gifted in a certain aspect of the horse. This is where you have to be very careful of who you choose to show you the way. There are never any wrong ways in my opinion. There are different ways. The instructor you choose must have your safety, and your horse's safety at the top of their list. If you feel at any point that this is put in jeopardy, then you must find someone else to work with you immediately.

The great riders have practiced through lots of repetition, and lots of hours. They know what works and what doesn't. They know what's safe and what is not. They have an outstanding team that pitches in behind the scenes, and that believes in their ability and talent.

You could take a lesson from five different instructors teaching the same topic or exercise, and each one would explain it slightly different. This is due to their educational background, the method they were taught, and what has worked for them over the years. Keep one thing in mind as you are looking for a system, method, trainer, instructor, etc. They are not all for you. Keep in mind what your goals are as a rider and what your plans are with your horse. Stay true to your needs, and don't allow prestige or dynasty to sway you into making a decision that is not suitable for you and your horse. Stay honest with yourself and your accomplishments. Bigger is not always better. The level you are currently at is where your journey needs to begin. I believe if the instructor is concerned with your safety and the welfare of the horse, then they will put you where they think you should start, not where you want to be.

There are many capable trainers and instructors who can help you reach a higher level. Once you reach that level of higher expertise and the education has run out, then you can venture out and look for a more specialized type of training. Do not over face yourself, or your horse. This will leave you feeling defeated and frustrated. In other circumstances it may leave you hurt.

As I was learning new skills, and moving up the ladder with my riding, I wish someone had given me a written map of exactly what I needed to do with my body to satisfy my instructors. I wanted to do well; I just wasn't a quick learner. I could not feel it. I became frustrated with myself, and for my instructor, because I knew they could do what they were asking me, but I couldn't. I wanted to help them, and help myself and my horse.

I hope to be that ideal instructor for you. To help you find a direction to get to your destination. I can be your navigator, your map, and I can help you to maintain and sustain the goals you are aiming towards. I hope to possess the one simple phrase or group of words that may help lead you to success. The pinnacle point that helps you get over the plateau in your riding career.

"A true teacher is a mentor who guides you to a far better understanding than what they have ever achieved."

IT'S JUST A WARDROBE

When searching for the mentor or teacher who you are turning over all your trust to it is my opinion that the saddle is just a wardrobe. You will go through many costume changes throughout your riding career. Whether you ride western, english, dressage, trail ride or various other disciplines, know that riding is not set in stone. I am going to give you ideas to make your riding better regardless what discipline you ride. There will be small differences in the position of your body for each discipline, but across the board, riding comes from a firm foundation and an understanding of how your body works along with the horse. There is no instructor out there who can teach you every move that you need to make during every moment of every ride. You will learn to adjust your body, and to adjust your horse's body. There is no perfect rider, and there is no perfect horse. It's a constant adjustment. You will learn new things everyday of your life for the rest of your life, regardless of what discipline you ride. As I said before, take what works for you and your horse. You will always hear differing opinions, but it is up to you to determine what is worthy of change and what is not. Be open-minded, and don't back yourself into a corner of riding one way because you ride english, or another way because you ride western. Some of the best riders can ride all disciplines because they know how to adjust their body, and ride with their mind, as well as their body. Think about it!

"Adjust your mind as well as your body, after all we all have one thing in common and that is the horse."

WHAT PARTS OF MY BODY DO I CONCENTRATE ON FIRST?

There are so many intricate pieces to the body. The difficult task lies in what sections we tackle or teach first to allow the body to flow in unity as we ride. Let's face it we all have flaws. Even the top riders in the world struggle with certain parts of their bodies that don't always cooperate. Every rider has a side of their body that is stronger, or more dominant. This will always affect how the horse travels. We are not machines. Our muscles must memorize certain feelings in our bodies in order for them to become automatic over time. The only thing that helps us become consistent is a build up of correct alignment, posture, and balance. It is also time and hours in the saddle.

It is a huge topic of discussion about what part of the body you should actually realign first when you are teaching. My opinion is that it all starts from the bottom. We need a solid base to build upon. Just like the foundation of a house, you need the basement before you can have a floor, walls, and a roof. As we progress through the pieces of the body, you will begin to understand what to think about. You will have a checklist to run through to make your learning easier. Keep this checklist in mind as you ride, and enjoy your new discoveries.

As I teach horse and rider teams, I am always finding new ways and new ideas to make learning both fun and educational. It is important that you are always learning in a way so that you will progress when the pressure is gone. There are moments when you will have to buckle down and challenge yourself, or your learning will never progress any higher than the level you are currently at, but it is also important that the rider enjoys the learning process, and finds it fun and enlightening. If you don't find joy in your riding, then you need to change what you are currently doing. I am a firm believer that if you are not having fun, then your horse is not having fun either, and that makes the process dull and stagnant. Brighten your horizons and look for fun, simple, easy ways to succeed at any level.

"Foundation is the fundamental skill that allows a new beginning; it gives you a starting point to build on."

HOW DO I DEVELOP FEEL?

The invisible ride is just that. It's invisible. It's the rider who has figured out how to harness a feeling that the horse and rider connect and are in constant communication. Every trainer, rider, and instructor is seeking that ride, a ride with feel, harmony, influence and timing. Some trainers will throw gimmicks and gadgets on the horse so the student can catch a glimpse of what the feel is. In reality these gimmicks only serve as a band aid to the solution. The feeling will be gone once the gadget is removed, and the rider will be left with the improper feel.

If an instructor has learned to feel while riding or schooling a horse, the next challenge is to teach that to their pupils. Upper level riders develop feel and maintain it which is why they sometimes become frustrated with their students. They wonder why the student cannot just do it automatically. But to ride with feeling can take months or sometimes years to master. Just be patient" feel" comes when you least expect it. With determination and focus, you will eventually harness the "feel" and capture those magical moments. When you realize that you have had that 'feel', try to recall that sensation. You have discovered what the great riders know instinctively. The need for feel will become addicting, and you will seek it every time you ride.

"Feeling is an illusive instance that you will harness from moment to moment; eventually it will become yours to capture eternally."

WHICH IS MORE IMPORTANT THE HORSE OR THE RIDER?

Each time I start working with a new horse and rider combination it's like the chicken or the egg scenario- which comes first? Is it the horse that needs the training, or is it the rider who needs the training? I always look for what the main issue is with a horse and rider combo then go from there. You will need to be your own worst critic in practice. Get a cheap full length mirror, and look at your progress. Sometimes what you feel and what you see are two totally different things. Analyze what your body is doing, and how your horse is reacting. Sometimes a disorganized rider can disorganize an organized horse, or vice versa. While you are riding ask yourself a simple question,

"Is the horse carrying me, or am I carrying the horse? "You will figure out the answer immediately and know what direction you need to head in next.

If, at any point in the learning process, you feel your horse needs the help of a trained professional, then, be the bigger person and realize that it will not help you to ignore the fact that you are just not ready to pursue the issues your horse is currently displaying. There is no harm in asking for help. Your horse will thank you for the wise decision to further its education with a seasoned professional who is familiar with fixing problems. You can then resume training after you feel confident on a horse that is well behaved and respectful. That is what will build your confidence as a rider. You will learn more from the experience, and it will allow you to set higher goals for your future when you are more experienced.

"The majesty of the horse is a kingdom that shall never be taken over but rather a safe haven for all greatest moments to arise."

I WILL BE YOUR CHEERLEADER

As you read through this book, practice the exercises, and find humor in the way I teach, know that I am writing this book to help you. I can help any rider even if it's one small issue that is keeping you from reaching a new level. I say that with confidence because I have watched high level riders struggle in a warm up ring. I have watched timid riders shed tears out of fear, and I have watched everyday riders find joy and solitude in spending time with their horses. I can help you seek improvement. The rider's faults now are the horse's failures later. We will all be at the bottom at one time or another and we will all rise to the top. Realize that we all struggle. You are not alone.

I am your cheerleader, and I am in your corner no matter what. I will help you, and guide you along the way. Every time you say something isn't working or you feel as though this book is a big joke, I want you to try to change three things with the way you ride. Pick only three "imagery essentials" out of this book, and practice them while you are riding your horse. Look for an improvement with your horse's behavior. I am training you and your horse along the way. Work with me. Humor me. Create that smile that is hard to wipe off your face after you have mastered a skill you have so desperately wanted to achieve. You can, and you will do it.

I remember when I was going through hard times or times of frustration with my riding. I look back now and think that I am the luckiest person in the world because through all of my struggles, I became a far better teacher. I never was a natural at riding, so for me it was easy to identify with my students frustrations when something wasn't quite attainable. Think of how much better you will become if the riding did not come easy. You will be able to help the next friend, student, or loved one seek acceptance in your words of encouragement. Never stray from learning. Never be afraid to try. And most of all, never be afraid of mistakes. Mistakes are always opportunities to learn and become better. Horses are in our lives for enjoyment. Enjoy the learning process and know that you will improve. Just relax and enjoy the ride.

Systematic Awareness to Begin the Reconstruction

SIMPLE THOUGHTS TO PROCESS BEFORE WE REBUILD

Riding Riddles

Riddles are like enigmas or puzzles. The art of riding well can sometimes be tedious, and confusing just like the start of a puzzle. It's complex and difficult to think about all those pieces coming together to become one picture. But take time to look at the whole picture. Don't procrastinate any longer. 'Back time' until you can find a reasonable place to start. Then build piece by piece until the puzzle is manageable, then doable, then easy. The movement and positioning of your body can be extremely complex at times. It's sometimes frustrating to understand how to gain control of specific parts in order to operate in a fluid and effective fashion. By changing parts of your body, and magnifying the placement and tone of each specific piece, you will learn how to better control your body parts, and create symmetry, harmony, alignment, balance and tone throughout your frame. This will help you become a better partner for your horse, no matter what discipline you ride.

Imagery Essentials

It is essential when riding your horse to think of using metaphors. This imagery training technique will condition you to reexamine specific body parts, and the order in which to use them. By creating an analogy, your mind can process the information more quickly. Your reaction and timing become more accurate. Using this technique will help the rider to make sense of phrases used in the equine world. Keep in mind we all learn differently. Use what works for you and develop a program to fit your needs. Throughout this book you will find imagery essentials that you can refer to. They can be used as a quick reference guide to check if you are on your way to better form and correct technique.

Riding Realities

Not only is it important to practice the correct way to ride, but it is also important to practice riding incorrectly. This will allow your body to experience the feelings that you will experience on days when your riding is in need of certain fixes. Riding well is truly an art, and the top level riders spend a lot of time developing each piece of their body to hone their skills, and magnify the use of each piece. You are going to mirror your horse eventually and build to the point where you can take responsibility for your own balance, so the horse can then move fluidly underneath you. If the horse needs to constantly compensate for your balance as well as its own, it will become difficult for the horse to reach its full potential, and for you, to ride in harmony. Riding Realities will help you to transmit all you have learned into form and function

Familiar Faults

When you ride for a prolonged period of time you are bound to pick up habits, both good and bad. It is important to note that mistakes are always learning opportunities. The more mistakes you make, the better rider you ultimately become. To learn through trial and error can be your biggest asset. By recognizing faults when you are watching another rider, or learning yourself, these mistakes make it more obvious to someone who is trying to fix their technique, and ultimately get better. It can also help to understand where these mistakes are stemming from so you can be sure to fix the problem, and never revisit old habits again. Keep in mind the familiar faults mentioned in this book are for you to recognize, store in your memory, and dismiss as you learn a better more effective technique.

Essential Puzzle Pieces

In this book I use the concept of puzzle pieces to represent specific parts of the body, and allow your mind and body time to digest the ways to use each piece individually. You will learn to gradually put the pieces back together so you can build to the finish line. You will then have the dexterity and tone necessary to be a better rider. Throughout this book you will find sections which will explain in great detail the use of each section of your body. Practice the exercises both off your horse and on your horse until you feel comfortable. It is an ongoing process. Be patient with yourself. The muscle building and strengthening exercises will help to build the tone and stabilize your muscles in order to operate correctly. Divide your body into pieces. These pieces will give you designated sections to work on as you follow the system to bring all the puzzle pieces together to create one beautiful picture.

Coordination & Strengthening

The muscles of the rider's body will only tone and strengthen when the rider decides to dedicate time to develop them. We all require a certain amount of exercise daily, and riding is a very demanding sport. Not only must you think of yourself, but of your horse as well. It is important to become an athlete if you decide to take riding well seriously. Timing is a skill that is a game of reaction. You must remain one step ahead of your horse at all times in order to stay safe and become productive. The more strength you build, the more confidence you will have because you will know that you are able to stay with the horse when moments arise that are surprising or unexpected. Your coordination in those moments will help determine the next few moments of your ride. Take great strides to improve your athletic ability both physically, and mentally. It will make a huge difference in your riding long term.

Putting together the pieces

Some common errors are apparent with each rider. Everyone is unique and carries their own set of flaws which make riding unmanageable and difficult for each individual. This becomes the nucleus of where your journey begins. Keep in mind that your riding errors will not keep you from your highest goals, but, instead, give you a stepping stone to start with. Think of riding as a giant jigsaw puzzle. At first, it is hard to imagine that all those pieces are going to eventually come together and form a masterpiece. Your body operates in the same fashion. You will use the pieces to build the border, and then gradually piece by piece fit together to form a gallery of images to create your final project. Like any puzzle, you can tear it apart, and build it back up again. Each time you begin to rebuild you become more efficient and quick, at how to fine tune what you are doing.

Your responsibility as the rider and trainer

Remember to practice these exercises on a well broke horse that is seasoned, and safe. Your safety is always your responsibility. It is important that you use common sense and practical judgment as you are working through this book. Do not skip chapters or pages. Each page is set up to go in a certain order to better the system, and keep 'you' the rider, moving at a steady pace. Your horse is of utmost importance, and you need to take responsibility and lookout for the welfare of your horse, and for yourself.

This riding system is no substitution for good training. I work with problem horses, as well as young horses, and by no means will this take the place of teaching a young horse the basics and foundation for safety, and control. This riding system will enhance a horse that is already safe to ride. If you are experiencing difficulties with your horse, then seek the help of a professional who can help you deal with behavioral issues so you can safely enjoy, and enhance the riding process with this system. There are no quick fixes. Be smart about how you handle and ride your horses. You owe them your dedication to pave the way for future success. You are the coach, the leader, and ambassador of your horse's training. Play that role to the best of your ability.

Tara Jones

"May all your Riding and Training puzzles always find a *"Pieceful Solution"*

Using our Mind to Help Our Riding Regimen

IDEAS TO OVERCOME THE OBSTACLES YOU WILL FACE IN YOUR TRAINING

USING OUR MIND TO HELP OUR RIDING REGIMEN

Once you begin your system of teaching yourself to ride you will experience different moments of frustration, panic, confusion, and self realization. You will also be happy, confident, diligent, hard working and coordinated. Here are some tips to read through before you experience the difficulties of riding. Remember you are training to become an athlete. You are also training your horse to become more athletic. You will go through the same emotions as a professional athlete. Here are a few things to remember.

"Stay safe, use common sense, and always listen to your body & to your horse."

RIDER'S BLOCK

Have you ever tried really hard to learn something that is really important to you? You keep trying and trying and to your dismay, you find that you have blocked yourself from the learning process entirely. This is what's called rider's block.

All riders experience this at one point or another. This can stem from different emotions as you ride such as the anxiety of not performing perfectly, or frustration because you can't 'feel' what the instructor is explaining, or self doubt. Your emotional stability is what will keep you learning. Be confident even if just for a moment. Tell

> *Embrace the chance to become better. Hard work and determination are always followed by a moment of adjustment before you can enjoy what you have learned.*

yourself that you can do it. Become determined to gain a positive result for a single moment, and then build upon it. Remember your validation as a great rider does not depend solely on this one movement that you are trying to perfect. You will have many things that you will learn with your horse. Take a deep breath, sit tall, and fill yourself with a smile. Pat your horse for helping you get this far, and ask your horse to help you. You will be amazed at how refreshed you will feel in that moment. It will cleanse your mind, and help you laugh at yourself for ever thinking that at that moment, your actions were going to make or break you as a rider.

"What you think in your mind, is what you achieve through your heart."

PLATEAUS

All riders will reach a plateau in their riding career. This is when progress slows down or stops completely. Sometimes you lose motivation, or life gets in the way. You find that our drive to run out and ride has become a thing of the past. This is normal in riding, and you must learn to set small goals that are attainable, and easy to achieve. This will keep your motivation strong, and our will to keep going alive.

A plateau will also take place when you are ready to emerge to the next level. As you are approaching the brink of improvement, you may feel defeated, almost as though you are losing ground instead of gaining ground. This is only a riding plateau, and like many you will experience, this, too, shall pass. Challenge yourself to reach that higher level.

I remember when I would reach a riding plateau I actually learned to look forward to the moments in my riding when everything just seemed to crumble and I felt like I was not achieving anything at all. Shortly after that, like clockwork, I would ride into a whole new realm, and my teaching soared as did the progress of my students, and horse's progress.

Plateaus are not a bad thing, they are something to look forward to since you have learned all you can and, now, are hungry for more information and a better way of communication with your horse.

As you learn to relax your body and accept the changes within, you become open to new feelings. This will allow you to readjust and keep your body functioning so that it can memorize the new feelings you are experiencing. Sometimes, when we think it's never going to happen and are just about to give up on the whole process, that's when we learn the most.

Keep in mind, Rome was not built in a day, and the spectacular riders we watch today have spent countless hours on their skills, and have overcome a lot of frustrating days.

"The peak of the mountain may pale in comparison to the journey of the climb."

BECOME FLEXIBLE

Becoming flexible is a process that is hard to learn sometimes, but can be a tremendous help. Give yourself praise. Receiving praise from someone else can lift our spirits higher in an instant. Now you can understand why it is so important to pat our horse. But did you ever think that just becoming flexible would be so much more helpful in the long run.

How many times do you wake up and have a strict schedule? We are all so busy in our daily lives that it becomes harder and harder to find time for our horses. If you are on a time crunch, maybe the answer isn't rushing to the barn and trying to squeeze an hour lesson into a fifteen minute time frame. Maybe, the answer is to be flexible. Become willing to change the routine, for yourself, and for your horse's sake-No monotony. Add a dash of fun into your riding and training. Just be flexible in learning something new. Have a recipe, so to speak, before you go to the barn and work on what is important in your learning process. It doesn't always have to be work, it can be fun. Just be ready to adjust and change the routine. Once you have accomplished this you are well on your way to changing your riding.

This also is important when learning something new. Don't dismiss a new idea because it sounds silly or because you haven't dedicated enough time to the entire learning process. Give yourself a chance to learn something new. The ideas in this book may sound a little "off the wall", but it helps to think of riding in a different light. Remain flexible to becoming educated in a new way.

"Let passion fill your sails and let reason be your rudder."-Kahil Gibran

ATTITUDE ADJUSTMENT

It is so simple to play the blame game. I find countless riders who blame their horse when something goes wrong. A horse will only perform what they think we are looking for. If we are constantly taking every mistake, every bad day, and every frustration out on our horse, then they will generally develop that same attitude.

Make it a rule to greet your horse with a smile no matter what kind of day you are having. Tell your horse about it. They are always willing to listen. Your attitude is everything while you're riding. Someone once told me that the horse will resemble the owner. In my travels I have found that to be so true. If you are a hard worker your horse will show qualities of proficiency. If you are high strung, your horse will be energetic. If you are stressed, your horse will be able to feel it and become tense and stiff as well. If you are timid, your horse will be spookier. If you are confident, your horse will be brave. If you don't believe me - try it. Give yourself two weeks of an attitude adjustment. Show your horse how pleasing, gentle, kind, sincere, and devoted you can be. I guarantee you will see a change.

Your body speaks for your mind. If you are riding your horse is feeling it all. A tense of stiff joint can point out fear, or uneasiness. Horses can feel anger and frustration, and they can also understand the sternness in your voice. Take a breather, and be the rider that you would wish to have if you switched places with your horse. You might look at it differently that way.

"Every ride may not be good, but there is good in every ride."

CONQUERING CONFIDENCE

A fearful rider, or a rider who lacks confidence when riding is very common. It is not a pleasant feeling to climb on board a horse who has hurt you, or frightened you in the past. You must be honest with yourself about what the fear you are experiencing is stemming from. Is it based on reality or is it something that you are fearful may happen. Your gut is almost always right, and if you feel a situation is unsafe... it probably is.

When dealing with a rider who has confidence issues, it is important to identify the root of the problem. I know all too well that you can't just relax if you lack confidence. You also can't just climb on your horse and hope it will all go away. In my experience fear is a bi-product of lack of knowledge. When you are unsure you lack confidence. The more you learn and experience, the more confident you become.

As you read through this book, you, will discover new ways of learning to coordinate your body with the horse. This will give you a whole new outlook to help you feel as though you are more secure in the saddle so you feel balanced and safe, which will, in turn, increase your confidence. Be strong, and take it step by step to conquer your fear once and for all and slowly become brave. Do not rush, however, or you will find that the confidence you gained can disappear in an instant in a bad situation. "You are not taking any steps backwards; you are always running forward with your riding and training".

"A rider who thinks with their hands, reacts with their heart, and rides with their soul creates confidence in their companion."

RIDE SMARTER

It is always better to ride smarter not harder. Riding smart and using your mind means not allowing your emotions to get in the way. You will be thinking as you learn to ride in new ways, and the imagery in this book will help you think about riding differently. Do not allow your thinking mind to take over, however. Be smart about what you are attempting to accomplish.

An obstacle is something in the way of your intended path of travel. There is always a way to get through it!

As you ride, your mind will learn to think in pictures. The pictures that you create in your head are the mental images that will allow your body to capture a movement. That is why I call them "imagery essentials".

I made a rule for myself as I climbed the ladder of riding. I made a promise that I would surround myself with the riders that I admired, and that inspired me. By watching those riders, and what they do with their hands, body and seat, and how they handle the situations on a horse, I would slowly process those pictures and try to emulate them. I could pick up on little aspects without ever practicing them. This can be both a blessing and a curse. For obvious reasons, if you are surrounded by harsh riders, or riders who are making things happen, then you will do the same as you ride. If your goal is to be a truly invisible rider, then look at those riders who are invisible. You will notice that they are barely doing anything visible to communicate with their horse. The adverse fact about that is they are doing everything in every moment to communicate with the horse; we just don't see all the subtle cues and aids they are using.

As I began to work for different trainers in my travels, I came across one of the best dressage riders in the world. I had the honor of working with him for three months. His riding was truly a sight to see, and I would sit on a bench and watch him work with a horse every chance I got. I studied how he used his seat, how his legs moved in harmony, and his hands were merely there to direct the movement. The horse would float across at the arena. It was never forced and never looked mechanical. It was beautiful. I realized that as I rode, I was positioning my body and riding more and more like him each time I got on a horse. I was learning to ride smarter by watching his actions and reactions on a horse. It was a pinnacle point in my training. Now, when I feel like things are not going well on my horse I envision what he would do and it helps me work through it.

Thinking in pictures will help you start riding smarter. You will envision the freedom of movement and your body moving in time with your horse.

The Imagery Essentials & Riddles of Riding

DEFINING THE ESSENTIAL DETAILS TO PUT THE PUZZLE TOGETHER

The Riding Borders

Throughout this book you will see "imagery essentials." Use these visuals to help you feel what the effective position is, Or where your riding riddles originate from.

When you open up the box to a jigsaw puzzle that holds 1,000's of pieces what is the first thought that enters your mind?Are you overwhelmed? Does it look like such and incredible task that you feel as though you don't even want to take the time to sort through the pieces? Do you close the box back up and wait for another time when you have more patience and can dedicate all of your attention to that task? Or do you start by assembling the pieces that have a common feature?

This is how learning to ride, or relearning a certain task can be for riders. It sometimes seems like you are never going to get that one little piece to make all the difference with your horse.

When you look at the jigsaw puzzle, this time look for the pieces that will make up the border. Build your framework, and then, work your way towards the middle. Before you know it, the pieces start to come together, and what seemed like it was never going to end, has now become something that is attainable.

Look at your riding in this light. You always need a solid border to start with. This is your foundation, so to speak, and a place to start your puzzle. We will refer to your body as the borders. These borders will give you a starting point. You can build your puzzle piece by piece from there.

There are three parts to the borders of your body.

THE TOP TO BOTTOM BORDER

This border is how your body aligns from the top of your head to the bottom of your feet. It is also easy to think of it as your up and down border. The top to bottom border will keep you stacked up. It allows your body to center itself over top of the horses center of gravity. This border is responsible for the up and down movement that the horse generates. You must be still in the saddle and not overkill the need to stretch up and away from your horse or push yourself up out of your stirrups. You must also be careful not to sit too deep and allow your body to bounce heavily along the horse's back.

A good rule of thumb to follow is that if you slid your horse out from underneath yourself by magic would you land on your feet? If the answer comes back "yes" then you are keeping your top to bottom border properly aligned.

The most common phrase you hear in riding terms is that "the rider must be aligned from the shoulder to the hip, to the heel." This is very true and a good rule of thumb to follow. The shoulders, hips, heels lines up when your body is aligned providing a solid load for your horse to carry. This will become important later on.

This is an example of the top to bottom line from the shoulder, to hip, to the heel of the foot. If Jiggy wore a cape, and suddenly flew out from beneath Tara, she would still land on her feet. A slight flaw in the alignment is that Tara's ears should be positioned over her shoulders, and her shoulders should be back a bit more over her hips. The pelvis could also be slightly elevated so her belt is more level and even. We are all a work in progress. Pictures help the rider to gain a vision of what needs to be corrected.

Throughout the course of this book it will be wise to develop your eye as well. See the slight flaws in the body positions. And decide what you would do to fix them?

To keep the line of shoulder to hip to heel, you will, basically, be standing with a little bend in your knee. On a moving object, it becomes more difficult than it sounds.

THE FRONT TO BACK BORDER

The front to back border will comprise the entire front side of the body, and the entire back side of the body. This border is responsible for the transitions and the movement that the horse will generate when speeding up or slowing down. You must stay with the horse, and not get ahead of, or behind the movement.

The front to back border is also responsible for the horse's balance both forward and backward. This will greatly affect the pace and footfall of the horse. If you have heard the term "half halts" this is the border responsible for execution of that movement.

To check yourself at any point during the ride, imagine if the horse spit the bit out and you were left holding the reins with no connection, would you fall backward or forward? If the answer comes back "yes" or "maybe", then you need to work on the alignment of your front to back border.

This is also the main border for jumping and for fast paced activity such as barrel racing or reining. You must become aware of how your muscle tone and core strength affect the balance and stabilization of you and your horse.

Often, this border is responsible for the stabilization of the rider's hands. Since stability comes from the core, all appendages including arms and legs will become stable if the center is still first. If the core is floppy, then the hands will be forced to use other means of balance. Often the bit, or the horses mouth will come into jeopardy during this phase.

The front to back balance plane is resposible for holding the body in place. As Sattui canters, Tara's core and back will help to balance the body to stabilize the movemet, and give her hands the freedom to allow Sattui to use her body, and make a connection with the bridle.

THE SIDE TO SIDE BORDER

Finally, we need to take a look at the side to side border. This border is responsible for your entire right side and your entire left side. This becomes a major turning aid, and is used mainly in circles and changes of direction. Later, it becomes a key ingredient in maintaining the lateral balance within your horse as well.

This border becomes a one-sided issue for most riders because we all favor one side over the other such as you being right-handed or left-handed. We always have a dominant side or a side we are stronger on. This border must line up evenly or else your horse will begin to show signs of "crookedness" or inability to turn with the four parts of it's body. The result will be a horse running through the shoulder, or worse, running through the bit entirely.

It is important for the rider to keep the ribcage open and not allow the body to bend, or collapse. Even dropping the shoulder will create adverse effects, and cause the horse to follow suit with their body. Be concious of how you use the turning aids. Leaning or tilting is forbidden in most instances.

The side to side border should be the right to left side matching evenly. No collapsing or uneven weight shifts. Ideally the horse's ears should be lined up in front of the rider's shoulder's. Loops and Tara have fairly good line up as they are beginning a slight change of direction to the left.

"BORDER LINES"

As you read throught the imagery essentials in this book keep in mind which border needs to play the appropriate role in order to benefit both you and your horse. You will be developing all three borders in the following series of exercises. Become aware and pay attenion to the line up and the impact each exercise has. You will develop correct lines as you ride, and become better balanced. When the border lines unite, you will feel a difference with your horse. Most of all you'll feel a difference within yourself. The strength and tone you develop will help in all aspects of your life.

STUDY: SHOULDER, HIP, HEEL, ALIGNMENT

Let's begin this study before we dive into all the information that follows. This is an area of great debate. Many instructors and riders will argue this point. I have been on both sides of the fence. I have learned to ride 4 different ways, and I will add my opinion into this discussion. I am, personally, a rider with long legs and a very long torso. I have longer arms than the average rider. I ride all disciplines, and sit in different saddles every day. Some of the saddles are not my own, and I must adapt my body quickly, and easily, to accommodate the horse I am sitting on. I am not going to sit here and say that you must have a perfect fitting saddle to ride your horse correctly. In my opinion there are no" perfect fitting saddles." You adapt to the situation to the best of your ability, and balance. That's what good riding is about. I am

personally going to say that your own genetic make-up, and how you are built has a lot to do with where you are comfortable riding. I've had instructors that have contorted me like a pretzel to the point that my body was in incredible pain. They were looking for textbook lines, and to make a long story short, they should have been looking at how I was built and the horse's way of going to determine what was needed for the appropriate moment.

There are many horses that I sit on that do not have enough back strength to hold them up let alone hold me up. I may have to keep in alignment, and raise my seat out of the saddle in order to accommodate their back and to allow them to lift, and travel without my weight on it. I am always riding in a way in which I can travel politely and correctly for the task at hand.

Riding correctly can be demanding on the body. I am not saying there will be no pain associated with learning to ride in alignment, but if the pain is uncomfortable, and your horse is showing signs of being uncomfortable as well, then, maybe you need to look at how you are being asked to ride, and judge and form an opinion for yourself.

The shoulder, hip, heel line up debate is a basis for all riding. It makes sense to align the body properly in order to function with balance and tone. The top riders in the world for any discipline are in this alignment. The secret is, you can give and take a few inches here and there. Judge what works for you and your horse. You will be adjusting along the way.

Introduction to Body Building Piece by Piece

THE OVERVIEW BEFORE YOU BEGIN YOUR STUDIES

What to look forward to

In the next few chapters you will find specific body parts that you will be studying, and making yourself aware of. It is important to allow yourself time to develop these pieces. You will gain ground by letting this information digest through your body, however it takes some time before it will become part of your muscle memory. Keep in mind you might gain and then lose ground here and there. It is perfectly normal while trying to climb the ladder of riding that you overkill certain parts for lack of understanding. Or maybe you are trying too hard to accomplish what you are reading about. Be gentle with yourself, do not give up. Read, study, and use a mirror or a ground person to help you. What you feel, and what you are being told to feel, are sometimes two very different things.

All riding scenarios cannot be written out word for word. I am giving you a broad over view of what you may encounter and what I have encountered over the years. Don't just think because it is written down that is the be all and end all of your riding journey. Feel for yourself, and come to your own conclusions. Your horse and body will speak to you. Listen to them.

Use the checklists in the following chapters as quick reference points to help you when you are practicing. Mentally replay the checklist recording in your head as you ride. The studies are to help you figure out and translate common riding terms thrown around by instructors and also top level riders who are trying to convey what they feel in the simplest of terms.

Remember, the greatest riders make it look as if they are merely sitting aboard their horses and doing nothing. In reality they are doing everything to stay as balanced as possible to allow the horse to give the maximum effort and to keep their bodies aligned and toned.

The degree to which you learn, and how far you decide to take this depends on your own goals, and your determination to take your riding to a whole new level.

I wish you all luck. This is the beginning of a great new plan for both you and your horses. It changed my relationship with my partners. I hope it does the same for you.

So let's get started

Puzzle Piece #1
Foot

Imagery

Essentials

The Foundation and Pedestal

Checklist for Proper Alignment of the Foot

✓ Five nails through each toe on both feet.
✓ Keep the tripod level.
✓ Toes remain relaxed like you are playing the piano.
✓ Wear roller skates, and be sure that all four wheels are on the ground.
✓ Keep the heels level as though you are standing on a diving board getting ready to do a backward dive
✓ If I put my finger between your foot, and the stirrup don't flatten my finger.
✓ Remain on a balance beam with the balls of each foot prominent.
✓ Stand on a spinning top.
✓ The bars and balls of the feet of the little toe and big toe line up.

TAKING THE STAND

The foot is the base of support for all riding disciplines. In many ways, it becomes like the pedestal and the foundation for all we will learn from the base to the top. Both feet should be evenly balanced and should remain steady. The placement and security of each foot in the stirrup becomes important, as well. The stirrups are the secure base of support we will learn to rely on. If the weight in your stirrups is not evenly distributed or balanced, the result could be crooked riding, loss of stirrups, or even joint pain and stiffness. Your stirrups are an important ingredient when jumping and the pedestal on which to remain balanced so the horse can safely carry you over a jump. If the lower leg begins to move as you ride, then the hands, the main tool used for communication with your horse, will suffer dramatically as well.

When you were an infant you had to learn to stand up and balance on both feet. At first, you probably wobbled about and needed the assistance of a parent. Once you could stand and balance on your own, you learned to put one foot in front of the other and walk for the first steps in your life. After some practice, you were able to walk without thinking about it and displayed natural balance and poise. Relying on someone or something to hold you up and help you balance became a need of the past. This is similar to what happens to the horse and rider.

Think of how many intricate parts of the foot make up your balance. Become aware of all ten toes and the placement and of each toe. How are they aligned across the stirrup? Are they relaxed? Are any of your toes stiff or curled under? Think of a gymnast or a ballet dancer. How important of a role do their toes play when they are performing? A rider must become aware of their feet, as well. The balance within the rest of their body depends on it.

Think of what happens if you are wearing shoes that are uncomfortable or too small. You develop a blister or a sore in a very short amount of time from the friction and the constant shift in weight. That blister will affect how you walk and bear weight on the rest of your foot. You end up using different parts of your body to compensate for that change in weight-bearing in order to walk without thinking about it. This is how we must think of our feet in the stirrups. The whole foot must bear weight evenly and take responsibility for balancing the rest of our body.

Think now of the horse, and how your balance or lack thereof will affect your weight in the saddle and your evenness on both sides as you ride straight or perform bending lines or circles. Maybe, you are to a point where you are performing lateral movements. Your precision will depend on how you place the weight of your feet in each stirrup. Let's take a closer look at some common errors with the rider's foot placement and then take a look at how we can correct the foot using some imagery essentials to give you good solid mental pictures to go by.

A Fun Foot Fact: There are 52 bones in the feet which make up one quarter of all the bones in your body. When they are out of alignment, so is the rest of the body.

Riding Realities

Common errors and enigmas

We all have witnessed riders who are riding with the feet in many different positions. Some ride with their feet outwards so the toes are pointing away from the horse, some ride with their toes pointing down so the heel is lifted too high, and some ride with their toes forward or pointing up. In extreme cases this is what is known as heels down. So what is correct? Instead of looking at what's correct, let's call these errors riding realities. Riding realities are essentially the cause and the effect of the rider's position. It will force you to examine the intricate changes in your muscles and what your skeletal system has resorted to because of the position of your feet.

Familiar Faults

Fault 1

The rider rotates the foot so the toes are turned out. The majority of contact with the horse's sides is held with the back part of the rider's calf. This will almost always cause the horse to run forward, and to constantly run through the rider's rein aids because the rider is signaling to the horse to move forward off of both legs.

On the other hand it may also create dullness to the leg aids and a delayed reaction to move forward since the horse feels constant pressure along the barrel. It may also put the rider behind the motion of the horse, as the lower leg slips forward, the upper thigh rotates outward and begins to lose contact with the horse's back and ribcage.

The rider must, instead, bring the angle of both feet forward, and straight. The inside of the upper calf is what will be "touching fur" with the horse's barrel.

Fault 2

We have all heard of the very famous line "heels down." I am a strong supporter of keeping the heels down as you ride, and in some disciplines, such as jumping, it is imperative that the heel is the lowest point of the rider's foot. But what happens when the rider over does heels down? In most cases, this will cause the rider to stiffen the ankle joint as well as the knee and hip joints. The rider will brace against the stirrup and cause the lower leg to swing forward, and the seat and upper body to roll backward. This results in a chain reaction causing the hands and the upper body to pull on the reins for balance. While you want the heel to be the lowest point, the entire foot should remain balanced in your stirrups.

When the heel is lower than the toe as a result of the rider pushing it down against the stirrup, the shock absorbing joints will lock. In this picture you can see the area in front of the ankle is locked. The area behind the knee has opened and is stuck, and the hip joint is in a holding pattern as well. The whole leg will move as a unit now due to the lock up created by too much heel pressure.

Too much heels down will actually put the rider at a higher risk of losing the stirrups, as well. If the front portion of the ankle is locked, then the back edge of the foot will be reclining backward and more weight will be placed on the back edge of the stirrup instead of across the middle of the stirrup. If a helper on the ground were to try to slide the riders foot out of the stirrup they would succeed with minimal effort. That is why riders with improper heel placement tend to turn the heels in too much. They need to be able to grip with that portion of the leg due to improper heel placement.

Tara's Test Stand in an "on horse position", and put all your weight in your heels. What happens to your body? In all cases, you will lose your balance and fall backward. This is true for riding as well. If there is too much weight in your heels, then you are going to fall backward. This will cause the rider to be behind the motion of the horse.

> *Throughout the book you will find riding tests to let you experiment and feel what will happen with the rider's balance if it is challenged*

Fault 3

The "ice hockey push off" is how I refer to the rider bearing too much weight on the inside of the foot to keep their balance. The sole of the foot will act as a hockey skate, and push away from the horse's barrel with each stride. The rider will have to grip with the knees and the lower calves will create unnecessary bumping along the horse's sides. A view from behind will show that from mid calf down, the rider has no contact with the horse's sides. This is a common mistake made by a rider who is trying to deliberately ride with no lower leg on a horse that is oversensitive to leg cues. This will also cause stiffening in the joints of the leg, and the rider will become rigid.

Fault 4

To the contrary, we also have 'outer rim' riders. Instead of rolling to the inside of the foot, the rider does the opposite and rolls to the outside of the foot. This causes the rider to lose the connection with the inner thigh, and most often will result in gripping with the lower calf. The rider will also experience intense pain down the outer part of the ankle, and possibly, up the outside of the calf.

The rider may also experience pins and needles in some of the toes, especially the little toes. This is not common with most riders' style, but may be the result when a rider tries to reposition the lower leg, or redistribute weight while in a corrective mode. This form of overkill may be necessary for a short period to fix a rider who bears no weight to the outside of the ankle, or the outer section of the balls of the feet.

The rider has pinched with the knee and fallen forward closing the hip angle. The lower leg has slid behind the girth and the toe is now pointing down with the heel rising. (Photo courtesy of Emilie Frede Photography)

Fault 5

The "ballet point" is common for rider's who tend to lean forward in the saddle. The toe of the rider points down and the heels rise up. This can be dangerous because, in extreme cases, the rider can lose their balance and the foot can slip through the stirrup. This fault takes away the rider's stability and causes the rider to grip the horse's sides with their lower leg. The lower leg will almost always swing backward toward the horse's flank which will cause the horse to move forward at a faster pace, and a vicious cycle could quickly develop.

We will be fixing the heel in various stages, and at some point, for the rider who has excessively pushed their heels down, they may need to actually practice riding in "ballet point" in order for the rider to find a happy balance of equally distributed weight in the stirrup. It's called relevé in dance terms. Do not confuse this term with ballet point.

Fault 6

"Straight leg stepping" is common for riders who try to brace against the cantle of the saddle. The rider looks as though they are straight-legged, but their legs are angled towards the shoulder of the horse as opposed to stepping straight down. If a smiley face was drawn on the sole of the boots we would be able to see it if we were standing in front of the horse. Riding like this will cause the rider to lose the feel of the entire leg. It will also hollow the horses back because the rider is causing their seat to dig into the loins of the horse. As you ride more, you will want to develop a floating seat, which is a seat that is not fixed in one position. Rather, it moves about and brushes the saddle because of how the foot is pushing against the stirrup in front of the body.

Note: When I begin to talk about "stepping on the brake pedal at a standstill", it is different than this fault. "Stepping on the brake pedal at a standstill" is an exercise meant to help you learn how to redistribute weight through your foot. "Straight leg stepping" is the rider allowing the leg to push forward and brace off it as they ride.

Tara is demonstrating how a rider may brace on the platform of the stirrup for balance. This is not good for the joints of the body as you can see that the hip joint, knee joint, and ankle joint are now in a locked position. These joints need to be soft and mobile so the ride can absorb concussion sent through the feet by the horse's movement.

Fault 7

The "toe clench" is what nervous riders do. If they feel they are in danger they will grip inside their shoes with their toes. Think about what happens when you try to make a fist and then move your arm. Your entire arm becomes stiff; the same holds true with the feet and toes. The toes should remain relaxed and free to move. If you stiffen your toes, then the ankle joints will lock up and you will begin to brace against the saddle and your whole leg may lock up.

TIP

If any of the above faults sound familiar, recognizing what needs to be tweaked is the first step in correcting it. You may go into other modes, and even experience another fault at some point as you journey through the various stages of riding. All riders go through different stages. Once you begin down the right path, your riding will improve dramatically.

Picture Perfect Pieces

Now envision your picture perfect pieces for the improved ride

Imagery examination:

Even weight distribution of both feet while riding

Further Explanation

The position of the foot in the stirrup is the key to success. Just placing the foot in the stirrup is not going to keep the rider balanced. The significance of weight distribution will help determine how well the rider can keep the stirrups, and dictate how to use the rest of the leg effectively.

Here are some tag lines to remember and put in your checklist.

Essential Details of each Imagery

Five nails

One of the biggest controversies' in riding is how much weight is put into each stirrup. You could ask ten different riders and get ten different answers. The secret really lies within the correct biomechanics. How does the body measure up? This literally means what it says. Your foot is the most important aspect at every moment during every ride. Realistically you will never be correct 100% of the time, because the horse creates a pulling/pushing force that challenges the body's stability every second. The key is to do your best with your own genetic make-up. To begin, just think about standing on the ground. Practice just allowing the foot to rest upon the ground; do not try to push your foot into the ground. The pink tape across the sole of the foot on the previous page shows the area of the foot that should be weight bearing.

The rider's foot needs to align across the stirrups evenly. The weight should not exceed 5 pounds in each stirrup. Basically, this means that the foot of the rider bears only 20 % of the weight. It is important to remember that the stirrups are to rest the feet on, *not to push against*.

To help the rider understand how to distribute the weight evenly across the platform of the stirrup, visualize a line across the ball of each foot that runs parallel to an imaginary line connecting the tips of the toenails on that foot. This line will be relatively straight from the big toe to the little toe on each foot. Imagine this line is a tightrope. Distribute your weight across the bar of the stirrup as evenly as possible remembering to have the foot remain along the tight rope with pin point precision. This will give the rider a guideline to follow regarding foot placement, so the rider does not allow too much of the foot to slide through the stirrup. The rider also needs to keep the foot positioned on the stirrup so that the toes do not support any weight. The balance point is behind the balls of the feet. Accuracy is important each time the rider places their feet in the stirrups. The balance point of the foot needs to be on the platform of the stirrup so that as the horse moves side to side or forward and back the rider can maintain balance and control. The momentum of the horse must not leave the rider behind, or push the position of the foot too far over the edge of the tight rope. This will help the rider to feel secure and set the foundation for the base of support. The soles of the feet have a huge burden to hold up the rider, and the heel and the arch of the foot are responsible for stability, as well.

It is true in any sport that finding the 'sweet spot' is a challenge. This is where forces meet to accomplish a maximum effort with what feels like minimal force, striving to do so in the most effective manner. Make this your goal as you study this book. You will gain strength and begin to strive for nothing but sheer excellence.

Tripod level

In some cases the rider's foot acts as the balancing rod. If it is not stable, the rest of the body will always be playing catch up to try and compensate for the lack of balance. There are three major points of balance. They are the point of the heel, the point of the hip and the center of the knee. These three points connect together when the rider is sitting in the saddle and form a triangle. This triangle must remain strong so the angles do not become too acute. There are also three points on the bottom of the foot that help keep the rider stabilized. This is what I refer to as the "tripod."

The angle behind the knee plays an important role in riding. It should resemble a triangular shape that is even throughout the ride. The bottom of the foot should be level, much like how a camera would sit on a tripod.

Keeping the tripod level will help the rider keep the heels level, instead of lowering the heels to an extreme which will lock the ankle joint. Instead, the area in front of the heel of your boot is the area which we are going to focus on keeping level. The three points are the ball of the big toe, the ball of the little toe, and the area directly in front of the point of the heel. These three points resemble a triangle if they were connected. This is the tripod.

If the rider relates this to a video camera tripod with three legs, all three legs are level and even on the ground. This visual helps the rider understand why they wouldn't want to lock the heel or put excessive pressure through the back of the calf to position the heels lower than the toes. This will cause the two front legs of the tripod to lift up. The result is too much weight backwards. The same happens under saddle. The upper body will tilt backwards, and the rider will bear too much weight on the heel. The rider who is at the other end of the spectrum may put too much on the front two legs of the tripod, and allow the heel to lift up. This will cause the rider to tilt forward, and rely on the reins and the horse's mouth for balance. They will shift weight to the horse's forehand and cause the horse to topple weight to the front two legs instead of the horse elongating the body and driving forwards from the hindquarters.

If we are looking at an English rider who is jumping it is extremely important to position the heel at a slightly lower angle then the toe. If the weight is not shifted to area just behind where the balls of the feet distribute weight while jumping, then the rider risks tipping forward on takeoff, or falling forward on the landing. The heel must be lower in order to distribute the weight through the whole lower leg.

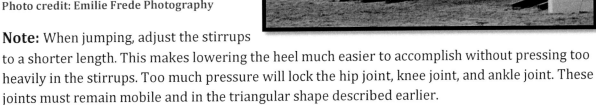

Kate Gerhart is displaying a lovely foot position over the jump during the take off phase. There is even weight distribution with the sole of her foot lying across the stirrup iron. There is a slight shift in weight towards the heel, and her foot remains her base of support beneath her hip. She would still land on her feet if the horse vanished beneath her.

Photo credit: Emilie Frede Photography

Note: When jumping, adjust the stirrups to a shorter length. This makes lowering the heel much easier to accomplish without pressing too heavily in the stirrups. Too much pressure will lock the hip joint, knee joint, and ankle joint. These joints must remain mobile and in the triangular shape described earlier.

Piano playing toes

Technically, the toes cannot move as freely as the fingers so the analogy of actually playing piano would not be possible. Envision Mozart, however, or Beethoven, or one of the classical pianists, and think of how their fingers floated across the keys. There was no tension, and pure rhythm within the music was within their joints.

Riders who lock their toes will, in turn, lock all the body parts above of the toes. Often a rider will concentrate so hard on the position of the ankle or the foot, they literally pull the foot up along with as all ten toes. This causes the weight to push against the tongue of the boot. It is imperative to keep all ten toes spread apart with even spacing between. They should be relaxed and free to wiggle. Let the toes flatten against the sole of the boot, while playing the piano keys as Mozart did to create beautiful music.

Pay close attention to all ten toes. Do they all relax? Or do you have specific toes that tend to stiffen or lock up? While it seems small, this is extremely important when it comes to relaxation throughout your feet, ankle, and legs. Pushing or stiffening the toes will result in one of the major joints becoming stiff. The toes must remain moveable and the ability to move each individual toe is good for coordination.

Some riders will experience difficulty with one specific toe, or one specific foot. Pay attention to this area when you drive your car, walk around, or even rest. Become conscious of relaxing that specific area of your foot. If you are having trouble relaxing, a good massage will help alleviate muscle strain and encourage relaxation. Muscle strain can happen when you are riding and using muscles that are being awakened and used in ways that are not a part of daily activities.

 Roll a tennis ball under each foot while sitting and relaxing. Practice curling the toes around the ball and then letting go entirely so that all ten toes are relaxed and free to move. This helps the muscles of the bottom of the feet relax, as well. Over time, the soles of the feet can develop tension from riding; this exercise will keep the muscles pliable and relaxed.

Wear roller skates

There are so many angles and rotations that the foot and ankle may try to incorporate into riding on their own. Many riders deal with different weight shifts, or positions of the foot with one foot dominating and the other having a mind of its own, so to speak. Riders often have difficulty figuring out where the blockages or tensions are and how to keep them in check while trying to remain balanced. This suggestion may help solve those problems.

When teaching someone how to actually roller skate the method of walking like a duck with your toes pointed out and heels together so the skates are in a "V" position is how a student is first taught. Gradually, they begin to step to the left and then to the right until they are confident enough to transform each step into a glide. If the wheels of the skates are kept directly beneath the body, the skater can add more pressure on the heel wheels, which will propel the skater forward with each glide. If the skater changes to pushing on the toe, then the skate will begin to roll backward. Once the skates are moving then the skater changes the angle to 12:00 with each skate and glides along evenly on all eight wheels. This is, ironically, how a rider begins to ride and where, at moments of the ride, the balance over the foot may change.

If the rider uses the toes too much, they run the risk of pushing the momentum backwards while they are falling forwards. If they use the heels and push, then the momentum rushes forward and the body falls back. The use of the feet in the "V" shape will resemble how a rider may clench or hold too firmly with the lower calf when in reality they need to release that pressure. Turn the "skate" towards 12:00 and glide along on all eight wheels.

When the feet are level and evenly balanced it is definitely less of an issue for riders to hold the stirrups, move the lower leg, and distribute weight through the entire leg and keep the whole body over the center of the balance point in the foot. In order to keep your feet laterally balanced as you are moving on your horse, pretend you are wearing roller skates. The four wheels of each skate must glide smoothly. Skating on the inside two wheels will cause the foot to roll inward towards the horse's barrel. Skating on the outside two wheels will cause the ankles to roll to the outside of the stirrup. Excessive pushing through the heel or back of the foot will cause the rider to do a "wheelie", causing the front two wheels to leave the ground. Pushing weight into the toes or the front of the foot will cause a toe stop where the back two wheels leave the ground. Keeping all four wheels (and your feet) level and even is an important piece of the riding puzzle, and becomes even more critical when you begin to perform upper level maneuvers in any riding style.

Correct lower calf position is a by-product of good, stable foot positioning. When both legs are used to signal to the horse to move forward, imagining wearing the skates will help alleviate the heel dig or lift that happens when a rider uses the toe stop.

Instead, keep all four wheels on the ground, and drag them along the ground as if they were your parachute so they are always parallel to the horse's sides. Imagine creating a set of parallel lines that would form if you were on the ground traveling in the same direction as the horse's belly resembling an equal sign (=).

This position will also help to teach the horse to be on "cruise control" which is, no lower leg to encourage the horse to keep moving every stride. Basically, ask the horse to move forward and they keep going with no leg pressure until you ask the horse to turn, stop, or change the speed. This saves your leg cues for higher level work when you are asking for lateral movements or movements where you will need to add leg to signal to the horse to change direction, or gain control of the ribcage. Keep in mind there will still be very light contact pressure along the horse's sides. There will just be no gripping or holding firmly.

Tara's Test

Have a helper stand next to you while you are mounted. Have them place their hand against the outer portion of your heel. Let them apply slight pressure in an inward direction towards your horse. You, as the rider, are going to use your upper thigh and

heel and push out against that pressure they are applying. This feeling of stabilizing the entire leg on the outside portion is what you want to become accustomed to in order to keep a stable lower leg, and to give effective leg cues. It will also strengthen the abductor muscles of the legs, which are equally important in riding.

Backwards dive

Balance for the feet can seem like such a simple task. In reality the most difficult part of riding is learning how **not** to push down into the stirrups, but instead balance on the balls of the feet while the rest of the foot is, literally, hanging in the balance with a feeling of suctioning pressure pulling the foot downwards but not beyond the point of the stirrup.

It is easier to capture this feeling if the rider thinks of standing on the edge of a diving board. The board is a spring board with lots of bounce. The diver must harness that trampoline effect by bending the knees, almost as if the legs are in squatting position with a 100lb barbell strapped across the back, and across the shoulders. The weight of the barbell is making the body heavier, but the legs and knees must keep the concussion within the joints. The bounce from the board should not rebound through the body, and knock the diver off the balance points. The same holds true for the rider. When the horse creates the bounce as the diving board will, the rider must squat more through the thighs and knees in order to counter balance all the weight so it doesn't shift to only the feet, and create an imbalance that shifts the body to bounce backwards or forwards.

Picture standing on the edge of the diving board and positioning the body for a backwards dive. Where is the placement of the feet? How much weight is distributed through the sole of the foot? Stay very grounded, and be careful not to add too much weight to the heel or to the toe. Imagine feeling as though you are balanced with the ankle and calf.

Transfer that same feeling to the stirrups. Be very sturdy in the stirrups as you are riding. The slight bounce of the board and the spread of your toes will help you visualize the gentle absorption of the horse's movement as it ripples up through your body. The balls of each toe should be weight bearing.

As the rider begins to distribute more weight through the thighs, there will be moments when the heels rise up slightly higher than the toes. The angle behind the knee will become more acute and the rider will become puzzled about how to move the lower leg back far enough to keep the position of the heel under the hip, as well as keeping the angles correct. Visualize the spring board, but imagine we added an extension to the board and it's now longer for you to reach the edge. In order for you to line your toes up perfectly and teeter on the edge, you must move your entire leg back from the hip joint at the top of both thighs. It is then that the rider will be able to allow the knee to drop down lower and the squat or bend through the thighs will become more intense resulting in a greater angle so the rider can stabilize the leg more.

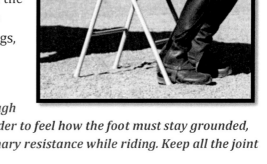

Tara's Test Practice the feeling of using the outer portion of the heel, or foot by sitting on the edge of the seat of a chair. Place your feet to the inside of the legs of the chair. Take each heel and push out against the legs of the chair. Imagine using your strength to break the legs off. This experience is similar to the high tone that is felt through the muscles in the outer portion of the thighs, and down the lower calves. This is a good exercise to strengthen the legs, while using the tone of the legs and angle of the foot.

By pushing both heels outward against a slight resistance, strength and muscle awareness will begin to develop through the outer leg muscles. Most importantly, it will allow the rider to feel how the foot must stay grounded, and the heel must push outward slightly against an imaginary resistance while riding. Keep all the joint angles pointing forward toward 12:00 while practicing.

Squashing fingers

A baffling question to me as I was in a stage of really coming to conclusions about the nuts and bolts of riding was… how much pressure do I apply to each stirrup? I experimented to great lengths to answer this question. In retrospect, the answer to this question was really pretty simple. There is a well known law of physics that most everyone has heard of at one time or another and that is Newton's law."For every action, there is an equal and opposite reaction". This means that if you push down in your stirrups, you are going to get an equal and opposite push back up, unless you soften your joints. If you don't soften your joints, the whole scenario begins to crumble with each body part losing stability. Balance is the first key to riding, but the second key is support of your own body weight throughout the body. The rider is not meant to sit on the horses back, and squash down all the carrying muscles, making themselves a heavy burden to bear. Support of the riders' own body is key, and it begins with the feet.

If a volunteer were walking next to the rider, and they were brave enough to position their hand or fingers between the foot and the stirrup, would the rider squash their hand due to excess pressure? Is there an overabundance of pressure or dead weight across the stirrup, or is the weight equivalent to a bathroom scale reading five pounds per foot?

During riding changes, or advancements within the body, there may be a stage of ignorance regarding weight across the stirrups. Keep an object of reference under each foot. The rider may become too light and grip with the knees, or some other part of the body that will compensate for the lack of even weight distribution. Think instead of having a marshmallow under foot, or maybe a pin cushion, or thumbtacks. Whatever the object may be, the foot must bear enough weight to decrease weight, or increase weight in the appropriate place, and distribute it evenly. Every step a horse takes is an adjustment of weight and balance for the rider.

You will be learning how to distribute weight through your thigh instead of your foot. Excessive weight in the stirrup leads to braced joints. If you needed to, could you slip your feet out of the stirrups, and travel around in the exact same position? If the answer comes back no, then you are putting too much weight into your stirrups.

If you are a rider that loses sensation in the toes as you ride, then you need to pay careful attention that you are not applying too much weight to your stirrups. This is usually a direct result of bracing or pushing. You will lose contact with your seat, and this almost always results in a loss of contact with your horse's back.

Strive to become skillful with your stirrups. If worse comes to worse, practice dropping your stirrups and riding without them for a few laps. While holding your feet in the position you would use if you had your stirrups. It allows you to drop the thighs down and open the hips if they begin to rise up. It will also help to build strength in other areas of the leg and seat.

The ratio between the thigh and the foot should be 70% of weight taken through the thighs and only 30% of the weight in your stirrups through your feet. This may be a vast difference and needs to be the basis of how you ride with your weight rearranged, so that it is as though the knee cap is pointing towards the ground. This extends the thigh down, and opens the hip joint. This will always lighten weight in the feet.

Tara's Test Practice dropping your stirrups then picking them up again without looking down. This may happen while you are riding. You need to be able to react, and find your stirrups without skipping a beat. It will also train the muscles groups that are attached to the foot to let go, and not grip so hard, or push down on the stirrup.

Stand on the balance beam

There are several similarities between a gymnast balancing on a beam and a rider balancing in their stirrups, which is why this exercise is suggested. The balance beam is only 4 inches wide, which is about the width of the foot and also very close to the width of many stirrups. A gymnast spends years perfecting their balance and the precision needed to perform on the beam. Before a maneuver, a gymnast will gaze at the feet, and be sure that they are centered to help even out their body weight so they can stay on the beam. Once they are centered, they will lift their head and perform the maneuver. A rider must think in the same way. If a gaze down toward the feet in the beginning stages will help reassure a rider that they are on the correct track, then go ahead and look down to take a quick peek. Once the position is established, however, lift the head.

Once again, imagine that line drawn across the ball of each foot as described earlier and pictured with pink tape on the rider's boot. This will be the line of concentrated equal balance. A gymnast that rises to the balls of the feet along this line with the heels rising does not topple forward on the beam. If they were to perform a full spin they would be centering their body weight over the balance of one foot. This is how the rider can envision using the heels to their advantage at moments during the ride. When a gymnast lowers the heel, or allows the heel to make contact with the beam, the rest of the upper leg and the seat of the gymnast are centered over the foot. You will never see a gymnast rock back onto the heels; the result would be a fall backwards or sideways off the beam.

This is why the balance of the foot is so important in riding. You must think of walking a chalk line, and paying careful attention to how the width of the foot is being used. Where is the weight being transferred as you balance over your foot? The gymnast has one advantage, and that is that the beam does not move while they are trying to balance. The rider must not only balance, but keep the forces of the push of the horse in check, and under their center of gravity. As we study different parts of the body you will begin to realize why the core, the seat and the upper body play an even bigger role to help the body become a stable load.

Spin the top

As the rider begins to find the balance point, the concentration of a specific spot becomes more and more evident. It's the 'hot spot' to teeter upon. Most riders only think of an entire stirrup to balance on, but what if we made that spot of balance as wide, and as round as a yoyo. Your foot will rest upon that yoyo as the toes begin to relax slightly, as the sole of the foot takes shape. That yoyo is positioned in the middle of the stirrup in the center of the chalk line.

Now, imagine making that point more precise. The hot spot is now as small as a pencil eraser, and the rider is balancing on the eraser with the entire body. The weight should not be so great as to break the lead tip of the pencil. If we challenge the rider even more, we could say to balance the pencil along the tight rope across the stirrup. The balance and thought process for this are so great, that the rider can think of only that spot in order to shift the balance. While this is not humanly possible in reality, understand my point. You must think of the foot as your base of support. It is not to push down on, or you would break the yoyo or snap the pencil. These are the moments when weight will shift slightly to the rest of the foot which is resting behind the yoyo or the pencil.

There are also moments in riding when the foot will have to rotate a few degrees outward or inward. This depends on the previous experience of the rider and their body build. Imagine a spinning top beneath each foot. The rider touches the spinning top with the sole of the foot to stop the top from spinning, but keeps the top upright so it doesn't fall over and lay on its side. The point of the top is centered along the stirrup, and teetering beneath the rider's foot. Without the momentum of the spin, the top will fall unless the rider holds the point of it along the stirrup directly in the center.

In order to change specific rotations with the foot, think of turning the top a few degrees while it remains balanced beneath the foot on its point. The right foot will rotate counter clock wise, and the left will rotate clock wise. This means that the center of the foot needs to remain over the wide part of the top along the best possible balance point. This allows the rider to make small balance changes and adjust the foot according to what is needed for the ride at particular moments, or for differing riding disciplines.

The Bars

Have you ever wondered why your stirrup is never in the same place twice? You see some riders with their feet far through the stirrup, and some riders with just the toes through the stirrup. So, which is correct? If you use your small toe, and big toe as guides, it will help you become more consistent with the placement of your stirrup.

The area of the foot that lies in a sturdy position across the bars of the stirrup is shown in the picture below.

Imagine the feet resting on each stirrup barefoot. The rider is trying to avoid the feeling of kneading the toes like what a cat would do when they are scratching. If the tip of the toes curl in and essentially wrap around the stirrups, then you take on the feel of a bird that is  gripping as if they were perched on a tree branch. This will affect the balance points of the feet. Instead, think of the cat stretching all toes forward, and spread the toes apart so they are past the platform of the stirrup, and the rider is further back with the balls of the toe along the stirrup iron. The smallest toe should line up, and be parallel with the outside bar of the stirrup. The ball of the big toe should line up and be parallel with the inside bar of the stirrup. This makes the hole of the stirrup line up parallel along the horse's side.

The big toe plays a little bigger role, and is often overlooked in riding. The big toe affects how the arch of the foot functions, especially in shock absorption. When the toes lower the arch flattens, dissipating shock in a controlled manner. If the toes are flexed upward, then the arch lifts much like the action of suction cup. The toes must be flat against the stirrup so the suction of the arch is not too high. When the toes relax, the suction and the energy is displaced through the foot. This helps the rider to stay balanced and the sole of the foot to stay level while riding each movement.

Stand on one foot and try to shift to the side to balance. You will feel the big toe activate and touch the ground. You will also feel the outer portion of your buttocks stabilizing the hip preventing the pelvis from tipping. Stabilization of the big toe plays a big role in riding.

With different riding disciplines you will discover that you need to change your leg position slightly depending on the variables of the ride. Be adjustable. Riding is not set in stone. You will need to practice all variables in case you are in a situation where you need to adjust your body to stay safe and create the best possible ride-a ride that is better for your horse and will help them balance. That is why you are learning to become adjustable one piece at a time.

Once you have mastered the position of the foot in the stirrup with even weight distribution, you can then go on to think of the big toe rotating for further control in downward transitions. The right toe will rotate slightly towards 11:00, and the left toe will rotate slightly towards 1:00. This is all done with a level foot, and no rising of the heel. This goes hand in hand with pushing the heel outward against a resistance. Practice in small increments. That way you will learn to have an adjustable foot rotation that can change, if needed, in a riding scenario.

Use the following exercises to help strengthen your puzzle pieces for the foot. They will help to create body awareness, and will aid in developing dexterity with your riding. Off horse exercises are necessary to allow your body to get used to the new positions.

Coordination and Strengthening Exercises

Pick up the rolled towel

Roll up a hand towel so it's in the shape of a long tootsie roll. Lay it on the ground in front of you, and practice picking it up with your toes and feet.

This will help you gain coordination and dexterity with all ten toes and the sole of the foot. Allow the towel to roll under your feet, as well. This is actually a good massage to give tired aching feet after a long riding session.

Roll the cylinder under the sole of the foot

Use a small cylinder or a rolling pin and allow the sole of your foot to create the rolling sensation under each foot. Let the muscles relax. Feel the arch of the foot, as well as your toes, spread apart and stretch.

Walking in the arena

In daily life, when walking or running we distribute weight differently through our feet. It is important to learn how evenly you walk in your daily routine.

Stand in the arena-footing doesn't matter. Step down into the ground as if you where on your horse riding. Then, take a step back and study your footprints. What do they say about how you distribute weight through your feet? Where is the footprint most prominent? Where is there hardly any mark of the foot at all? This can tell you a lot about how you ride with your feet in the stirrups. Strive to make the footprint even in depth. Even depth equals balance.

Elevé and relevé

This was personally a revelation in my own riding. This is a dancer's terminology for standing on the balls of the feet. An elevé is a gradual rising onto the balls of the feet, using control to rise up. This is the feeling that results once the rider has taken control with the balls of the feet on the stirrups.

A relevé is like a elevé but is executed with a spring like action. This is the same as a rider who needs a little spring to the rise in posting trot. Or if the rider is used to pushing down in the stirrups and squashes the horse's movement. It will be to the rider's advantage to stand in an "on horse" position, and practice elevé by rising to the balls of the feet and lifting the heels off the floor. Learn to balance for longer periods of time doing this. It will help under saddle. You will also feel the calves building muscle tone as well.

Puzzle Piece #2

Imagery Essentials

Ankle

Extension of the Foot

Checklist for the Proper Alignment of the Ankle

✓ The water glass in your ankle should remain full, not allowing any water to tip out forward, backward, or either side.

✓ Wear the ankle bracelet, keep it level and even.

✓ Achilles tendons stretch like a rubber band to maximize the heels being slightly lower than the toes.

✓ Ice skate with the blades straight to prevent the ankle from rolling to the inside or the outside.

✓ Fill your tall boots with concrete to help stabilize the lower leg in order to give a solid communicative leg cue.

✓ Snow plow with your skis.

✓ Headlights on your shoes help to keep your foot away from the horse's sides, and the angle of the ankle perfect.

✓ Exhibit the proper position of the ankle.

✓ Keep the shackles stretched, and keep the chain tight.

The Ankle

Extension of the foot

We have gone into great detail about the foot and the ten toes. We have learned to pay careful attention to the smallest intricacies of the feet in order to keep our stability and balance strong. As we progress to the next section, which is the ankle, it is important that you understand that the ankle is a major shock absorbing joint along with the knee and hip. The ankle will help the rider to remain fluid with the horse's movement. It aids in controlling the thigh and the lower leg. If the rider is tensing the ankle, then the rest of the leg will suffer. This will continue to travel up the body into the rider's seat. Once the rider begins to pay attention to the ankle, then they can go back and think of the foot, as well. The rider will lose some pieces of the foot placement as the thinking process begins. This is normal. Just assemble the missing pieces and go back and review what is needed in order to gain control of the two sections of the body before moving on.

> *The ankle is the continuation of the foot. Once you have mastered the position of the feet you can then move onto the ankle.*

Riding Realities

Common Errors and Enigmas

The ankle of the rider may pose differing issues for each individual. What is the position of your ankle? Do you ride with your ankle rolled to the inside or to the outside? Do you create stiffness in your ankle so that you cannot use your ankle as a shock absorber? Are your ankles braced, locked, or holding tension? Let's take a closer look at some familiar faults that may inhibit movement in one of your major shock absorbers.

Familiar Faults

Fault 1

Often issues that lie within the feet will carry up to the ankle. When riding, which toe is higher? The outside toe or the inside toe on each foot? If you ride with your little toe raised higher than the big toe than you roll your ankles to the inside. This is known as "inner rim riding" it will cause the rider to keep the lower leg in constant contact with the horse, which may result in the horse becoming dull to leg cues. It can also create a disconnection with the thigh. If you ride with your ankles rolling to the inside you will experience stiffness in the outer rim of the ankle joint. The rider will not be able to use the ankle as a shock absorber while the horse is in motion. The foot should remain level and even, so the ankle is level as well. It is important to experiment with your ankle and to make the ankle strong enough to maintain the stability of the entire calf.

Fault 2

If you experience the opposite issue, and ride with the big toe higher than the little toe, then you roll your ankles to the outside of the stirrup. This is known as "outer rim riding" This will cause immediate tension not only through the outside of the ankle rim, but also through the calf all the way to the knee joint. It will cause the rider's lower leg to swing, especially in the canter. The stiffness will create a rigid feel in the motion of the ankle. The rider will also lose the connection with the thigh and have no even pedestal to stand on creating an imbalance through the entire leg.

Riders sometimes complain of pain along the outer portion of the ankle and the top section of the foot. The foot must balance along the stirrup in order to help the ankle stabilize.

Fault 3

Every rider learns early on that they must keep their heels down. Riders work extremely hard to make the heel lower than the toe. This can be both a blessing and a curse. If the heels are forced down, you create a block in the front of the ankle joint. When you have your heels lower than the toe, it is stemming from the rider's hip elongating and the back of the leg stretching. You will never accomplish this by bracing the ankle alone. Too much weight pushed onto the back edge of the stirrup will not only lock joints, but it can also push the rider up and out of the saddle. In the beginning, you will actually learn to distribute weight though your whole leg. You will learn that the heel is the bi-product of correct alignment.

Fault 4

When a loss of balance occurs, the most common error that happens to a rider is the ankle joint will open in the front, causing the heel to rise and the toes to drop. The rider will be in a vulnerable position, as this creates a downward spiral of gripping to hang on when the upper body topples forward. This is known as 'ballet point'. Once the rider can build strength in the ankle joint and the surrounding muscles, the heel will become level first, and then begin to drop lower than the toes as the rider progresses. In some stages of riding, however, you will need to lighten the weight in the heel, and it will feel as though the toes are dropping down. This may have a similar feeling to ballet point, but, instead, I like to think of my feet resting inside of big fuzzy slippers. The slippers are soft just like my foot, and ankle joint. This reminds me to keep the joints solid and tone, but with little resistance. (Do not confuse this with relevé. If the exercise of raising the ankle is deliberate and controlled, then the result will be strength built in and around the ankle.)

Fault 5

The ankle must be a shock absorber. I cannot stress that enough. If you hold the entire ankle to try to keep it still, you will lose the quality of the mobility in the ankle entirely. You must think of coil springs that bounce as the movement of the horse is compressed, and stretched. If you hold against the movement with the ankles, your body will find a way to absorb that concussion most likely in the seat, or in the hands, causing other unwanted issues. Movement must ripple through the ankle much like how the bounce is absorbed when standing on a trampoline.

Picture Perfect Pieces

Now envision your picture perfect pieces for the improved ride

Imagery examination:

Accurate ankle angle

Further Explanation

Level, even, shock absorbing ankle joints are a major extension of the foot. You will learn how to keep your ankles stable, yet able to absorb concussion. The mobility in the ankle will determine how the heel can become the lowest point as you further your riding. It will keep your pedestal immoveable, yet pliable.

Essential Details of each Imagery

Water glass in your ankle

Once you have established the position of your ankle, you are then going to keep the muscle tone of the ankle relaxed, and free. As you read and practice these exercises, remember that we are discussing the area of your body that is in your sock if your socks were pulled up and stretched to the maximum height, so the material is not bunching.

This section tends to make contact with the horse's side or come into play without intention and it sometimes can feel as though the back part of your sock is always somehow sneaking in when it's not wanted, and trying to make friends with your horse's ribcage.

Think of a water glass inside your ankle, or even your sock filled up with water. It is filled to the brim and any shaky moves will leave the water to slosh and probably spill. This is often the case if the rider is trying really hard to keep the lower leg still, and not allowing the ankle to be the shock absorber. The 'give' in the ankle will help keep the rest of the leg steady and still. The water should not spill out the front from lifting the heel, or tip out the back of the glass from trying to force the heel down. The water should not spill out the left or the right side of the glass from the angle of the ankle. This holds true if the lower leg needs to move in order to give a leg aid as well. It's done with delicate precision.

In the beginning stage of learning to distribute weight correctly, any rider who has excessively pushed the heels down will need to think of the lightness in the feet by bringing the heel out and away, and also of gently pouring water out of the front of the cup like a pitcher with a spout. Once the rider has established the feeling of lightness in the stirrups, and the weight through the thighs, then the cup will become more level again. There will be adjustments here and there depending on prior riding experience and muscle habits.

The ankle bracelet

The ankle joint forms where the foot and leg meet. This joint allows for movement through the ankle both up and down, and side to side. The ankle joint tends to be more stable if the foot is flat on the ground. This is why so many riders are so particular about having a level foot in the stirrup. When the toes begin to point toward the ground, the ankle will be more susceptible to injury because the joint becomes dependent on soft tissue and ligaments to support, protect, and stabilize it. This is an excellent reason why the rider must imagine wearing an ankle bracelet that keeps the ankle securely in place.

Imagine the bracelet is thick like a watchband, and has an 'elastic' feel to it. It is positioned directly above the two boney protrusions on both ankles. I will refer to them as your "ankle knobbles" The links of your bracelets must remain closed not open. If you feel as though you are beginning to stretch those links as you would if you were removing a watch or putting it on, then you are not evenly distributing weight through your ankle. This is a big tattle tale sign for the rider. It's time to check and determine which part of their ankle is 'leaning', so to speak, or bearing more weight. If the ankle knobbles were replaced by a small tennis ball under your skin, in which direction would the ball be rolling? For some it may be to the inside, and for others, to the outside. In rare cases the front of the ankle may open too much and the ball would pop out the front onto the top of your foot, but more than likely it will try to roll out the back of your foot and sit behind the heel of your foot. If this happens then you are riding with too much "heels down" and most likely you are drawing your toes up toward your knee cap. Always keep the ankle soft and elastic.

Symmetry of the ankle joint is equally important. The circle of the bracelet must always be level. Think of the ankle knobble becoming the planet Saturn, and the ankle bracelet is Saturn's rings. The rings of Saturn float around the planet and do not make contact or touch at any point in time. Gravity keeps the rings from floating away. Rolling the ankle left and right can sometimes be an issue for some riders so be sure that you feel all five toes along the stirrup.

Helpful hint:

The use of ankle weights can help the rider to feel solidness throughout the ankle, but do not exceed 5 pounds each with the weights. The ankle weights will help the feeling of the weight dropping down like a plumb line through the body, but they will take away the temptation to push the feet into the stirrups or worse, tensing the front of the ankle joint when trying to bear too much weight in the heel. They will also aid in keeping the ankle straight as opposed to turning the ankle to the inside or outside of the horse's ribcage. If you warm up with the weights, you can remove them after a few minutes. You will be left with the weighted feel that you can sustain throughout your ride.

The use of a 5 pound ankle weight can be very helpful in developing the use of the ankle while riding. It is gentle reminder to keep that section of the leg away from the horse's sides. Practice taking the leg away, and then brining it close to the horse's sides. Keep the whole leg in an "on horse" position.

Achilles tendon stretches like a rubber band

Tendons within the body join the muscles to the bone. They are connective bands of tissue that transfer the force of a muscle contraction to the bones to help align them and allow for movement and balance. The most well known tendon is the Achilles tendon.

This tendon joins the heel to the calf muscle, and feels and looks like a thick rubber band. Its main purpose is to transmit the power of the calf into the foot. It is needed for any upright movement, so riding reinforces the use of this tendon tremendously. Abuse of this tendon such as excessively pushing the heels down, or stretching this tendon can cause damage over time.

Have you ever watched those riders who look like their ankles are like "Gumby"? They stretch down so far it's as if they had chewing gum there instead of ankles bones. The Achilles tendon is the thick cord that lines the back of the foot. If the Achilles tendon where a rubber band, that rubber band should feel as though it had enough tension to make the rubber band taught, but not enough to actually stretch the band too much that it would snap. If the rubber band feels as though there is absolutely no stretch to it, then the heels are lifting.

In early stages of riding, especially if you had pushed high amounts of weight in your stirrups and are now trying to reverse those effects, you will need to relax the tendon completely. Wipe the slate clean and begin again. In practice stages you may look as if you have a lifted heel and your weight in on your toes. This may be necessary to redistribute weight into your thighs, mainly the quadriceps, which are the front of the thighs. Once you reach a relaxed state, begin to re-train the muscles and the tendons to add the appropriate amount of stretch and allow the heels to become more level.

We are all striving for that beautiful long elegant leg that so many high level rides have. They have not achieved this excellence without working through various stages with their body. It is possible to keep the tendon stretchy like an elastic band, but never to the point of snapping. It must be able to stretch, but not beyond the points where it discourages the proper weight distribution throughout the foot and calf.

The riders who exhibit the long elastic heels have worked on it for years. Don't expect to go out and get this tomorrow. Be patient with yourself and allow your body time to stretch and become acquainted with this new position. Proper weight shifts in other parts of the body will help you take the burden off your foot. Each of us has a threshold for how far our ankles will stretch. Some riders are more flexible. Work with what you have and make it the best it can be.

Ice skate with the blades straight

In daily life we walk, stand, and shift weight in all directions in order to keep our balance, and stay in alignment. The sole of the foot must maintain a certain balance, and distributing weight will have a direct effect on the ankle joint and the other joints above it. Often riders will experience a "rusty hinge" joint. The joints of the ankle will become stuck or rigid. Other riders will feel overly oiled in those joints creating a "sliding" joint or too much mobility. The rider must find the in-between place where the joints have been greased, and can move with ease and lack tension. This feeling is similar to an ice skater who glides along the ice.

In order to find the correct angle for the ankle while riding, think of lacing up a pair of ice skates. If you have ever experienced ice skating before, you know that the laces need to be tight around the area of the ankle in order to help sustain the balance over the blade. Use the center of your foot evenly, and pay careful attention to where weight is being distributed. You don't want to be able to roll to the outside or the inside of the blade. You need to remain inside your ice skates with your blades gliding along in a straight line and with both ankle joints equally stable.

The alignment of the upper body should remain even over the ankles so not to cause too much weight to fall on the front of the ankle, or the back of the ankle. The feeling of the blades will help the rider to judge how much weight is needed in each stirrup.

Use the center of your foot evenly, and pay careful attention to where weight is being distributed. How is the weight being applied to each blade as you are skating along the ice? There is another reference that will keep the rider's heels slightly lighter in the stirrup. You would not be able to skate correctly if you were trying to skate off of the back edge of the ice skate first. The balance would throw the front of the blade down in a hurry, and you would roll to your toe. This is another reason why lowering the heel too much will cause the opposite action within your body. Think of the balance of the foot in a different light. It doesn't make much sense to drop the heel lower than the toe when you think about this scenario.

A word of caution: Do not think of an ice hockey player that pushes off their skates to skate faster when they need more power. They use the inside edge of their skates to push off of the blades. Think of the beautiful figure skater who glides along effortlessly in a straight line.

Fill your tall boots with concrete

This scenario helps the rider keep the entire lower leg as well as the ankle in a "fixed" home position. You will later be moving the lower leg to ask the horse to move the haunches or the shoulder, or to ask for lateral movements. The "boots filled with concrete" image will help to keep the legs as one stable unit. Words of caution to the rider-do not take this imagery literally. You are stabilizing the leg, not stiffening the leg to the point of over kill. A locked hip, knee, or ankle joint will create stiffness in the whole leg making it hard to move each section independently. Sometimes, you will need to break the concrete into separate pieces if needed.

Concrete is a consistency that is not forgiving. It is solid and permanent. If you think of a statue, you envision stability. This keeps you in a state of tone. That tone is what is needed to keep the leg set, so to speak.

In addition to the imagery of the tall boots filled with concrete, there are some other things you can do to help stabilize your lower leg. If you have a lower leg that is sometimes jelly-like and moves about along the horse's barrel, then firming up the muscles will help to keep the leg more stable. If you have a leg that bounces and wiggles about because you have stiffened or locked the joints, then you are adding the effect of bouncing because like a statue, you have become too stiff, and are working against your body to develop the tone needed to carry the stirrups.

You want your ankle to stay in one place as you give the horse a leg aid. The "concrete boot" will help hold the leg in position. Later, we will discuss how to give an effective leg aid and to teach your horse to become obedient to leg cues. This leg position will become more useful as we venture into the sequence of forward movement, and how to properly cue the horse to move forward with all four feet.

By no means however are you to stiffen your calf, or your ankle joints. This image is merely to help you to keep the ankle stable. You are not using your heel to ask the horse for forward movement, instead, you are using your entire lower leg combined with the ankle and the foot.

Snow plow with skis

Controversy is always an issue when discussing exactly where the heel placement is most efficient. In my experience, in the early stages of riding, I was taught to keep my heels down at all costs. This is the known rule and the most common phrase shouted while taking a lesson. As I rode more over the years, and rode with some top trainers, I realized that professional riders really don't push on the stirrups, or lock the front of the ankle joint. They use muscles of opposition which means for most top riders they are pushing the heels out, and away from the horse's sides, and never in a downward motion where the angle in the front of the ankle locks, or closes drastically.

To learn how to properly position the foot in the stirrup, the rider will need to train new muscles along the outer rims of the legs. By thinking of the ski's and the heels pulling out, and away from the horse's sides, the rider will learn to use the foot in another position to help free up the calves and use their legs independently.

Envision you are flying down the slopes in Aspen and you have to make sudden stop. You crisscross the front of your ski's to form an "X", and kick the back end of the skis out and away to do a maneuver called a "snow plow". Never, however, will you lift the back of your ski's up off the ground as you form a slight "X" formation with the front of the ski's or you can imagine the outcome. You would be doing a nose dive head first into a snow drift. Keep your heels flat and light, to allow the ski to glide over the surface area of the powdery snow until you come to a stop.

This feeling will tone the top portion of the outer thigh. By toning this portion you will begin to feel more contact with the upper portion of the inner thigh. Once again we have muscles of opposition working together to form a suction that is sticky. The feeling of suction should resemble the consistency of tacky glue that hasn't dried, as opposed to a vice grip that fatigues muscles, and gives you the opposite effect of popping up, and away. Keep thinking of the snow plow position as you ride to train your heels to be light in the stirrups, and buoyant in the steady security with the stirrup.

The rider should strive to keep the foot straight through the stirrup. This neutral position will allow for the rider to conform into different positions once this is achieved.

Headlights on your shoes

While you are riding there are several different positions the feet may be in depending on what discipline you ride. Whether you are conditioned to ride for long periods of time, or you are just starting out looking for the most effective safe position, you will begin to understand through hours in the saddle why the rotation of the ankle is a giant piece to the puzzle. We will review some different positions for the ankle rotation, and the degree to which you will turn your foot in order to influence the horse's ribcage, and gain forward movement.

Imagine headlights directly attached to the pointy part of your boot. The headlights are bright, and streamlined to form a perfect reflection of light that passes by your horse's shoulder in a parallel line to the ground. These headlights can become very important as you attempt to determine whether you are using your feet to the best of your advantage.

Your goal is to slowly move into the position of 12:00 with both lights shining directly in front of you. This is a hard task to accomplish in the beginning. You will need to gradually work on this over time allowing yourself enough time to stretch the muscles, and align the body correctly.

The position of 12:00 can be a goal to strive for, and it's often a surprise for many riders that they must struggle for this extreme angle. As an instructor I have found that when a rider learns how to use the ligaments and tendons to master this angle, if a moment should arise that the rider needs to slightly change the angle to an outward rotation away from the horse's ribcage, then it is easier to accomplish.

If you switch disciplines, or if you ride for pleasure this angle may not always be ideal. For the rider who jumps or rides English the headlights will point more toward 1:00 on the right, and 11:00 on the left. This will help the rider secure the body as they are going over jumps, or working on the flat. A higher level rider can keep the toes pointing towards 12:00, and can keep the lower leg in position before, during, and after the jumping effort. All this is done with the ankle absorbing the shock before take-off and landing.

For the western rider, the headlights can also point more towards 1:00 and 11:00. The use of the thigh needs to be more mobile especially for the reiner who is performing a spin, or a sliding stop. A western pleasure rider will use the lower calf to gently bump the horse's sides to initiate movement.

A trail rider will look for a comfortable position for long hours in the saddle. It is more important to keep the center of the toes under the center of the knee, and the hip sockets wide. Long hours in the saddle can affect the seat bones, and the rider may feel as though they need to push in the stirrups to relieve the uncomfortable feeling. Try to distribute the weight evenly to keep the horse comfortable, as well.

Pay careful attention as to whether or not you are pointing the beam of light in a straight line directly in front of your feet. If the beam of light shines down to the ground, the heels are rising and you are putting too much weight on the balls of the feet. If the beam of light is shining up towards the sky then the heels might be too low or the angle behind your knee has become obtuse. Keep the lights shining in a straight line toward 12:00.

Many top riders have slight angle to their foot and ankle. The best riders will be able to adjust accordingly to what the horse needs at the moment. If you are riding a horse that's a little unpredictable then you want to be able to adjust your body according to what the horse needs.

While you are riding it is important that you never go past the point of 1:00 and 11:00 with your headlights. The only time you will ever use this position is when you are using an artificial aid such as a spur to momentarily give the horse the aid. Then, you will immediately go back to the position of 12:00. Otherwise you will falsely touch the horse's sides with the spur which will make them dull to the aid. This, in turn, will create other unwanted behaviors.

Stretch the shackles and keep the chain tight

In many areas of riding often times the rider has to make a decision as to how much contact the lower leg can sustain in different stages of the horses training. If the lower leg is always in contact with the horses side of the belly, then the horse may become confused as to whether that is an aid to move forward or transition to the next gait, or, if you are just holding to keep your balance. A higher level horse with more refined cues will learn that there is a slight variation in pressure and knows the difference. However, that horse may also mistake a rider who is holding to keep up with the movement of the horse, for an actual cue to move forward faster. Nonetheless, you should be prepared to be able to balance, while keeping the foundation of the lower body set.

It is useful to think of a maximum security prisoner who is being escorted to a different facility. When they are asked to walk they have steel shackles on both ankles with a heavy duty chain in between. The weight of the shackles is fairly heavy, and causes the prisoner to shuffle in a sense so they cannot make a quick getaway. The chain drags between. The rider must think of holding those shackles away from the horse's sides, and not allow the heavy steel of the "shackles" to touch the sides of the horse. Imagine that the chain between the shackles passes through your horse's belly, and must remain tight, not loopy or loose. If you give way just a little, you will create a weakness in the links, and the result will be the shackles making contact.

This imagery can be practiced to varying degrees. Once you can hold the shackles away completely and still function, then, you can begin to ease your way to touching ever so slightly against the horses fur.

When you begin to gain enough control that you can advance one leg forward and one leg back, think of the chain forming a diagonal line instead of a parallel line through the horse's belly. That way you will be using the two legs in unison and involving the hip flexors to help steer the horses back as opposed to griping with one leg more than the other.

When asking the horse to move forward you can think of adding a gong or a symbol from a drum set to your horse's sides. If you are asking for forward movement make the chain tight by bringing the shackle out to the side and then letting it fall onto the gong or symbol as if it were the drum stick. Immediately put tension in the chain again, and rebalance so you are able to stay with the horse as it moves forward in response to your driving aid.

The key is to be able to change the rotation of the ankle in all directions so you have more tools for your toolbox.

Pronation and Supination of the Ankle

The ankle joint can take on various angles. It is important to be aware of what pronation and supination are in order to help form a healthy balance.

Many riders may find it difficult to change the angle of their foot in the stirrup due to how they walk around in their everyday lives. Pronation of the ankle is the inward roll of the foot. Supination is the opposite and outward roll. When one part of the body is out of alignment, such as ankle position, other parts of the body such as hips, knees and lower back, may be affected. It is important that you realize what rotation your ankles may display. If they are excessively turned inward or outward, you may cause blockages or stiffness in other parts of the body. Use all the imagery essentials above to help gather data in order to achieve the position best suited for your body and your balance

Coordination and strengthening exercises

The dumbbell raise

In order to strengthen the ankle joint use a lightweight dumbbell. Attach a piece of bailing string to it, and practice raising and lowering the dumbbell with the toe of your foot. This will allow the rider to use the correct muscles, and tone the area in front of the ankle. You can do this by counting in reps of 10 first. Practice daily until you feel like you can hold the dumbbell without dropping the heel too low.

This picture is showing the raising phase of the dumbbell. It is important to allow the foot to lower as well without allowing the dumbbell to slip over the top of the foot. Do these reps slowly, and keep complete control of the foot.

Rotating the ankles out of the stirrups

Briefly remove both feet from the stirrups and allow your whole leg to stretch down and relax. Rotate both ankles around in a few circles going clockwise; then rotate both ankles counter clockwise. Keep your thighs and calves still. Only move the ankles. This will help to relieve some stress and tension that may have built up while you were practicing and bring your ankles back to a relaxed state. Once they feel like they are attached by a string and they are part of a puppet, then you are ready to reposition your foot through the stirrups and resume riding.

Point toes/ pick toes up

Remove both feet from the stirrups once again. Begin by pointing all ten toes towards the ground just like a ballet dancer on point. Really stretch and reach to challenge yourself to point your toes. Your end result should be a straight line from the knee down the front of the shin to the tips of the toes. Hold that position for a count five. Next, envision a friend placing two fingers under your foot just behind the balls of the feet, and giving you guidance to lift your foot up with the gentlest of ease to a riding position of both roller skates flat on the ground. Practice pointing your toes, then brining your feet back to riding position. This will help relieve tension in the front of the ankle, and will allow the rider to become more flexible in the movement. This is the first step to getting the spring-like action you have been searching for.

Heels against a wall

You can do this exercise on the ground after you have finished your ride each day. Go to your horse's stall or a fence post, and position your body with your back to it. Take your right heel and

press it into the wall. Hold for a count of ten. Keep your foot in the riding position with the front of your ankle relaxed and all ten toes tension-free. Switch legs and repeat with the left heel for a count of ten. If you are doing this correctly, along the back of your hamstrings, behind your knee and down the back of the calf you will feel a sense of strength and stability. This will help to keep your leg still while you are riding.

By using a fence post to push the heel against it will activate the muscles needed to help secure and hold the leg in place while riding. This will keep the hamstrings strong, and also keep the front of the ankle in position.

Stepping on the inside rim of the stirrup

To aid in keeping the ankle straight, it is helpful to place the foot on the inside rim of the stirrup, so the little toe is resting on the ledge. When balancing becomes easier, practice standing, and even posting in this position. It will also aid the rider in feeling the "breathable" position of the calves barely touching the horse's side.

Engagement ring exercise

In order to retain the proper feel throughout the foot and toes along the top surface compared to the amount of weight needed in the heels, the following exercise using plastic rings will help. The engagement ring exercise will help the rider develop the correct angles.

The rings used in this exercise are used as a pool game called the ring toss, and come in sets of 6 and can be purchased at local pool supply stores.

They are lightweight, and easily come off the rider's foot. They can be used with the foot out of the stirrup, or with the foot already through the stirrup. The purpose is to ensure that the rider places the foot in the correct alignment and also has the weight distributed through the whole foot. This will keep the ankle in the correct position while riding. If the rider uses too much angle or drops the ankle to the inside or outside, then the ring will bounce off the foot. The rider must learn to keep the foot buoyant. It cannot retain stiffness. This is wonderful exercise, and should be able to be performed at a walk, trot and canter.

By placing the ring in this area of the foot, the rider can learn how to distribute the weight evenly, and correctly. If the rider loses the ring (which will happen often in the beginning,) attach a small piece of sting to the ring, and tie it to the stirrup so the rider does not need to keep dismounting in order to put the ring back on the foot if a helper is not available. They can reach down and reposition the ring back along the top half of the foot just in front of the ankle.

Puzzle Piece #3

Imagery Essential

Lower Leg

The Hallway of Aids

Checklist for the Proper Alignment of the Lower Leg

- ✓ Zipper down the front of the shin faces forward.
- ✓ Keep the smiley faces on your knees facing forward.
- ✓ Hold a soft ball behind the knee.
- ✓ Center of the knee remains over the center of the foot.
- ✓ Hold the sponges with the inside of your calves.

Connection with the Calves

The lower legs or calves of the rider form the hallway in which the horse is expected to follow through with the ribcage and back. This hallway will help to initiate movement in both a forward, and sideways, or lateral direction. The calves are to help guide the horse, lift the back muscles, and create rhythm and impulsion, or spring in the horses stride. The rider's calf can also create activity within a gait. It is essentially the turn signal to let the horse know what is coming next so the ribcage of the horse can stay behind the shoulders and in front of the hips.

The calves become the connection and the gas pedal to initiate forward movement in a straight line, as well. Eventually the rider will teach the horse to move around the lower leg, and to bend gently with the back when an aid is given with the lower leg. In later work, the calves will also encourage the horse to keep the back mobile, and moveable, and to help with the connection in assembling the horse for collection for upper level work.

> *The calves and lower leg become the gas pedal and the hallway to help initiate forward movement and guide the horse.*

The calves also are connected to two of the main shock absorbers, which are the knees and the ankle joints. As you progress through the puzzle pieces of your body structure, you will realize how your calves start to develop stillness while you're riding. You will be able to position the calves along the horse's barrel to signal to the horse the direction and speed. You will also have the ability to lift the horse's ribcage up for collected work. You will be assembling your body just as you piece together the horse's body as you advance.

Riding Realities

Common errors and enigmas

The lower leg is the hallway of your aids. The calves become the accelerator and the gas pedal for forward movement and will also tell the horse to move laterally (sideways). They will gently hold the ribcage upright, and delicately advise the horse of all upcoming maneuvers. They aid in balance, and teach the horse to maintain speed. If the calves or lower leg are used in a disruptive manner, it will result in refusal to move forward or ignorance to the obedience to leg cues. Let's take a look at some common faults that disrupt the flow of forward movement.

Familiar Faults

Fault 1

If the rider cannot hold the lower leg still, and the calf swings with the horse's movement, then, the horse will find static amongst the cue, and become confused. This is referred to as "leg swing" which happens when the rider stiffens behind the knee, or locks the hip joint or knee joint. The direct result will be a rigid lower leg, and the horse will immediately either speed up in response to the leg cue, or slow down, as he begins to ignore the leg cue altogether. Concentrate on keeping the lower leg in a neutral position. It must hang like a curtain draped along the sides of the barrel. Keep softness throughout the leg.

Fault 2

A "gripping calf" is common with riders who are jumping, or who have learned to depend on the lower leg as a means of balance. Turning the calf so you are holding with the back part of the calf and becoming loose at the upper thigh, will only result in a loss of seat, and a deterioration of balance. Practice keeping the calf and foot facing toward 12:00 as you ride. If you need to rotate around to the back of the calf for added hold if your horse performs and unexpected maneuver, then you may do so, but promptly return to the home position. You will be changing the angle of your joints as you need to for each situation that arises. Remember that riding is not set in stone. You must do your best to adapt to all situations that will arise by becoming flexible.

The rider pictured is showing signs of a gripping calf, as the toe is excessively turned out beyond 11:00, it puts the calf in a holding position. This can also morph into the extended stay calf which is too much dependence on the inner area of the lower leg. Photo Emilie Frede photography

Fault 3

It is important that the lower leg does not rise as you ask for movement. This is what I refer to as a "floating leg". The lower leg will become less firm, and resemble the consistency of feathers or sifting sand. Instead, we are working towards the consistency of wet sand. You are not squeezing upward; your intent is to allow the lower leg to drop and wrap around the horse, as if you are giving the horse a hug. You will eventually learn to lift the horse up and create a forward willingness. Pay careful attention to minor details now, so when you are ready for upper level work the fundamentals are already in place.

Fault 4

The "extended stay calf" fault refers to the rider who leaves the leg on for a prolonged length of time. If you signal with the leg aid too long, the horse will learn to lean against the lower leg, and push against it. In extreme cases the horse will move into leg pressure, instead of away from it. Always add the lower leg in a series of touches, or gentle bumps so the horse learns to move off of the leg. Adding your leg for a long period of time will not make your horse light to it, it will make your horse resent it, or in most cases, completely ignore it. Your leg is not on a week long vacation against your horse's side. Ask, and then dismiss the pressure when your horse gives you the slightest gesture that the thought of moving the feet in the desired direction entered their mind.

Picture Perfect Pieces SOLUTION

Now envision your picture perfect pieces for the improved ride

Imagery examination:

Locomotion of the lower leg

Further Explanation

The lower leg plays a key role in riding as it is the number one ingredient to tell the horse to liven up the motion or move forward. The more stable the lower leg is, the less guessing the horse will have to do in order to have a clear signal to move the feet, either in a forward motion or a desired direction. To achieve this practice making the lower leg active only when you are looking for something specific to change with the horse's body. Otherwise, the lower leg remains stable and quiet keeping a feather light touch I refer to as "frictional contact".

Essential Details of each Imagery

The zipper

The position of the calves can be tricky. The calves of most riders become stiff due to excessive pushing against the stirrups, or bearing too much weight. A rider must learn to keep a steady and following contact with the feet so the calves can remain in alignment. There are many intricate movements that happen at differing angles. The calves are a major functioning part of the system to help create forward motion in the horse. That forward movement may be one of the most important creations that we generate upon a horse.

> Always strive to keep a quiet and effective lower leg. Your horse will remain extremely responsive, and your riding aids will become lighter.

The angle of the front of the shin will be facing forward as you ride in a passive position about 80% of the ride. It is helpful to think of a heavy weight zipper that runs from just below the front of the knee following your shin bone down to the front of the ankle. We zipped it up tightly as to not let any contents leak out. Each link of the zipper is fully closed so that the seal is not weak from the top of the knee to the front of the ankle. It is useful to keep the zipper pointing towards 12:00 as you ride forward. It may also be helpful to think of an opposing zipper down the back portion of your calf that is equally as strong, and zipped tightly to keep all the contents trapped away neatly in its compartment. In some cases as you begin to experience this strange feeling, the back of the zipper may feel as though it is pointing out and away from the horse's ribcage. It may help to think of the snow plow with the skis and the feet remaining light and lifted in the stirrups.

Smiley faces

Where are your kneecaps pointing? This is a big question to ask yourself as you sit in the saddle. Not only what direction are they pointing in, but are they even. A twist in the rider's hip can have a direct result on the placement of the knee. This may trickle down into the rider's feet as well. The rider needs to pay careful attention to the shock absorbers, which are the joints of the ankles, knees, and hips. Think of a smiley face directly in the center of both knee caps. These bright yellow smiley faces must remain in a position where they can catch a full glimpse of the ride. In other words, if your eyes were part of that smiley face, what would be your view from your kneecap? Would you be looking up at the horse's neck, or would you be looking more towards the horse's front feet? In some instances your smiley face may be staring at the ground. As funny as it may sound this plays a big role in how the rest of the thigh and foot will be in reference to the whole body remaining in good balance.

One place that the knee can start to point to in some cases, is toward the horse's shoulder which is a telltale sign that the rider is gripping with the knee or thigh. Do your best to keep a firm but relatively "tacky" hold. The faces should not start to gaze toward the horse's shoulder. This may mean that the rider has rocked back onto to the tailbone, lifting the pelvis up. The rider may round the lower back and begin to lean back in the saddle.

If the smiley faces are pointing outwards (away from the horse) then the rider will compensate by latching on with the calves and relying too much on the floor of the seat bones. The calves will end up holding too much like a vice grip. You are looking for the knee to remain flat against the horse's sides so that you could not slip a piece of paper in between the area of your knee and the saddle.

As you begin to progress with your riding, you will eventually want the knee cap to angle more toward the ground. This will resemble the feeling of kneeling down or falling to your knees. The angle of both thighs will change to permit more weight to be distributed throughout, and the knees will reposition once they are conditioned to pointing toward 12:00 first and are straight. Another key point is to try to keep the knee over the center of the foot, much the same as if the rider were doing a squat on the ground. Do not let the knee extend beyond the foot.

Tara is keeping her knee soft. The angle is enough that a softball could rest gently in the groove and remain steady as she rides.

Softball behind the knee

There's no bat involved; just a ball. Sometimes riders will experience difficulty when asked to move the lower leg back behind the hip. If the lower leg is the only section that is adjusted backward, you will never be able to keep the leg in position because you are using sheer muscle strength to hold it there. That muscle strength is not the secret, and trying to hold your position with sheer muscle will not work. By using sheer muscle strength you will cause your body to fatigue very quickly, and in some cases, you may ride into seize up, or freeze mode.

Instead, you need to become soft behind the knee. Often you will see a rider who looks like they are sitting in their recliner in the living room. There is no bend behind the knee, and the lower leg is outstretched in front of the rider's body, pushing heavily into the stirrups. This will make your leg become rigid. The end result will be the rider relying on the stirrup, and the seat will, in turn, push back against the cantle, or make the rider unstable during the trot or canter.

Another error is riders who ride with a stirrup length that is too long. The bend behind the knee is almost non-existent. In an effort to get the long elegant leg that all dressage riders dream of, these riders have made the common error of trying to make the leg too long which will only result in a lack of balance. Keep the angles behind your knee, and check your stirrup length to make sure that if you were to remove your feet from the stirrups and let your feet hang down next to them, the stirrup iron would touch just above your ankle knobble. Any lower is, really, too long of a stirrup.

Instead, think of a softball that is placed behind both knees. You are gently holding the ball in place, keeping a gentle bend behind the knee. Do not grip onto the softball and allow your lower leg to swing back too far. It's not like a golf ball where the bend in the knee would be extreme or a basketball where the bend behind the knee would be more toward a straighter position.

Keep the bend of the knee going more toward the ground instead of up toward the horse's nose. Think of a small arrow on both knees, and that arrow must point down more toward the ground. This will pull the softball in a backward direction, which will ground your leg, and open your hip angle wider to allow for more absorption of the horse's movement.

Important

Helpful Hint:

The elegance of a long leg always comes from the rider learning to elongate the leg from the hip joint and to use the entire leg effectively. It never comes from making the stirrups too long to start with, and trying to ride with the length of your leg under your hip. You want to create angles, and use your muscle tone to hold your alignment in position. This gives the illusion of the long leg that beautiful riders have.

> *You can think of kneeling on a stool to help direct your knee into an effective position.*

Knee remains over the center of the foot

For any weightlifter or athlete, careful attention is always a factor when dealing with the ankle joints as well as the knee joints. Any motion that requires a bend in the knee (like a squat) or lowering their center of gravity toward the ground with the buttocks, will involve the calf. The calf needs to be either toned or at moment's notice relaxed.

Aligning the knee over the foot is like putting a roof over walls with the walls set on the base or ground. They all go hand in hand, and must stay stacked, or the result will be one joint overriding the other, causing the structure to topple over. If the toes begin to turn away from the knee, the body will be forced to use the lower calf for balance, and the gripping begins, much like a clothespin. Another problem is the knee floating outward, leaving the rider in a position where they will be weighted heavily on the seat bones, and will remain behind the horse's motion. Part of the battle is knowing what your alignment looks like aboard your horse, and there is no better way to gauge it than with duct tape.

By placing duct tape on the knee and over the center of each foot, the rider can gauge how much the joints align while riding. There is a small gap between Tara's leg and the side of Loops. Keep this light frictional contact as your end goal.

Place a small piece of duct tape over the center of your boot. Then place a small piece of tape over the center of your knee on both legs. If you played connect the dots you would be able to connect those two spots easily and the result would be a straight line between points. As you ride, glance down periodically to see if your alignment has changed. Do you move your feet before your knee or you knee before your feet? This is a great way to check yourself without an instructor present to remind you.

If it is difficult to align your spots while on the horse, sit on a barrel. It's always easier to sit on something that is not moving beneath you first, and then get your balance and alignment on the horse.

This technique will also show the rider if one leg tends to float forward or backward more than the other. This is a common problem with all riders. Identify it first then fix it piece by piece. Remember you must still keep the correct shoulder, to hip, to heel line up as you connect the dots.

Hold the sponges

When learning to add pressure and give an appropriate leg aid, it is difficult to find the correct mixture to make the recipe just right. An "incredible hulk" leg will leave the horse either dull or ignorant to forward movement, or will cause the horse to "get out of dodge" and run away. On the contrary, if the lower leg is swinging like a rag doll, then the horse will be forced to make judgment calls on his own, as confusion may arise with the communication breaking down between a swinging leg that just doesn't have enough "stuffing", or a bumping leg that is explaining the go forward cue over and over. Eventually, the horse will become frustrated, and begin to shut down as the answer is never clear. The rider goes on to believe that graduating to other means, such as spurs or a crop, will do the trick, when in reality, they just need more stable control of the lower leg. The best fix to help with position of the lower leg and the stability is the exercise of using two carwash sponges.

Place the sponges along the inside of each calf. Always start off with the gentlest of squeezes, as if those sponges were just dunked in a bucket of water. You are adding a feather light squeeze—just enough to cause a trickle of water to run down the horse's ribcage on both sides simultaneously. By gently holding the sponges in place, you can begin to train your calf to move in motion with the horse.

As you practice this exercise, it will soon become obvious how you use your calf on each side of the horse's belly. If the sponges slip forward or backward, it tells you that you tend to move your calves while riding. If the sponges become flat, it indicates that you are most likely a gripper. Excessive hold on a horse's sides is a myth; it is not how you stay on a horse. In fact, once you have mastered the correct hold, your lower calves should hardly make contact with the horse unless you are asking for something specific.

By holding the sponges, the rider will learn to keep a soft feel and to leave the leg in the same place. The sponge will have strange indents if the rider bears more weight on the back of the calf, or the front of the calf.

If this exercise shows you that you are not using your calves correctly, it is time to figure out why. Does your lower leg swing with each stride? Do you tend to roll on to the back of your calves so the sponges are pushed forward? Do the sponges roll out the back because you grip with your knees? Are your calves so far from your horse that you lose the sponges completely?

As you continue to practice, you will eventually learn what neutral leg position is and the "home" spot for your legs to naturally hang down so that your horse is responsive to your requests.

Ride in different gaits and practice using your legs aids ever so lightly to receive the forward motion. Your sponges will be your guide.

Coordination and strengthening exercises

Walking with an exercise band

The calves are going to become a highly developed piece of your anatomy. They need to learn how to maneuver and become useful on their own accord. An exercise band is useful to practice with while you are on the ground. It will help you gain control of each calf. This exercise will also strengthen the outside of your upper thigh which we will discuss later.

Position the exercise band around your ankles. Spread your legs hip distance apart and slightly bend your knees. Relax your lower back, and keep the pelvis under your hips. Keep the band so it is tight enough that it is not loopy. Take small steps forward, carefully walking while keeping your toes pointing forward toward 12:00. You will begin to feel the wall your calves create. Picture your horse's barrel in between your legs. You can now feel how important your hallway of aids becomes. Practice a few steps at a time. Before long you will be able to walk down your barn aisle and keep your position. You will feel the difference when you ride as well.

Holding the ball between the bulb of each calf

Use a ball that is small enough to position between your calves. You will be placing the ball just below the knee and low enough that you can touch it with each bulb of the calf muscle. You may sit in a chair to practice this exercise. This will strengthen the lower leg and teach the rider to feel how to use varying degrees of pressure.

Keep your toes pointing forward toward 12:00. Keep a bend in each knee and try to keep your legs in an "on horse" position. Work in reps of ten. Squeeze and release the ball for ten reps. Do not allow the ball to drop. Think of the ball being a balloon instead, and you do not want to pop it. Once you have finished your ten reps, squeeze the ball gently and hold for a count of ten. You will feel your inner thigh muscles working hard. Try to practice differing degrees or pulses and vibrations with the ball. This will help you gain control of the movement of your calves. Too often riders hold too long when they ask the horse to move forward. You can practice asking with authority using the ball, and not dropping it all together. Keep a light frictional contact.

If you look at Tara's left foot it is slightly turned in more than the right. The same is true as she rides. This is an asymmetry issue that requires her concentration. She does not want to roll to the outside of her foot when giving a cue for the horse to step forward. It also puts a slight unevenness in her body. Even those who ride everyday struggle with correct body position. It is always a work in progress.

The speed control center

Let's Look at Leg Aids

How to effectively use your leg aids to develop a "go forward" cue with your horse

You have practiced controlling the position of the lower leg. Now, it's time to train the horse using a system that is simple in philosophy. It may seem like foreign territory when you actually begin to ask for the horse to move forward, but as you feel the softness of the cue versus the forcefulness used a majority of the time by riders, you will begin to understand why you are asking in the following sequence. You will, more than likely, have to teach your horse again to move forward in response to your leg cues. This is a useful session that will later be extremely beneficial when beginning to teach your horse other movements where one leg at a time is required to move the horse laterally (sideways) and to create activity within the gait.

Teaching a horse to effectively move off a leg aid is rather difficult at times. You must think like a horse. If you are a rider who constantly bumps with your lower leg to ask for forward movement you will be faced with the situation of a horse becoming extremely dull to your aids and resistant to go forward. This is an instance where you will have to teach your horse again what a leg cue means. Take the time to go through the four phases of cues so your communication with your horse can grow.

If you are a scared rider who constantly holds with your lower leg without consciously knowing you are gripping, the horse will feel no difference when you actually add the pressure needed to ask the horse to move forward. You may be a rider who has ridden for years, and are now ready to increase the language with your horse to include lateral work or even canter transitions. If you have used too much leg in the past, how are you actually going to tell the horse to move sideways when you have used up all your leg aid to tell the horse to move forward? These are important questions to ask yourself, and teaching your horse to effectively move off of light leg pressure will solve a lot of common riding errors and issues you may be having with your horse.

If you stop and think about it, forward movement is the most important ingredient needed in training a horse. You're "whoa" and "go" issues are exactly the same. Let's think about a rearing horse. If it has time to plant its feet, stop and then rear, what aid is it not obedient to? The answer is your leg. If you have a horse that begins to buck, what cue is it not being responsive to? Why do you think you hear the term "buck a horse out?" In my opinion, bucking a horse out will never solve the problem, but it certainly will teach the horse to move forward. A horse that is bucking in place is harder to ride than a bucking horse that is going forward. What about a spooking horse? If it has time to stop and look at imaginary objects, or time to pick and choose when it will spook to get out of work, then the answer is lack of forward movement. Even a bolting horse is not being obedient to leg cues. That can be the opposite end of the spectrum with the horse fearing the leg cue instead of ignoring the leg cue. All in all, it is the same issue and you need to take a closer look at how you are asking for your forward movement.

Your horse has two options when leg is being added. They are; 1.) Move all four feet forward in response to the aid, or 2.) Stand still and ignore the cue. In some cases horses who have felt leg pressure constantly on their sides are no different than the rider who goes out to a really nice dinner. You are waiting to meet your friends and in the lobby of the restaurant they are playing this really irritating music. You begin to think that you will never make it through dinner if they keep playing this music. As your party arrives you begin to greet everyone and realize that ten minutes after sitting down to eat, the music that was playing is a thing of the past, it becomes like back ground music. That is what your leg cues become to your horse if there is a constant squeezing pressure. Your leg pressure becomes like background music. If the horse feels the leg bumping, nudging or irritating his sides constantly, why would that additional little nudge or kick mean anything different just because the rider is looking to move forward and it makes sense to them?

This is what riders struggle with every day with their horses, and in my opinion, a majority of behavioral issues stem from the fact that the horse has never been taught to respond to leg pressure and to feel the sensation of "cruise control." This is when the rider totally relieves their legs from the horse's sides, and remains touching the horse with only light frictional contact. They feel the horse's fur instead of digging into muscle or bone. Be kind in your requests. After all, a horse can feel a fly land on its skin. Do you really think they can not feel your leg aids?

A horse will choose to ignore our leg aids sometimes, but it is up to the rider to teach the horse to be responsive, and obedient to leg cues 100% of the time. I use a system called the four phases of leg cues. The end result is going to be an invisible cue that tells the horse to move forward. Once this is established, the rider must make a promise to the horse. The leg cue will release and lighten and the rider will take responsibility for their own balance and not clench the sides of the horse to hold on, nor will the rider keep nagging the horse to move. This is a learning curve for both riders and horses. It takes a lot of concentration when you first start out. Some riders will want to give up and go back to their old ways. But I promise you this will work if you are patient enough and guide the horse through it. Something new is never easy, and it is tempting to resort to your old ways of training and riding. Stick with it, and the outcome will far outweigh the sweat it took to get there.

When can the cue to go forward be taught?

Another important tip to remember is that this is never fully learned. By that I mean, you will teach your horse to be obedient to leg aids and rein aids everyday of their lives, for the rest of their lives. Unfortunately, your horse will forget from time to time how to move forward, and it is your job as the rider to remind the horse of the four phases of leg cues.

Each time you teach your horse something new you will have to review the basics. It's like being back in school and learning how to add and subtract. You had to know basics before you could multiply and divide. If you are looking for too many things at once while you are riding, you are going to confuse the horse and defeat the purpose of your training session. Keep it simple. Use the K.I.S.S system. Leg means go, and hand means whoa. Once the horse is moving they learn all about cruise control.

Do not try to use one leg for lateral movement until the horse firmly understands what two legs mean. If you are using one leg at a time to signal to the horse to move the barrel or move the hindquarters or shoulders, the horse may mix the cues. They must firmly understand both legs mean move forward and change your speed before you add any other aids.

What do the two legs mean?

When you begin to teach the meaning of leg cues to your horse it is important to remember that both of your calves mean two things to the horse:

1. Move forward
2. Change the speed of the horses legs

It is that simple. Both legs mean GO! We can be more specific and say that all four feet must first begin to move, and then all four feet must move consistently which is 100% of the time. In other words, every time you use both legs to cue your horse it will move all four feet consecutively and keep marching on. After you have established the fact that your horse will move its feet, you are ready to ask the horse to move the feet when and where you choose. This means that you can start to ask for the horse to walk at a specific spot such as a cone or marker. This makes the cue more accurate. It also allows the rider to see how responsive the horse is. Does it take your horse five steps to actually respond to your cue and change the leg speed? Or does the horse instantly change speed at your request immediately after you have asked? This becomes important. The reaction time is a big factor and in the beginning you just worry about getting the cue. Then you will be ready to move on to getting it quickly and on the mark. After the response time is shortened, you are ready to ask the horse to move the feet in a specific direction. This will mean stepping to the left or right, or changing directions. It is important to note that if you are adding pressure on both reins to ask the horse to turn you are in fact slowing the speed of the feet down. If you slow down the speed of the feet by picking up both reins it just gives you another moment to train the go forward cue. Each time your horse makes a mistake it becomes a training opportunity for you as the rider.

Understand that rein contact will almost always slow the feet down because the horse will naturally want to stop when rein pressure is applied. When training your horse to go forward, try to keep your changes of direction to a minimum so the horse will not become confused until you have taught the go forward cue well. Once you have established your change of direction you are then ready to start speeding the feet up and slowing the feet down. This is often a problem when riders are teaching the horse to be responsive. They instantly want the speed they want. You have to be a little more lenient in the beginning. You are looking for the horse to go forward and that is it. Once that happens, then you can start to ask for a slower step or a faster step but you never want to overdue that step in the beginning. You as the rider should change the speed of the horse's feet before they get the chance to change it themselves.

In review the sequence of how to get the horse's feet to move are:

1. **Get the feet to move**
2. **Get the feet to move consistently**
3. **Get the feet to move when and where asked**
4. **Get the feet to move in a specific direction**
5. **Get the feet to change the pace and speed up or slow down**

The four phases of leg cues

When asking your horse to move forward it is important that you use a system of cues and you keep that sequence exactly the same as you ask for the horse to respond to your leg pressure. You can use any phases of cues you like. I am going to share my cues because they are what have worked for me over the years. Just remember when you are picking and choosing your cues, the first cue is the absolute lightest cue you will use so it must be invisible to the onlooker. The last phase must be a reinforcer. The horse must move at all costs when they know that this cue is coming. The in-between phases must gently increase in intensity until you are to the reinforcer. **You must stick to your guns on this. Do not become a push over. Be firm and immediately forgiving when the request is answered.**

Phase One: The light leg squeeze

This phase is the lightest of all four cues. This is your goal-the cue you will want to eventually use every time you cue your horse to move the feet. It is a very light squeeze that is completely invisible to a person standing on the ground. Imagine how easy riding would be if you could successfully use a cue that would resemble that of touching a piece of wet toilet paper that is draped between your horse's sides and the stirrup fender or leather. Don't break that sheet of paper. The bulb of the calf is all you need to signal to your horse to move the feet. The lightness would be amazing. Now you know why you will have to constantly review leg cues with your horse. As you ride your legs may bump or touch the horse's sides without your knowledge. This will dull out your light leg cue. Keep reviewing. Once you teach the cue it will only take a few moments to revamp it and revitalize your horse's responsiveness to it. As your riding progresses, you will be able to keep your lower leg still and only use it when you are asking for a meaningful cue to step forward or change the speed of the horse's feet.

Phase Two: The leg bump

In most cases the horse will not move off of the light leg squeeze. If the horse does respond immediately go to"cruise control" with both calves. If you have already added the leg squeeze and you got no response, then immediately up the intensity and move into the leg bump. This is not necessarily a hard kick, this is a bump. You are not begging the horse to move forward. You are going to ask with a two bump limit before moving onto the next phase.

Use both calves in rhythm and add them at the exact same time. Use the bulb of your calf again to add a tapping that is quick and sharp. Do not prolong the bump or leave your leg stagnant along the horse's side. You are allowing your lower leg to rebound off of the horse's barrel. Say out loud "go" for the first bump and "forward" for the second bump. This will help to not prolong the action of your leg cues. You want the horse to feel the bump. Raise the intensity and awareness, and look for something specific. If the horse moves forward, release the pressure and allow your lower leg to relax along the horse's sides, keeping it still.

Phase Three: The leg slap

Notice I have not mentioned kicking yet. I do not kick horses with my heels. If you use your heels and raise your legs you run the risk of losing your seat position. If the horse were to move forward, it would take you a step or two to catch up and you would risk bumping the mouth with your reins accidentally signaling to slow the feet down. You would, in essence, be riding with the gas pedal accelerating while holding the hand brake.

The leg slap is exactly what it says. You are literally slapping the horse's sides with both calves. You are now moving onto the higher phase of cue. The leg slap is a promise to the horse to move or else. Use both calves. Take them away from the horse's sides while you keep your thighs in contact with the saddle. You do not want to lose your contact area with your seat and your thighs. Your legs will swing and hit the horse's sides like a pendulum. Immediately, after the two bumps take both calves away and add both legs so you can hear the slap along the horse's sides. Remember you only get one shot so make it count. This is not an aid you keep repeating one after the other. One good one and then it's on to phase four.

Keep your upper body still as you use your legs. Often riders will push with the seat or use their upper body. Only involve your legs. Do not lean back. You need to be balanced so if the horse does jump forward and move the feet quickly you will be balanced and ready to go with the horse.

Phase Four: The dressage whip

I like to use a dressage whip instead of spurs at this point because spurs have a tendency to get overused. I have a rule for my riders that no one gets spurs until they can show me that they can walk, trot, canter and never touch the horse's sides with the lower calf. If they can demonstrate a solid, still lower leg then they can graduate to spurs. But, technically, spurs are to enhance a movement not disrupt a movement.

Using the dressage whip means that you have reached the end of the phases. The horse has ignored all your previous suggestions to move forward and now you are going to have to reinforce the behavior you are looking for. Use the dressage whip on the hip and begin your series of tapping until you feel the horse want to surge forward. Immediately stop tapping once you feel the weight shift forward.

Discontinue the use of the whip once the horse is responsive to leg cues. If you come across a day when the horse is lazy and unresponsive, pick up the dressage whip and be ready for action. It does you no good to allow your horse to ignore the cue. You will end up in a battle. Always be able to follow through with your requests. This will lead to an understanding between horse and rider to be compliant to the very light leg cue 100% of the time.

Important notes to remember when going through your phases

★ Always go back to the lightest cue of phase one each time you have to ask for a step. Even if your horse walks forward only for a step or two you must release the pressure of both calves and let the horse walk out on cruise control. This will teach your horse to be trusting of your leg aids. When you perform a little retest of the lightest aid the horse will begin to understand that the leg along the barrel means go forward. Once they move all four feet forward they will be given a reward and a release of the pressure for a few steps until asked for something different.

★ Do not hold the reins and try to collect the horse or put it into a frame. You are only teaching one thing-move forward. The reins stay loose with an elastic feel. Do not try to control the speed right away.

★ Make sure you are in a safe environment to begin asking. Do not go to an open field and practice this exercise. A fenced in area works best for the training portion of this session until your horse learns to move forward willingly.

> *Each time your horse stops after you have added the leg cue and are practicing cruise control, think of it as a training opportunity. You can now go through your phase of leg cues again, and confirm the phases.*

Anytime you are adding a cue or signal to obtain a reaction out of your horse and you are in the training phase you can expect that the horse's body will react with an even or opposite push back against your cue. The horse's body may stiffen. This may cause a small reaction. Keep in mind as you practice with your horse that you are going to teach the horse to respond to the lightest of cues, gradually returning to a phase of feather light signals. The horse's response will become much quicker and much more pleasant.

Obtaining the desired speed at each gait

You have now worked extensively at asking the horse to move forward in response to both legs adding pressure. By now, you should be able to add the lightest squeeze possible and the horse will move forward energetically within one step of asking with the aid. Now it's time to ask for a change of leg speed.

When you are looking to move into a different gait you will ask the horse to move with the same sequence of cues that you used to ask the horse to move forward. The most important note to remember is that you are looking for a *noticeable* change of speed. You are not looking for the horse to necessarily transition to the next gait. When both legs add pressure, the horse must respond by marching forward with a "happy walk", not a sullen, "sad walk". The horse is not out for a Sunday afternoon stroll. A be-bopping walk so the rider can feel the swing of the horse's back through the seat is what is desired.

The leg of the rider will match the feel of electricity to the horse. It will shock the horse to move forward. You want that sudden surge of power that comes from the horse's hind end where the engine lies. You want to start it up and give a it a rev...VROOM VROOM. Both of your legs act as the accelerator. Maximize the forward. Keep your horse ready for action.

Once this is mastered at the walk, then move into the trot. Practice adjusting the speed of the horse's feet. Ask for the legs to speed up and move faster. At first, the horse may idle out, or in a sense, stall like a car that has no power in the engine. The feet will slow down and become lazy and flat. The horse must learn that it is up to them to hold the speed until asked for something different. We must remind the horse to start the engine. Each time it stalls out, we must start it up again. That way the horse will learn to leave it idling.

Using one leg at a time

Once the horse learns to move off of two legs, then teach the horse how to move off of one leg independently. It is important to teach the horse to lift the barrel and ribcage when working on turns or changes of direction, or else your horse will fall into the circle and drop down with the shoulder. This will feel as though you are riding a motorcycle and the feet of the horse will suddenly speed up instead of keeping a rhythmic tempo as you turn. The horse's front feet represent stilts. Those stilts must stay upright at all times or they will topple over and fall to the left or right, forward or back. The horse must learn to lift through the chest and bend the knees instead of kicking the stones with the front feet as if they are shuffling along.

The sequence of one leg will follow the same protocol as two legs. Remember that the horse will move away from pressure, but if you hold the pressure for a prolonged period of time, the horse will lean against that pressure and you will have the opposite effect. The rider must think of shattering any resistance offered from the horse. In simpler terms, adding a series of small gentle bumping motions will gain a bigger response from the horse. They will move away from that pressure quicker than from a constant heavy pushing pressure from your calf. Never add so much pressure that you begin to lose your balance. As we explore further pieces of the body you will learn that the seat and upper body balance play a key role in affecting your leg cues.

Opening and closing the door

When giving a leg cue to teach the horse to move away from pressure, the leg that you are adding will move the horse in the opposite direction. This means that the leg used against the horse's side is closing the door on the horse's movement so to speak. The opposite leg must open the door so the horse has somewhere to move. For example, if the rider is wishing to turn to the left, the left leg will open slightly away from the horse's ribcage. It is drawing the horse in that direction like a magnet would pull something to it. The right leg will move against the horse's side to signal to the horse to move the ribcage away from the pressure. If you are turning to the right, then your right leg would pull like a magnetic force and open the door while the left leg would signal to the horse to move in the desired direction.

Phases of pressure: Fur, skin, muscle, bone

A good rule of thumb is to think of adding pressure in increments such as this: The first phase of pressure is enough to touch the horse's fur. Its feather light pressure, as if a fly landed on the horse's skin and the horse is reacting by shaking slightly to remove it. The next phase of pressure would be as though you're touching the horse's skin. This would be the same as taking your index finger and gently poking the horse in the side just long enough to count to one. The third phase of pressure is to add enough pressure to feel the muscle of the horse. This is not necessarily hard; it is the different use of your muscles in a steadier, stable fashion. It's like a sweeping motion so you are getting down and around the horse to feel them glide to the side. The fourth phase is not attainable in reality, but if you think of pushing through bone you will increase the intensity without sacrificing your own body position. That is always the key factor. If you are losing your own stability, then you are asking with too much intensity. You should never unseat yourself or sacrifice your own riding position. This will put you in a position that is not helpful for the horse's training and also not safe for you as a rider. At this point in the training you will need an artificial aid such as a dressage whip to touch the horse on the rump so the legs of the rider are not exhausted or ignored.

Always remember when you are asking for a signal or cue to happen, you must be ready for the reaction of the horse. If you ask with the appropriate pressure for the situation that you are currently in and cannot keep up with the action that follows, then you had no business asking with that much intensity in the first place. I will go out on a limb and say I have no respect for riders or trainers who ask for too much too soon. If they are not ready with their body and balance, then the horse is not ready either. Seek the help of someone who can help you attain your desired response and hold their body position so they can adjust with the horse and the behavior that follows.

Frictional contact

Frictional contact is a phrase I use to help my students understand how to gently keep a light contact with the horse's sides. I also refer to it as a "breathable leg." As your horse travels you will feel the ribcage shift from side to side or one of the four feet moving beneath you. You must learn to keep a slight hold with the barrel but not interfere with the natural movement of the horse. Once you master this feeling, you will be able to move to higher levels of riding so you can influence the movement of the horse.

This is true with english riding and jumping since it requires a light hold with the lower part of the calf. If you were wearing tall riding boots or half chaps, the top section of the inside of the leg should have more wear than any other section. This is because this section of the lower leg is used for stability in the jumping effort and also to encourage a horse to open the stride or move forward at a moment's notice when searching for a distance to jump comfortably. It is also very important for higher level work when asking for collection and frame. The rider will ask the horse to lift the midsection in order to raise the back while keeping it pliable and loose. You can see why it is so important to know what parts of your body you have control of and what they are used for as you dive deeper into your riding career. Every aid used should have a purpose.

Puzzle Piece #4
Thigh

Imagery Essentials

The Contact Area

Checklist for Proper Alignment of the Thigh

- ✓ The thigh resembles a baseball bat.
- ✓ Sit in an imaginary chair to tone the thigh for light seat.
- ✓ Tighten the puppet string.
- ✓ Stop the bounce of the trampoline beneath the feet.
- ✓ Kneel in the sling with both knees.
- ✓ Ballet Plie' stance in order to open the upper portion of the thigh.
- ✓ Hold a pillow beneath each thigh softly, keeping it fluffy.
- ✓ Smear the ink spots evenly from the upper portion to the lower portion of both inside sections of the thighs.
- ✓ Imagine a horse stance from martial arts, and hold that position.
- ✓ Rubber band stretch.
- ✓ Spiral in the thigh from the top portion.
- ✓ Knees should be kneeling into the water bucket.
- ✓ Thighs shall remain in the middle of the horse.
- ✓ Wear an imaginary seat belt across the hips.

The Thigh

The thighs become the contact area, and also the way for the rider to support the upper body along with helping to stabilize the lower body. (This is the area between the pelvis and the knee.) Strong thigh muscles are important for balance and movement.

The thigh is comprised of the quadriceps muscle that lines the front of the thigh, and the hamstring muscle that lines the back of the thigh. It also houses the abductor muscles, which line the outside of the thigh, and adductor muscles, which are along the inside of the thigh. These are the prime movers and they extend and flex the leg, and also take the leg away from the midline of the horse, or the body, and bring it back toward the body. There are also rotating muscles that connect at the pelvis, which are responsible for rotation left and right.

As riders progress they learn how to encourage the horse to use their back muscles so the horse can connect the ribcage to the shoulders and hips. This is quite different from allowing the back of the horse to remain stiff and rigid. The thighs become a wonderful tool as you progress. They will support the body weight of the rider, as a horse in early stages of training begins to lift the back up, and strengthen those muscles in order to carry themselves, and to carry the weight of the rider.

Parts of the thigh

To take a more in depth look-divide the thigh into three parts upper, middle and lower. The upper part of the thigh is the section that connects to the pelvis and goes a distance of about 6 inches until it meets the middle section of the thigh. This section of the thigh is responsible for staying at high tone, and holding the weight of the rider off of the horses back.

The mid-section has the most muscle mass. It is often in the way of the rider and the inner thigh muscle which is known as the gracillis muscle, can be rotated to the back so the inner thigh lies flat and forms more of a triangular shape, rather than a round cylindrical shape.

The lower section stretches from the mid-section to the inside of the knee. This part of the thigh is often misused, because riders allow this section to rise, or crawl up the saddle. The knees will pinch as a last ditch effort to hold the body weight, and support the rest of the leg. The fix is to elongate the entire thigh, and allow the thigh to essentially drop away from the pelvis, and the hip joint.

Your end goal is to position the thigh so the kneecap is pointing down, and a natural contact from the top of your pelvis to the surface area directly above your knee is evolving. This will allow the hip to open bringing a whole new realm to riding. As the thigh elongates, it is important to keep the thigh as a whole positioned in front of the hip. Otherwise, too much weight will fall onto the middle of the horse's back, and this could cause the horse to hollow out the back muscles, causing tension and making it difficult for the horse to lift it back and use it properly under the rider's weight.

Riding Realities

Common errors and enigmas

The thigh plays a huge role in stability. It is also the steering wheel and the support system for the rest of your body weight. Once the thigh has made contact it becomes like a magnet to draw you closer to the horse and also to pull the horse's back out and away to remain under the weight of the rider. Stirrup length is a link to how well a rider can use the thigh to effectively support the weight of their body. Stirrups that are too short will result in the thigh peeling away from the saddle too much. A stirrup that is too long will create air pockets or gaps toward the upper section of the thigh. This may cause a loss in balance, resulting in the rider tilting forward to compensate. It is essential to get the right blend of holding pressure throughout the thighs to become symmetrical.

Familiar Faults

Fault 1

The "rolling pin thigh" is a common fault. When the rider rolls onto the back of the thigh they lose contact with the supporting section of the body. This will cause the knee to disconnect and raise upward, forcing the calves to squeeze through the horse's body instead of laying lightly against it. The rider will then fall toward the loins of the horse and bear too much weight on their seat.

Think of the rolling pin rolling forward along the horse's ribcage so the front of the thigh is making more contact than the back of the thigh. That allows for the rider to keep a consistent contact. The back section of the rider's hamstrings should remain visible as the rider makes contact. If the hamstrings are beginning to disappear then the rider has begun to open the thigh and lose contact with the inner section of all three parts.

The thigh is rotated outward and the foot has an excessive angle away from the horse's belly. Tara's belt buckle is no longer level as she has rolled onto her pockets and is sitting heavily in the saddle with her seat bones now.

Fault 2

The "locked thigh", or gripping thigh, acts like a clothespin. It will lift the rider's seat and pop the rider up and out of the saddle. Extensive leg grip instead of tone and alignment is over-riding the motion. Allow the thigh to maintain an even, steady contact through the three portions of the thigh.

Remain in a frictional contact with the horse's back. The thigh should extend down along the horse's sides as much as possible. The longer the better. The rider can then peel the seat away and move into a light seat, with weight distributed through the whole leg.

Fault 3

Often a rider will allow the thighs to rise up. In some instances it may be extreme. If a tabletop could rest atop your two thighs and stay balanced and upright, then your thighs are too high. Think of dropping the table top to the ground and allowing it to slide down each thigh so it would drop to the ground behind the horse's front feet. Another helpful tip is to think of a laser beam light that is radiating out of each kneecap. Keep the light pointing forward similar to the smiley face imagery, but also in a downward direction. The angle should aim behind the horse's front feet. This will keep the thighs in contact with the horse, the hip joints open, and the knees coming back with the softball. You will be able to make contact with a larger area of the horse's sides to become more effective with forward movement, steering, and stable contact.

> *Adductor muscles are responsible for moving towards the body. Abductor muscles will pull away from the body.*

Fault 4

The "vice grip" lower leg stems from the clench and squeeze with the lower leg. This will have a similar effect as the thigh rising. In some instances you will need added support from the lower leg. The key is the support to hold the rider's body weight should not only come from the lower leg. The hips will always open varying degrees, and move along with the horse's movement.

Picture Perfect Pieces SOLUTION

Now envision your picture perfect pieces for the improved ride

Imagery examination:

The support system of the three parts of the thigh

Further Explanation

The thighs do not just move the legs. They have a big responsibility with how the hips move. The hip joints are of big importance. The thigh must not lock into the hip joint. The thighs allow the upper and lower extremities to function and communicate with the horse. In essence the thighs become a steering wheel for higher level work. It is one of the only pieces of the body that will remain in a fixed position, and bear most of the weight of the rider.

Up to 80% of weight is distributed through the thigh. Pay careful attention to detail with each section so all three parts of the thigh can perform as one. They are also the key part of the body to control the speed of the horse's feet. Using the thighs will elevate the rider slightly to keep the seat above the hollow that the horse creates with the back muscles. With careful coordination, and strength, the rider can control the muscles along the horses back, and help the horse to travel with the muscles at high tone so it can support it's own weight. Once this takes place the rider can gradually add more weight to the horse's back. The horse will then be able to carry and support the rider. This opens up a whole new world to riding, and the beginning stages of collection.

Before we begin to dissect the thigh and figure out how to properly weight the thigh and use it effectively, it is important to know which part of the thigh is needed to make contact with the saddle. The muscle that lies along the inside of the thigh is the gracillis muscle, but more importantly it is known as an adductor muscle. These are the muscles that bring the leg toward the body.

The rider must reach underneath the hamstring muscles located at the back of the thigh to grab the inner thigh muscle. By pulling the entire mass of the muscle to the outside you are repositioning the thigh to the spot of most effective use while riding. I sometimes refer to this as taking the fleshy part of your inner thigh, and moving it to the back. The inner seam of the pants will make direct contact with the saddle. This is the section of the inner thigh that can now take over and reposition for maximum benefits.

Four major muscle groups of the thigh

The thigh is a complex mechanisim, and a huge piece to riding. It must bear enough weight so the rider can support the body. The thigh is often what helps the rider to dig their way out of the hollow or hole a horse creates with the back muscles until they are strong enough to withstand the weight of the rider's seat and gluteus maximus muscles, otherwise known as the rider's behind. It is important for a rider to get control and learn how to fire or trigger each muscle of the thigh. I use the clock to represent which section of the thigh we are referring to.

Twelve o'clock on your thigh is the quadraceps muscle, it is responsible for flexing the thigh at the hip joint. In daily life you activate that muscle when you lift the leg to walk up stairs. At six o'clock, which would be the back of the thigh, is the hamstring muscle. This is the weakest part of the thigh and it opposes the movement of the quads. Hamstrings are used to stop any forward motion with the legs. They also flex the knee and bring the heel toward the thigh. This is a very important movement for riders. At nine o'clock on the right leg and three o'clock on the left leg we have the inner thigh muscles which are the adductor muscles. They are the section of the thigh which is in contact with the horse the most. They also oppose the abductor muscles which are on the right side located at three o'clock and on the left leg located at nine o'clock. These muscles are responsible for moving the leg away from the horse's sides. This is important when giving a leg aid or when the rider needs to give the horse room to move the ribcage toward the direction that the thigh is pulling away from. Think of it like a magnet. All four sections of the thigh do their fair share to ensure the body is correctly balanced and aligned. Let's investigate each piece.

Quadraceps: the 12:00 muscle

The quads affect how the hip angle opens and closes. The hip is a major shock absorber for riding, and the hip angle needs to remain open. It is like a door hinge. If it closes all the way the rider will be at risk of falling forward. If the hinge is too open, the rider will fall backward. The quads hold that angle to a functioning degree so the rider can maximize the use of the thigh. The quads are a big part of your two point and jumping position. It is not the lower leg that holds a rider back from a jump when a horse is slowing down and is debating a refusal. The thigh bone, otherwise known as the femur(the largest bone in the body) must take control, and hold the rider securely in place.

Essential Details of each Imagery

The baseball bat

The femur of the thigh is substantial in size. The muscles surrounding the femur must help support the thigh from floating upward, so to speak. If any lift happens in the thigh, then the hip angle will close too much. It is important to keep the strength in the thigh along the quadriceps at high tone. A baseball bat is a wonderful image to keep the rider's mind believing the high tone that will need to happen in order to hold that quad in place during the ride. The handle of the bat is placed near the hip joint at the very top of the thigh, while the rest of the front of the thigh is the bat. As the bat drops down it gets wider is circumference, and also more stable. The end of the bat is the kneecap.

The rider must aim to point the thickest part of the bat, the tip, toward the ground at all times. In a sense the bat must try to touch the ground and rest softly there as if it were a kickstand or something to lean on. When the bat begins to lift, the rider loses stability. If we placed that bat in a pool of water it would begin to float to the surface. This is what happens to a rider as they begin to trot or canter. The stability begins to float upward. The rider must keep pushing against the resistance of the imaginary water to keep the bat down in position. If we think further, we can also use the bat scenario to think of how a ball player swings the bat to hit a ball. If we were pitching a ball through the horse's belly and it would pass through to meet the bat, the rider must aim to hit the ball and send it back through the belly to the other side of the horse, back to the pitcher's mitt.

This will help with the hold of the quadriceps. A firm secure touch inward, but also a firm secure push backward as well. It must push down, but also remain parallel to the horse's sides.

Sit on the imaginary chair

The quads are involved in all types of squats. One exercise that engages the quads the most is sitting down on a chair-but not so fast. Just simply sitting in the saddle puts the quads at rest. A two point position or a light seat involves the quadriceps muscles in a stronger way because they must remain at high tone, and work isometrically to keep the contact area, which are the thighs and seat, from making contact with the saddle.

The imaginary chair is a great exercise to hold the quad muscles and build muscle strength. This is also dubbed the"pain exercise". This is, ultimately, what give riders the correct posting trot mechanism to hold that tone so the legs do not swing in each rise and sit.

The weight in the stirrups is very light and the thighs will bear most of that weight to support the body. If there is a chair beneath the rider's seat instead of the horse's back, the rider will slowly (inch by inch) lower their center of gravity and close the knee angle. The hip joint and knee joint will feel like old rusty hinges that are going to break if the rider moves at a snail's pace to keep the angles set and steady. As the seat lowers, and just before it is ready to make contact with the chair, stop. This is your light seat. I often refer to this as the" roosting seat". If someone placed an egg beneath the rider's buttocks and the saddle, the rider would roost on the egg. The egg cannot roll away, and the weight of the rider can certainly never be too much to break that egg. You must sit quietly, and 'hover' atop the chair and the egg.

To make the quads stronger, add in a magnetic force that feels as though it will swallow you up if you lose the tone in your thigh. It is constantly trying to draw you in and pull you down, but hold your ground and keep the hover above the egg and seat. This will keep you at high tone which you can turn up and down when the situation arises for more power from the quads.

Hamstrings: The 6:00 muscle

Directly behind the quads is the home of the hamstrings. The hamstrings primary function is to aid in knee flexion-which is bringing the heel toward the buttocks and hip extension, which is moving the leg to the rear or behind the hip joint. This muscle is very overlooked with riding, and needs to be used in conjunction with the quads to balance the hold generated to keep the riders leg still and in place. Only this will take away any unwanted movement as it pertains to the rider's leg swinging forward or backward as the horse moves the body in a specific gait.

If, at any moment the rider's hip rises, the buttocks will take over and try to compensate. It is important to keep the hips down and the lower back heavy. This will isolate the hamstrings, and help the rider to keep the seat from floating up and away from the horse's back when trying to reposition the thigh or lower leg.

Essential Details of each Imagery

Tighten the puppet string

The hamstring is a thick, cord-like muscle located at the back of the thigh. For most riders this muscle will not be very dominant. The action of drawing the whole leg backward is a tough task to master. Combine that with the pushing power of the horse's body and it's a big thrust forward that the hamstrings must hold off in order to keep the leg in place. When the horse moves forward, the primary power source stems from the hips and hind legs. That movement will rock the rider's body forward and back with each step the horse takes.

The hamstring runs along the back of your thigh, from your pelvis to your lower leg. There are three hamstrings that all help to bend the knee and extend the hip joint. They will enable the rider to move the thigh back toward the buttocks. Imagine the hamstring was replaced with a string, like the string of a puppet. You are the puppet master who holds that string and decides how much tension is needed in order to lift the leg, pull it back, or to bend the knee. That slight bit of tension is what is needed to hold the hamstring in the proper place.

Once this string is drawn up tight, the rider must not cut the cord. If someone were to take a pair of scissors and cut that cord in half, the leg would drop down, become straight and swing forward. This is the opposite effect of what we are looking for with the rider's leg position. The heel of the rider must not stretch the cord forward and risk snapping. There must be a constant hold with the hamstring to allow for the legs to be still and steady, and keep the rider from adding too much pressure in the stirrups.

On the contrary, if the rider feels as though they are losing the stirrups, the feet begin to move about too much and do not stay on the platform of the stirrup. Then, the rider must think of letting some tension out of the string or cord. There is a happy medium with the hamstring muscle that every rider must find. Experiment until you feel the correct amount of tension that works for you.

Stop the trampoline

There are not many sports or other athletic activities that are comparable to riding. It is difficult to practice any exercises 'off horse' that will help the rider to simulate what will happen on the horse. A trampoline is similar to the bounce and the push upward and drop downward that will happen from time to time upon the horse. It is especially useful to use the thighs and legs in order to think of stopping the motion of the trampoline bounce all together.

With riding, the thighs and legs have a tremendous job. The rider must assemble the muscles in accordance to what the horse is doing. A trampoline with one person on it creates the feeling of what happens when the horse is in motion. Gently bounce on the trampoline while keeping your feet firmly planted on the trampoline surface. This feeling of sticking with the hamstrings while keeping a bend in the knee will help to reinforce how to keep the body still on a moving object. If you were to add in the mix of someone else bouncing on the trampoline while you are still on it, your feet would eventually leave the trampoline surface, and you would be fighting against gravity to hold yourself in place, or to get your feet back on the trampoline's surface.

The knees of the rider must remain softly bent. The joints are free to move about and accept the small moments of buoyancy and bounce that are generated from below the feet. The seat or buttocks may need to sink down a bit as the upper body remains above the center of gravity.

In moments when the rider feels as though the seat has peeled away, or the joints are fighting against the body and they begin to bounce about or lose the softness, then the rider must think again of the trampoline, and what it would feel like to create a gentle bob upon the trampoline. Ultimately controlling the bounce will secure the rider's position, and help the rider use their legs and thighs effectively, especially, the hamstrings.

The position of the quads and the hamstrings

The heavy feeling that must sink into the thigh is a tough concept. Most riders will spend an eternity just trying to situate the feet and getting just the right mixture of what will suffice in order to get the leg to become responsible for some of the weight. The secret really lies in the thighs. The muscles of the front and back of the thigh must work together in order to hold the position. It is then that the addition of the inner and outer thigh may be added into the equation to provide proper hold against the saddle.

Essential Details of each Imagery

Kneel in a sling

When a rider is positioned upon the horse's back, where are they bearing most of their weight? Most will sit too far forward and bear too much weight on the horse's forehand. They also tend to clench with their thighs similar to a clothespin, behind the horse's shoulders. This causes the thigh to ride upward and a vicious cycle begins. To break this cycle the rider needs to open the hinge of the hip to create a new feeling in their body, one which is similar to falling to their knees. The stability that follows, especially for those who jump, will be monumental once the thighs have settled into the middle of the horse's back. The following exercise is designed to help the rider experience this.

If the horse had a giant piece of material that resembles a sheet tied around them and beneath its belly, this would be the rider's knee sling. Imagine that the sheet was open like a hammock. The knee sling is used for immobilizing the thigh, the same concept as a sling used to keep a broken arm or shoulder of a person from moving about. The sling is there to allow the rider to drop weight into the center of the horse's body, and allow the weight of the thigh to fall into the material so the kneecap is pointing toward the ground.

This is foreign to most riders as they feel at this point in time they are leaning way too far forward. The reality of the feeling that is generated is that the rider will learn to open the hip joint and balance the weight of the upper body through the thighs. This is the contact that is necessary to draw a horse's back up, so it can use its back muscles in the most effective way. Once the feeling of heaviness is generated though the thighs the first few times, the rider will learn how to harness the weight and distribute it in different sections according to what is needed.

In order to feel the amount of pressure needed and the muscle strength that needs to be generated in order to hold the quadricep muscles and the hamstring muscles in place, the rider can experiment with the following exercise: Sit in the saddle with the horse at a standstill. Reach down with your hand and bend your knee so you are able to hold onto your ankle. Point your kneecap toward the ground as much as possible and push the weight of the thigh into the hand that is holding the ankle. You will feel a tightening sensation through the ankle joint and throughout your leg. This is the stabilization that needs to take place in order to hold the leg in position while riding.

The Adductor Muscles

Right thigh 9:00 Left thigh 3:00

When speaking of the adductor muscles the rider must think of the muscles that are along the *inner* thigh the adductor muscles move the thighs towards the center part of the body. These muscles run from the bottom of the rider's pelvis to the upper rear surface of the thigh bone. When the rider contracts these muscles it brings the thigh inward toward the midline.

To help you find the adductor muscle, sit with your ankle crossed over your knee and imagine a line that divides the inside surface of your thigh in half length wise. You will feel your adductor muscle near the upper end of this line. If you raise your knee slightly toward your face while feeling your inner thigh, these muscles will stand out. It is these adductor muscles that will make contact with the horse's back, and eventually become strong enough to be the kickstands that will hold you out of the sand trap that is formed by the horse's long back muscles.

Tara is holding her ankle as she positions her knee toward the ground. Be careful not to hollow the back, or tilt forward onto the pelvis. Keep a neutral spine

Essential Details of each Imagery

Ballet plié

Each rider is shaped differently. For many, the angle at which the toe turns in or out when walking in everyday life will affect how the legs and feet lie against the horse's sides or rest in the stirrups when riding. The end result is a far cry from the beginning stages of how we choose form over function to distribute weight evenly and comfortably under saddle.

The ballet "Plié" is a movement in which the knees remain bent, and the back is held straight. For a dancer, it is a position used in jumps and turns to provide spring and absorb shock, and as an exercise to loosen muscles and develop balance. The rider can use this to their advantage as an equestrian by thinking of its foundation for similar attributes to help with stability and balance.

Use the vision of the dancer to involve your inner thighs and the motion on the horse. The thighs must be in good position to absorb shock which is the same for a dancer when performing leaps and turns as they land.

The word Plié means bent, and the word demi means half. When performing a demi plié, the dancer will bend the knees as far as possible without lifting the heels off the ground. The feet are turned out to the point where they are comfortable, and centered beneath the knee. For the rider this would be similar to rotating the thigh outward and positioning the foot at an angle in the stirrup while retaining the feeling of keeping your feet planted on the ground. When the full capacity of bend has been reached, the dancer will begin to unbend the knee, moving back to the starting position with the feet still planted on the ground and the back straight. A rider would bring the feet to the forward position of 12:00 with the thighs and knees facing forward once again.

If the rider were to think of executing this movement, but freezing in the midst of the upward knee bend, this is similar to the position used when riding at all times. The rider does not fully straighten the knees, and the thigh and foot will not remain in an outward rotation, but the feel of the inner thigh against the saddle will be similar to a dancer. The slight bend will remain, and the adductors will be in position to support the rider. This is done with the toes facing forward, and the adductors rotated inward.

If the rider were to hold a 20 lb dumbbell in their hands, and allow it to drop down between the legs so it is even with the ankles this would be the position of the upper body. The rider must be careful, however, not to bend at the waist. Keep the back straight and allow each rib to stick together and become shorter while holding the abdominals tight.

It is a deep knee bend that is required for the adductors to do their job. This is often overlooked with riding because of the burning sensation that can be associated with holding these muscles at high tone. As you strengthen them, it will become easier to hold the legs in position.

It is useful to practice this movement 'off horse' to gain the feeling needed when riding.

Test your adductor strength by making a fist and pushing it against the pommel of the saddle. You will feel the adductor take full hold and the intensity is sometimes overwhelming to riders who have not discovered this muscle. If you are making a fist with your left hand, place it against your left side of the pommel and push inward as though you are going to punch through the saddle. You will feel the right inner thigh muscle take hold. Switch sides and do this on the opposing side. When you feel like you need strength just stop what you are doing on your horse and remind yourself of this technique to teach your adductors to engage.

Hold the pillow

When referring to the rider's inner thigh, there is always a struggle to explain how much contact, pressure, and feel, must remain against the horse's sides. Riders who are used to gripping with the knee find this concept a challenge because they need to undo patterns within the muscles that have been ingrained. It takes a tremendous amount of concentration at first to feel with the inner thigh. It is almost like a blind feel. You will become acquainted with different levels of hold or contact within different maneuvers on your horse. It is also slightly different depending on the shape of the horse's back and ribcage. A narrow horse is sometimes harder to gain a feel than a wider horse that is wide through the ribcage. The level which the back is hollowed or lifted also plays a role in the feel that you gain with your inner thigh.

Tara is pushing against the pommel in order to activate her adductor muscle.

The key is to find the balance point in the middle of the horse's back and to teach your thighs to hold you out of the trap until you can gently add more and more weight or contact onto the two long back muscles that line the spine of the horse.

The rider needs to think of a fluffy pillow that is full of feathers. This pillow is placed between the thigh and the horse and runs the length of the inner thigh area from the top of the groin all the way to just above the knee. If the rider only squeezes this pillow at the space between the knees, then the pillow will wobble about at the top of the thigh causing it to shift back and forth, or even to fall out from between the legs entirely. The pillow must have contact from the top of the thigh to above the knee. This will place the weight evenly, and you will have a fighting chance of allowing the horse to expand the ribcage and ready the back to be lifted in moments of correct frame and posture for the horse.

I often tell riders to think of the horse's back as a giant ball. This ball is the width and height of the horse's midsection. The rider must balance upon this ball with both feet in a spot that would place them on the ground. The torso and pelvis remain in a region where you would not lose stability if the ball were to roll forward or backward. It is here that you find the ultimate balance point.

On a horse that is moving this task seems monumental because of the constant weight shifts in all directions. The rider must learn to easily counteract those movements while keeping a steady balance that is centered over the horse's center. Believe it or not, this has a lot to do with the grip of the thighs. A professional rider will describe this as a relaxation through these parts. In all honesty it feels that way to them, but in reality they have a high tone that is constantly counteracting the horse's pushes and pulls to try to move them in a different direction. When your muscles are strong there is a relaxation that will follow, and it will feel as if you are virtually doing nothing.

You can also think of a gel pad or a magnetic force that pulls you inward.

Smear the ink and paint evenly

The rider must learn to use the whole thigh effectively. This can become confusing in the learning stages. If the rider thinks of the thigh split in three sections: top, middle and lower, they can become aware of the contact and feel that has developed. In english disciplines, the contact is very important, especially for jumping. The contact of the inner thigh must remain like the consistency of honey-sticky and tacky but moveable if need be. The forces of the other muscle groups, if all correctly doing their job, will help to hold the thigh. If the rider were to try to squeeze inward and hold that contraction to stay on the horse, it actually has the opposite effect because the body will stiffen other joints, and the rider will become easier to dismiss if the horse decides to become a tyrant.

Let's now imagine black ink. Take that black ink, and form a line of adjoining dots down the inseam of your pants on the right side. On the left side, from the top of your thigh all the way down to right above where your knee starts. If the rider were on the horse these dots should all make contact simultaneously, and begin to smear along the inseam of both pant legs as you apply your thighs to the saddle. Each thigh will have a pattern as to how it will smear those ink spots.

As the rider, you must determine what that pattern is, and begin to fix each section of the thigh that does not have an evenly smeared ink spot. Would it be even on both thighs? Or would you have one side that was very smeared, and the other side not so much? Would you have blank spots at the top of your thigh, and then as you went down the leg would the ink smear more, or vice versa?

Think about how you are sitting and applying pressure with your thighs. This can tell you a lot about what you are doing with each thigh while you are riding. Ideally, you should have an even smear of ink from the top of your thigh down to where your knee begins. This will enable you to keep adequate weight for balance and connection of the upper body with the lower section of the body.

The rider can also think of spraying bright pink paint down the inseam of each pant leg. This pink paint leaves its mark, and if you were to dismount, what would be the pattern that was left on the saddle? Compare each side and determine what your pattern is for riding. I will give you a small hint; no rider will have the same pattern on the first shot. It can fluctuate from horse to horse. This is your gauge to see how well you can suction to your horse's sides with each thigh. This will play a huge role in turning, making round circles, or later with lateral work. A leaky thigh is an escape route for your horse's ribcage, and some horses choose to take huge advantage of that opening.

Think of an Olympic dressage rider. Their thighs are beautifully immovable with tacky, yet tactile feel.

The Abductor Muscles

Right thigh 3:00 Left thigh 9:00

The abductor muscles are the muscles that run along the *outer* portion of the thighs from the top of the hip joint to the outer section of the knee. These muscles move the legs away from the midline of the body. This occurs during any athletic movement requiring you to move side to side. This is true with sports such as football and ice skating which we can draw inspiration from.

It is a huge asset to learn how to control the abductor, especially for turns, or when the rider needs to, literally, hang the butt in the air so to speak and stay off the horse's back. This is true with half seat or light seat in english disciplines, but is also used for training young horses. They need the rider to hover over the back until the back is strong enough to lift the rider and hold them.

Essential Details of each Imagery

Horse stance

In martial arts there is a basic stance called "the horse stance". In the old days of learning Kung Fu, students were made to stand in a horse stance for increasingly longer period of time before they were taught anything else. It was used as a way to show that the student was serious. It also was used to build leg strength. It makes you realize why horseback riding is claimed to be tough as you reach higher levels. It may have something to do with the difficulty of having to hold the horse stance for a prolonged period of time. Only strong riders who can withstand the challenge rise to the top of their game. That is true for martial arts as well.

In this stance, the feet are usually 1 ½ to twice shoulder width apart with the knees bent. You should not allow the knees to extend beyond the toes. The tops of the thighs should not be lower than the knees, and the feet should aim to point forwards towards twelve o'clock.

A rider may find themselves in a similar stance with slight variations in balance stemming from this position. Use this stance to improve riding position. Think of sitting on your horse, straddling its back. The legs are in this wide stance and you must think of keeping the legs in this position, but sliding them toward the midline of your body until your entire leg makes contact with the horse's sides. This is a great demonstration of the abductors working, pulling the thighs in toward the horse's sides.

Keep the knees from rolling over your feet as you slightly slide your legs closer. Pretend that there is a huge force that is pulling your legs through a thick substance such as thick mud or heavy rushing water. When you make contact with the horse's sides, you must hold your leg steady so the current of the heavy water rushing beneath you does not pull your leg in any other direction. This is a glimpse of abductors at work. It is a hold against imaginary resistance. The opposing muscle groups will need to work together to hold the strength and keep the body stable.

Isometric exercise produces faster gains in strength than traditional moving exercises such as squats or lunges. Isometric exercises will target one muscle group against another muscle group so the muscles can contract without shortening.

Rubber band stretch

The area of the thigh that is hardest to get to in order to have it firmly placed in position and ready to do the job of holding is the top of the inner thigh, (directly below the pubic bone area). While the inner thigh needs to remain in contact, the outer thigh is what helps that section have the correct amount of feel and hold.

A gymnast on the balance beam creates a good visual for the exact location of the muscle that needs to be focused on while riding. When gymnasts perform on the beam, they are required to do certain work where they are touching the beam. Some gymnasts straddle the balance beam before they do a handstand or another fancy move to stand up. The moment *we* are concerned with is the second that they have the beam between both legs, when the area of the inner thigh is making contact.

The reason we are thinking of a balance beam is because it is narrow enough to target the muscle group we need to focus on, and it is 4 inches wide. In some cases, we must shrink the inner thigh to help with the lifting process of the horse's back. The section of the inner thigh that is making contact with the balance beam is going to be harnessed with a thick piece of thera band. This stretchy elastic is what the rider must think of while riding. The band will stretch apart and the thighs will do their part to hold the band open while riding. As crazy as it sounds the more you can pull that band apart and hold it in that position, the more you will be able to bring the horse's back up. The muscles that will also be targeted are the hip flexors and the buttocks. It will feel as though the top section of the thigh and the hips widened. This is a key factor in learning how to harness the hips and the glutes to help with later work.

The band can also be useful to think of when making a turn. If you are going to turn to the left stretch the band by opening the right side and making the space wider. If you are turning right it would be opposite and the left side of the band would stretch slightly further outward. These are little tricks to help with the body position and the strength needed to harness your inner power to guide the horse.

Further Study: The position of the thighs

To keep the position of the thighs correct the rider must think of the following:

Clockwise and counter-clockwise thighs

The rotation of the thigh inward or outward will also depend on the horse you are riding, and the rider's build. As we discussed earlier, you want your thighs to rotate inward toward the saddle. The direction for the right thigh will be counter-clockwise. The direction for the left thigh will be clockwise. Think about your knee remaining stable and still, while you pull your knees down, and back. This will give you more contact, and sink the upper thigh deeper and closer to the saddle. We will discuss in more detail how to position the pelvis in later chapters in order to keep it from rotating too far forward when the thigh position is priority.

An english rider will ride in a more forward seat, or light seat, where the rider will rotate the thigh so they are making contact with the front part of the thigh. If your thighs were a roller that you use to paint walls, roll the paint from the back of the thigh to the front, not vice versa, or the thigh will open too much.

A western rider would remain more on the middle of the roller and not allow the thighs to roll forward or backward.

A dressage rider would really use the roller at the top section of the thigh and try to bring the paint to the front of the thigh. The thigh will be longer and more stable and still.

Spiral in from the top

This scenario is another way to look at using the thigh to rotate inward to get the maximum benefit and alignment from all three parts of the thigh. The rider will always need to move the thigh starting at the top first, then work your way down. This will instill that they are moving from the hip, not just the lower leg. Once the horse starts to move at a faster pace, it will be hard to hold the thigh with just sheer muscle strength. The rider will need to move the thigh from the top first. This is a common error for riders who think that if they grip and squeeze that they will be able to hold that position. This is false because the rider will fatigue rather quickly and become loose in the saddle. This is often when the rider will feel some of their greatest moments, because they begin to allow their body to align instead of trying to fight against the motion. When the body comes into a natural alignment, then we can become a force to be reckoned with. We will become immovable, and will feel like we are doing virtually nothing to keep it.

Caitie is positioning her knee so it would point inside the bucket. This helps the thigh to align properly.

Knees in the water bucket

This is a wonderful analogy to get the angle and the drop of both knees correct if the rider thighs tend to rise up or point away from the horse's ribcage. If the rider had a helper on the ground holding a water bucket beneath their knee, the rider must think of kneeling into the bucket enough that the knee, lower thigh, and upper calf would be wedged in the bucket. This section of the thigh needs to be weight bearing as you ride. The more the knee points down toward the ground, the better the chance that the rider will stay with the horse, and distribute weight evenly across the horse's back, and into the stirrups.

Imagine this water bucket is present on both sides while riding, and the bucket is even and not tipped forward or backward. You can also think that the bucket contains a substance that is bright green and you are dipping your kneecap into the bright green substance that suddenly molds to your leg and holds you in place.

Thighs in the middle

When positioning your thighs along the horse's back it is important to position your thighs in the middle of the horse. You need to think of your thighs as a giant set of tweezers that are going to come along and pick your horse up off its feet. The area in which the tweezers take hold of the horse will lift the horse up evenly, so the horse is not hind heavy from the tweezers being behind the shoulders, or front heavy from the tweezers being placed too far behind the saddle area. Pick the horse up with your thighs. All four of the horse's legs would be perfectly even, and the horse would then dangle in mid-air. In reality this is not what the rider is doing, but the visual of the placement of the thighs will place the rider away from the horse's withers. Do not confuse this visual with gripping tightly.

TIP Always adjust the upper leg or the lower leg by moving the hip and opening the joint. This will always help position your legs to keep them in balance and help promote stability throughout the rest of your body.

Seatbelt across the hips

In order to feel the security of the hips it will help the rider to think of a seatbelt over the tops of the thighs. The seatbelt will rest along the seam of the hip flexors. Imagine it is tightened it to its maximum, this will then be the guideline. Once the rider can feel the security of the hamstring against the saddle, then the hip flexor can open or close with ease.

As you progress, you may find you will need to lengthen your stirrups one hole. Once you achieve an open hip, the only way to keep it is to let your stirrups down a hole. This is a big achievement. Be proud of your accomplishment. Do not rush it, however. Only lengthen the stirrups when you are ready and feel secure. Once movement and stretch happens in the thigh, then the by-product will be opening of the hip angle.

Helpful Hint: The back of the hamstring must be exposed. By that I mean the entire length of the hamstring should be able to be seen by an onlooker from behind. The hamstring muscle must not roll toward the horse. This will start the downward spiral of losing the stability of the thigh. The opposing muscle groups of the quadriceps and the hamstring muscles must work together to hold the thigh still and keep the security.

Coordination and Strengthening Exercises

Alternating knee lift

This exercise will aid in opening the hip joint and elongating the thigh along the horse's sides.

Use caution when performing this exercise.

Have a handler on the ground hold your horse for you at a standstill until the horse is used to the movement so they don't become frightened.

The object of this exercise is to alternate lifting each leg for a count of three. You will begin by taking your feet out of the stirrups, but keep your leg in the correct riding position. Raise your thigh so you are closing the hip angle. Do not allow any part of your leg to touch the horse's sides. Hold for a count of three, and then let the leg drop and relax. Pick up the opposite leg and repeat the exercise. In the beginning, only do about 5 reps with each leg. You can gradually build to higher reps once you are used to the exercise.

Do not allow your upper body to lean back. You will feel the effectiveness of your ab muscles working just below your belly button. This is your core muscles beginning to work and strengthen in order to help hold your body stable. After a few reps you will feel your hip joint open up once you reposition your feet in the stirrups and begin to walk forward on your horse. You have experienced an open hip joint. Try to maintain this as much as possible when you ride at any gait.

Once you can easily lift each leg individually, then you can move onto lifting both legs at the same time, holding for a count of 3.

Straddle the saddle

You are now going to practice the feeling of allowing your upper thigh to make contact with the saddle. You are going to ask your helper to hold your horse once again as you practice this feeling of opening the upper portion of the leg. Keep your feet facing forward toward twelve o'clock. Keep a slight bend in your knees and don't compromise your riding position. Open your thighs as far as possible-right thigh towards three o'clock and left thigh toward nine o'clock. Hold both thighs away from your horse's sides for a count of five. Then allow both legs to gently come back and touch your horse's sides. Repeat the sequence until you can build the strength to hold it for longer periods of time. This will also aid in helping the rider develop a more stable leg in order to give a clear signal to the horse to move forward. The outer thigh will build more muscle tone and become steadier

Hold the stirrups away from the horse's sides

This exercise can be used as a means to strengthen the lower leg, the three parts of the thigh, and to help the ankle find its place. It will also help the rider's seat remain in contact with the saddle and give a sense of finding the connecting link in the saddle.

Start by taking your feet out of the stirrups. Position both legs underneath the stirrup fender for a western saddle, or under the leathers for an english or dressage saddle. It may help to lengthen your stirrups a few holes so they are resting below your ankle knobble on each foot.

You are going to hold the stirrups away from your horse's sides. Keep thinking of snowplowing with both ankles. Allow your knees to drop down, but keep both feet in the position you would normally ride in. You will be using the abductor muscles of both thighs. This will help your legs to feel the contact points in the saddle and help to strengthen your entire leg. When you become comfortable and strengthen your muscles, then build up to a trot, then a canter. It will do wonders for your canter

departs when the lower leg will not be able to move much when asking for the canter transition.

If you feel as though you are losing your leg stability, drop your stirrups, and practice this exercise for a lap or two. It will position your body once again, and give you the long lower leg without the gripping sensation of trying to make it happen.

Push the fenders back

This is the same principle as the exercise before. You are now going to position your foot and leg ahead of the leathers or the fenders, and gently hold the stirrups back. Slip your feet out of the stirrups, and hold your heel in front of the opening of the stirrup. Think of pushing your heels back against a wall and do not allow your knee to ride up. Instead, think of pushing it down and back toward the horse's hocks. Keep a gentle bend behind your knee. This helps for riders who tend to let their lower leg slip forward too much. It will also strengthen the hamstrings along the back of the thighs. This is often a hard to reach area for riders. Practice this exercise at a walk first, then when you feel stable, move on to a trot and canter for a few steps.

Keep the heel in the hole of the stirrup. Be careful not to lift the entire thigh. You will feel the hamstrings take hold. It is important to keep the foot level as if it were resting on the stirrup.

Imagery
Essentials

The Hidden Shock Absorber

Checklist for Proper Alignment of the Hip

✓ Keep the headlights positioned on the front of the hip joint on high beam.
✓ Hip lies above the heel.
✓ Keep your zipper ahead of your heels.
✓ The magic horse and the magic carpet must stay upright.
✓ The running water faucet that will divide and run down each leg must not trickle.

Extension of the Thigh

Equestrian sports like dressage and show jumping require strong hip and leg muscles to keep the rider stable aboard the horse, and to be able to pilot the horse through intricate movements and somewhat risky maneuvers because the hip is constantly flexed while riding, long or intense rides can leave the muscles strained and sore. Dressage riders will stress the hip muscles due to the outward rotation. A jumper will fatigue through the thighs and hips due to tremendous effort put forth on these muscles to stabilize the body throughout the jumping effort to keep the rider in place over the center of gravity. A trail rider will become sore due to long hours in the saddle.

The hip is the key ingredient to success for many riding disciplines. Riders must learn how to use the hip to their advantage in order to maintain effectiveness while riding their horse. An open hip angle allows the seat to remain in contact and become the platform for the rest of the body. A closed hip angle can cause turbulence throughout the rest of the pieces that must line up correctly. As you learn to ride different disciplines, you will learn how to use your hip to close the angle for a good jumping position, a half seat, or two point position when riding English. A western rider must keep the angle of the hip joint more open to allow the horse to lope under the body. Let's take a closer look at the hip, and how it will affect your ride.

The Hip

TIP

The hip is the main piece of the body used for shock absorbing while riding. It becomes extremely important while a rider is sitting the trot. The ripple of the horse's movement must be able to float through the hips. If it can't, the rider will begin to bounce in the saddle and become stiff with the thighs, calves, and feet. The rider's upper body will begin to fall behind the horse's movement and the hands will begin to hold onto the horse's mouth for balance.

Locating the Hip joints

The location of the hip joint is a key factor in determining how to use it effectively while riding. The pelvis consists of two bony hip bones along with the sacrum and the coccyx. As you are sitting in the saddle locate the hip joint. Use your index finger and follow the crease of your pants towards the seat of your saddle where your leg meets the torso. Keep your finger at his location and bend forward until you feel your buttocks lifting softly away from the saddle. You will feel movement in the area under your finger. Then slowly begin to lean back. This will open the hip angle. Move around between a slight lean forward and a shift of the upper body leaning backward. Find the feeling of a soft hip joint. Keep locating this joint as you ride when you feel like you have stiffened or locked this area. Gaining control of this section of the body will help to contribute to an effective riding position in conjunction with the lower abdominals and lower back.

At times, riders will experience a push backward from the horse or experience a lack of forward glow. This will cause the riders hip angle to close and the seat to slip backwards. Once the horse begins to power forward, the rider gets left behind, and the vicious cycle begins. If you learn to locate the hip and can keep it functioning as you ride, then you can keep the thighs strong and seat still.

Function of the Hip Joints

The hip joint is a synovial ball and socket joint. This means that there is a slippery membrane that lubricates it to aid in permitting movement about all axes. The head of the femur (thigh bone) fits snuggly into the pelvic bone. The hip is designed to stabilize and propel the body to move the legs. It permits flexion and extension (moving the thigh forward and back). It also aids in adduction and abduction, which are moving the thigh toward and away from the midline of the body. The thigh can rotate inward and outward and circumduct in a complete circle all thanks to the hip. It is extremely important to use the hip to your advantage during riding.

Riding Realities

Common Errors and Enigmas

There are a few different ways a rider can close the hip angle and cause a chain reaction to happen throughout their body. The main reason is fear. When a rider becomes scared, they tend to curl up into the fetal position because this is what is natural for the nervous system. The hip angle will begin to close from the rider tipping forward with the upper body. Let's take a closer look at some common errors to work on as you progress through the puzzle pieces.

Familiar Faults

Fault 1

Closing the hip angle by folding in half is the most common error. If the rider allows the top section of the body to fold in half by leaning forward which causes the seat to slide backward, the direct result will always be a loss of balance. The rider will be forced to pull on the reins for balance, and often the lower leg will slide backward too far. There is a difference when actually closing the hip angle over a jump or learning to perform in two point position. We will discuss this further in later chapters.

In this picture Tara has closed the angle of the hip joint too much. The wrinkles in her jean shows the hip angle more acute than it should be. Her seat has slid back, and her back has hollowed as a result.

Fault 2

The hip angle can also be closed if the rider allows the thigh to rise up. This is referred to as the "floating thigh". The thigh is not set, and does not have contact with the horse's sides. This will almost always result in the rider closing the hip angle in the front section of the body. The lower leg will no longer anchor, and the foot will not be grounded.

A rider can also grip too hard with the knee. This results in the knee closing the hip angle as well. A rider will fluctuate between gripping too much and letting go with the thigh. Once you find the happy medium you will feel the connection start to happen within your body and with the horse.

Fault 3

A" brushing seat" can also be a culprit causing closing of the hip angle. This results when the rider allows the seat to slide backward, and the pubic bone begins to rotate back toward the horse's hind feet. The seat of the rider begins to brush along the saddle like a broom, and the stability and stillness is lost. The hip angle will close, and it will be hard for the rider to re-open it until the pelvis aligns properly once again.

Fault 4

You can also open the hip angle too much. This can happen when the rider tilts backward too much with the upper body or the lower leg slides forward too much. This becomes a pushing seat, or also known as a driving seat. It can be misunderstood by the horse to generate more forward power to move on more quickly, often more quickly than the rider would like to go.

Fault 5

Leaning forward with the upper body or collapsing the shoulders can also ripple down through the hip joints. This can start by the rider looking down at the horse which is common for those of us who are training or with a rider who likes to see what is happening beneath them. If you think of picking your eyes up and rolling your shoulder girdle back so it is positioned above your hips, it will aid in keeping the integrity of your body lined up.

The arch in Tara's back will cause a tip forward onto the pelvis. From the point of the shoulders to her buttocks there is an arc which should be more aligned to neutral spine.

Fault 6

Often a rider will begin to hollow out the lower back, creating an arch in the back. This will result with a dropping of the pelvis in the front line up. It will cause a slight closing of the hip angle which can result in the seat sliding backward, and creating a chain reaction of loosening the lower body. This will make it hard to maintain your balance, and your body will naturally take over to keep from falling forward or backward.

Picture Perfect Pieces

Now envision your picture perfect pieces for the improved ride

Imagery examination:

The coil springs to keep the connection

Further Explanation

The hips are the coil springs or shock absorbers. They must remain open and upright for maximum efficiency. You will learn to use the hips like finely tuned pieces of machinery. They will be the connection between the upper body and the lower body. They will become strong and elastic in order to produce the desired results necessary as the rider progresses in different riding disciplines.

If a rider has stiff hips the timing of the aids may be off. This may result in the rider blocking the way instead of guiding the way.

With all the movement required in riding, the use of the hips helps to create stability in order to find balance within the movement. The muscles of the hip enable the rider to absorb shock and move the entire body forward, backward, sideways, upward, and downward. Gaining control of these different directions is one of the obstacles that take tremendous muscle building and strength.

Essential Details of each Imagery

Headlights on high beam

In order to keep a constant balance and maintain stability it requires excellent core strength. If this section of the body is lacking in muscle tone, the rider will compensate by gripping with the inner thigh. This will lead to sore hip flexors, fatigued thighs and strained lower back muscles.

In a motor vehicle, the driver has the ability of using the high beam or the low beam options to light the intended path of travel. A high beam headlight will not only shed light on the path directly in front of you. It will also cover the full spectrum inward and outward as well. It is a bright light that is open, not streamline and thin like a low beam light.

To keep the hip joints open and active, the rider must think of the head lights attached to the front of the hips. They begin at the lowest section of the abdominals, and extend to the tippy top of the thigh muscle. These lights need to remain open and bright, and on high beam. They cannot become dim. The head light needs to shine in the path of travel, and light the way in the direction you wish to go.

If the light begins to shine toward the ground or the horse's front feet, you are beginning to close the hip joint and switching to the low beam option. Often a rider will close this angle with the upper body and torso or they will close the angle by allowing the thigh to rise up toward the abdominals. This is a common issue as the hip flexors may become tight from prolonged time in the saddle and cause flexion in the hip hinge.

If the light begins to shine up over the horse's ears, the hip joint is too open and the rider is beginning to lean back. Keep a streamline of light evenly lighting your path. If you are thinking of your side to side border you will also want the lights to be level. You do not want one light to drop lower, or become crooked. This will allow the hip joint to stay open and functioning as you ride. It will also help to control your seat.

Caitie is demonstrating the angle of the hip joint that will be most effective during riding while Tara holds the flashlight in the area of the hip flexor.

A rider must keep the hip flexors stretched and in good working condition. This is the first section to become tight, and once these muscles fatigue they will begin to pull the pelvis forward in the saddle and close the angle. All the riding tips in the world will not fix this issue until you stretch this area. It will be as if the hinge has gotten rusty and stuck, and you must oil it to keep it in working order.

Hip lies above the heel

Over-developed or tight hip flexors can contribute to lower back pain by causing the pelvis to tilt forward. This is more common for women riders than men riders due to their genetic makeup. To counteract this, the rider must think of how they are positioned in the saddle at all times. Stretching the hip flexors and strengthening the abs will reduce pelvic tilt along with the thought of keeping the hip joint over the center of the knee.

Tara is holding the stick to show the area behind the knee that must remain in a triangular balance. The hip is positioned over the heel, and the knee has a nice angle behind it. If we slid the horse out from beneath Tara she would land on her feet.

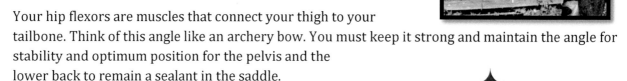

When looking at basic alignment within the body, the hip needs to remain directly over the heel. The rider needs to envision a triangular shape that will form behind the leg. If you connect the hip joint along the back of the thigh or the hamstring, and allow that line to extend along the back of the kneecap and along the back of the calf, it would, finally, reach its destination at the point of the heel. This angle needs to remain stable. If the line were then drawn upward it would extend from the heel to the hip joint in one straight line. This is the triangle that needs to remain when riding.

Your hip flexors are muscles that connect your thigh to your tailbone. Think of this angle like an archery bow. You must keep it strong and maintain the angle for stability and optimum position for the pelvis and the lower back to remain a sealant in the saddle.

Keep your zipper ahead of your heels

The hip flexors become active when the abdomen is moving toward the thighs. This is common when doing a sit up. It is not uncommon, however, for the rider to begin to over-develop this muscle, especially, when riding english disciplines and jumping.

> *Hip flexors, being a small muscle group, are often worked in conjunction with the abdominals for maximum strength.*

It is true that the rider must fold over and close the hip angle slightly, but the rider must not lose the hip angle entirely. The rider must make a compromise. It is either leave the thigh and bring the torso closer, or leave the torso and bring the thigh up. This scenario can be taken to extremes however, and the rider must never do so in a fashion that is visible to an onlooker. By this I mean this is internal. The muscle required to do this is so high tone that the body keeps the bones in alignment, and surrounds those bones with stability from the muscles. This is what keeps the rider still.

The rider needs to envision the zipper of their pants with the top section that is just beneath your button of your pants slightly tilting forward toward the horse's wither. This will keep the pelvis tilting in the direction needed to sustain the stable seat needed to hold the rider in place. As the rider becomes stronger through the thigh region and the hips, then they can begin to settle the seat, so to speak. The rider will slowly begin to allow the angles to change. It is as if we placed bubble wrap beneath the riders seat bones, and they must not pop any bubbles. The rider, in effect, will hover in mid air, all while the hip joints remain open and the angle of the zipper is slightly ahead of the heel. This will help to keep the hip angle open wider and keep the stretch throughout the hip so the hip flexors can do the job intended to stabilize the rider's body while moving.

The magic carpet and the magic horse

The position of the rider's body needs to remain in constant balance-plain and simple. The horse will be easier to ride once they find their own balance, but it is often hard for the horse to find their balance when we can't find our own. The horse will never be able to balance until we do. They must always compensate for us. If we shift our weight even though it will throw them off balance, they will shift as well to make up for our improper balance just to simply remain on their four feet. They must counteract our imperfections. Once we take responsibility for our own balance and we are a very stable load to carry, they will begin to change their own balance, and the entire ride will become easier.

Hip angle can be as simple as sitting on a horse and holding a balanced position. Imagine that the horse is standing on a magic carpet, and that magic carpet is pulled out from beneath the horse's feet. Would you be able to balance as your horse tries to balance on all four feet? This is harder than it sounds, but is, in a nutshell, what riding is all about. It is as if we sat on a giant ball and our feet were not touching the ground trying to balance while that ball keeps rolling about in different directions. That in itself would be super hard to do and the tiny weight shifts would feel as though they were huge. The body would work overtime to isometrically stabilize in order to balance the entire body.

Another way to determine the balance of the rider when in motion would be to imagine what would happen if the horse pulled out from beneath you by magic. Would you land on your feet and remain standing without toppling over in any direction? This is a big question to ask yourself as you ride. Check to see if you have your horse in balance and if you are in balance upon the horse.

Here are two different riding disciplines-one english and one gaming. In both pictures if there were a magic carpet under the feet of both horses, and it flew out from beneath their feet, they would still be standing. Tara also has good alignment because she would also land on her feet if the horse was not beneath her. This is body balance for the horse and for the rider. The hip angle can change but the balance must remain intact.

A horse can do a lot of pushing backward as you are riding. Sometimes, it is the horse that forces us to close our hip angle. The reality of the situation is that if your horse is more on the lazy side and you are doing a lot of seat pushing and kicking, then your hip angle will close and the result will be that the horse has taken away all your power to block the push backward that they are generating. Think of your hip like a shield. That shield will block any backward push the horse may try to get away with. Stand your ground and hold your body in this stance. The horse will realize that they must move forward and you will find that the lazy horse you once had is now moving forward much more freely.

The running water faucet

While a horse is in motion it will generate force and balance checks for the rider to sustain. The rider must remain organized with the hip. The hip flexor muscles are responsible for moving the hip joints. They activate when the knees ride upward or when bending over to touch the toes. The rider needs to organize the body and keep the lower back strengthened in order to help improve balance between the muscles of the hip region.

One of the most useful imagery essentials to keep the hip joints balanced is to think of creating a hole to allow water to pass through directly at the top of the rider's head. The rider must think of a water faucet with a constant flow of water passing through the midsection of the body and into the feet. Before the water flows to both feet, however, it must pass through the middle of your torso and separate. It will split in half and flow down through each hip joint and down the thighs to the rider's feet. The rider must maintain the flow of the water and keep it as even as possible once it reaches the hips.

The water must run evenly through the right and left hip in order to keep the seat and legs balanced. If the water would become blocked or stuck, then there is a closure or blockage within the hinge of the hip. A raised knee or thigh could be at fault, or else the hip angle has closed due to the torso dropping down towards the thigh.

If the water could rush freely down both sides and flow down through the feet and out of the toes, then the hip joints are open and the rider is on the right track. The rider needs to think of this analogy each time the rider expects a transition, or a change of direction. It will help the rider to keep a sense of feeling the body, and keeping the angles correct.

Coordination and Strengthening Exercises

Stand up and alternate bending each knee

This exercise is extremely beneficial in order to build balance and to stabilize the lower leg. Once you can stand up and balance without tipping forward or falling backward, you are on your way to better balance, and opening up your hip joint.

The horse should be at a stand-still. Use a still horse first, and then slowly build up to movement. Don't hesitate to have someone help you by holding your horse.

Keep the center of the foot, the center of the knee, and the center of the hip all in line. Look straight ahead over the horse's ears. Hold the mane if you need to in order to maintain balance. Bend your knee and hold your lower leg away from the saddle. Then switch to the opposite side and repeat. Your hip joint should remain open and the pelvis should remain level and even. Once you can do it at a standstill, then ask the horse to walk forward and try the exercise again while in motion.

You will find that before long, you will be able to balance at a walk and trot while alternating your leg and bending at the knee. This will keep the hip open and keep the rider balanced and toned. It will also help with the appropriate amount of weight across the stirrups.

Hold the heel up

Another good way to teach the hip joint to stay open is to actually stretch while you are on your horse. Ask the horse to stand still once again, and if you need to call on your helper to hold your horse while you practice, that would be valuable at this point in time.

Bend your knee and grasp your foot in your hand. Allow the knee to point down straight toward the ground and feel the stretch up through the hip joint. Hold for a few seconds, then switch to the other side. You will want that sensation to remain with you as you ride.

Sometimes riders who spend long hours in the saddle will actually tighten the hip flexors, making it difficult to open the joint. If you spend some time stretching, it will do wonders for your riding. Remember you are becoming an athlete. Take care of your body so it will last you through the many wonderful years you have with your horse.

Fold over and touch your toes

Do this exercise standing still on your horse. If you need a helper to hold your horse then have one to be safe. Be sure that the center of the foot is under the center of the knee. Keep the foot spread out across the stirrup, with the ball of each foot touching the stirrup bar. Without risking your lower leg swinging too far forward, imagine you are touching brake pedals on each side. You are going to practice folding your body in half to release the flexor tendon and close the hip joint. Allow your bottom to slide backward as if it were on rollers. Keep your feet positioned underneath you, and do not let your lower leg slip back. If you do begin to lose your lower leg, then ask your helper to hold your calf in position as you fold in half with your hips.

Bend forward, releasing the flexor tendon so your nose is lowering toward your horse's neck. Keep the back flat, not arched or braced. Allow all the muscles in the upper, middle and lower back to relax as you fold over and touch your toes. Allow your torso to touch the upper thigh as you reach down to touch your feet.

As you advance, you can begin to grasp under your foot for a deeper stretch. In the beginning, just allow your muscles to settle and relax. Do not strain to try to reach further. It will naturally happen over the course of a few sessions.

This will help immensely with jumping position, and you can advance by pulling yourself back up to a sitting position without using your hands to help you. Your lower leg must remain stable and

steady. You cannot arch or pull up with your chest. You will be using your thighs and lower legs to lift your body again. Do a few reps each day to release the tension in your hip joints and help your hips to stay mobile and usable.

This exercise will also help with stabilizing the lower leg so you realize which muscles are used to hold gently for the frictional contact.

Reach down and across and touch your toes

Another exercise that will help to release the hip joints and help with coordination is to have your horse stand still again with the use of a helper if needed. Take your right hand and reach across the body so you are reaching down to touch your left toe. Allow your hips to fold, and your back to become flat. Do not allow your back to arch. If that does occur, your hips will not close at the correct angle and your buttocks will not slide back and release the tension. Hold this stretch for a count of three. Switch sides and take your left hand and reach across to touch your right toe. Keep your lower leg on both sides still, and do not allow them to swing as you reach across and alternate sides. Be careful not to grip with the lower leg either, or your horse will probably move forward unexpectedly because of your previous work to make them more responsive to your leg cues. Do this work slowly, and do a few reps each time as a warm up. This will help your leg and hip muscles. It will also help you find the appropriate sweet spot for the seat.

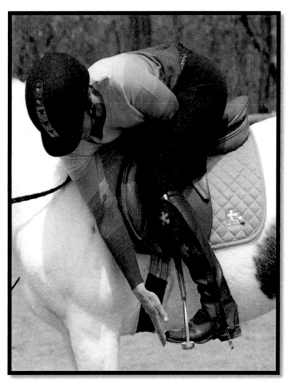

We will talk about how to close the hip angle for the two point and jumping position in later lessons. We will also discuss in detail the light seat and the different angles that the hip can obtain through opening and closing the joint.

Putting Pieces & Position into Practice

The hips can play a key role in turning and steering the horse. It is important to remember that the hips, when opened, help to lower the leg. If the leg lowers, it enables the rider to encompass more of the horse's ribcage which can help draw the back up when working on more collected work.

Hips to help steer

When opened the hip joints become elongated and useful in the effort to help turn the horse's body. As we have discussed, imagining a high powered beam of light shining from your open hip joint can help improve your riding. Picture this light as a steady stream to help aid in directional control. The angle of the beam of light becomes extremely important. If the beam of light is facing forward and the rider is sitting balanced and correct, then they will be able to determine if the horse has fallen onto the forehand. This means the horse is bearing most of its weight on the front two legs instead of the desired hind legs. If you are wishing to pick up the horse in the front end so it doesn't feel as if you are about to slide down a sliding board, you will need to point the beam of light in a horizontal line that is shining past the height of the horse's shoulders. If the beam of light is shining in a diagonal line more toward the ground, then, either the horse has chosen to bear more weight on the front and you will need to correct through proper riding, or you are allowing your hip angle to close slightly.

On the contrary, if the beam of light shines upward in a diagonal line then the rider may be opening the hip angle too wide and leaning back slightly. In any case the angle of the hip will help you to promote a more balanced seat through proper alignment and body mechanics.

The beam of light and the direction in which it points is important when turning, as well. If you are turning to the left use both hips and point them in the direction of travel. Use your hips and thighs to point towards eleven o'clock. Keep the high beam lights on. Do not let them become dim by closing your hip angle. If your hip angle closes even slightly, the thigh will rise and less of your lower leg will touch the horse's side. This will also cause a disruption with the longitudinal balance of the horse, which means the softness from front to back over the horse's back muscles. When turning to the right you can think of pointing the beam of light toward one o'clock and keeping the high beams on so the angle remains open.

It helps to think of a figure skater that is skating on one skate in a circle. If they are skating on the left skate the majority of the upper body will be facing to the outside of the circle. They must do this in order to keep their balance. You will never see the skater take the upper body, and face it to the inside of the circle. This will result in a twist with the torso, and a major loss of balance and possibly a fall.

The figure skater's hip angles would be open with one leg extended out behind them and the other leg almost straight with a slight bend in the knee. Now picture that the skater has dropped the extended leg down behind her, but kept skating to the left. Think of the position the hips would be facing in. This position of the hips would resemble the direction of the rider's hips as you ride a circle, or turn. The same would be true in the opposite direction if you were skating on the right skate instead.

Avery is skating bearing weight on her skate blade with her hips following the same line.

When riding in a circle, be sure that the hips are even so the thighs can remain in the downward position. If the hip begins to close, then you are going to lose the position of the hip and lower leg. The result will be a loose upper thigh. You will begin to disconnect as you circle and centrifugal force, such as what happens in a washing machine during the spin cycle, will take over. Your body will naturally fall to the outside of the circle.

The Seat

The ideal seat can influence the horse significantly. A strong secure seat is a sensitive one. Through practice a sense of feel will develop into a harmony between horse and rider. The classical seat put simply, is when the rider's center of gravity is perfectly positioned and aligned in the saddle. The foundation arises from the pelvis which should be upright with equal weight on each seat bone and the pubic bone. I often go a step further and add in the tailbone as a point of reference for the seat, as well.

It is often a point of controversy of how exactly to use the seat while riding. It can be rather tricky to balance and maintain the motion with the horse while keeping the seat intact. The rider can vary the degree of connection while riding above the motion, with the motion, and into the motion. These are all influential seats which need to be part of a rider's position. Many horses will call for differing degrees, and levels of how to sustain the hold, or the communication through the seat receptors.

We often talk of differing seats used in riding today, and some ideas become a little confusing. The important point to remember is no matter what discipline you ride, it is important to know various ways to adjust your position to be helpful for your horse's balance, whether riding on the flat, over jumps, on inclines or declines, and through and over obstacles.

When riding a young horse, should the rider put unnecessary pressure on the horse's back? In most cases the horse's back is not yet fully developed. I believe that, basically, you must work with the athletic ability of your horse. A young horse does not have the muscle strength to sustain weight for a long period of time, and it can be a little more uncomfortable for the youngster to carry your weight, plus balance his own body weight on his four feet. In most cases, I will begin with a posting trot as opposed to a sitting trot on a young horse until I build up the framework for the horse to carry me comfortably. Working in small increments to introduce the sitting trot for a few strides helps to build strength, then returning to the posting trot for the duration of the ride.

When working in a canter, I try to free up the back as much as possible when cantering in longer increments. I often use a half seat position to help the horse learn to move the back muscles without the added weight of my body. This is a more polite gesture for the rider training a young horse. If I am riding a horse that is rather unruly or unpredictable, then I want to feel the back as much as possible, and will stay sitting so I can plug in and feel what the horse is thinking.

In early stages in training, I will often teach the horse to go forward with the absence of the seat bones or with the weight of the seat bones. In english riding this helps with jumping. When reaching higher heights the rider will adjust the stirrup length shorter. This will bring the leg beneath the rider and the hip joints are able to close more allowing the seat to slip back over the center of balance in the jumping effort.

Be a good judge and listen to your horse's needs as you are learning. Practice different seats for that one day when you are ready to advance or take on a new riding discipline. Let's talk about all the differing seats and what your seat is comprised of.

What parts of the body comprise the seat?

Think of your seat as resembling the shape of a diamond. The "top point" would be your pubic bone. It tells the horse to increase speed or maintain a particular gait. The "bottom point" will be where your tailbone is, and is used to communicate to the horse to steady a gait, to slow the feet down, or to stop moving entirely. The side points will be your left and right seat bones, which will be used in conjunction with other parts of the body to signal the horse to turn left or right, or to bear weight on one foot more than another.

When fully developed, the points of your seat can be used to communicate direction, speed and timing to your horse. At this point, your horse will be following what I call a "magnetic seat." You will be able to use your seat to "pull" the horse in the direction you wish to travel as well as use it to brake, speed up, or determine the length of your horse's stride. Your aids are, essentially, invisible at this point.

DIFFERING SEATS USED IN RIDING

The full seat or "3 point" seat

When riding different disciplines you may hear different terms used to describe the same ideas. A full seat is the diamond making contact with the saddle as you ride at the walk, trot, and canter. We refer to this as three point position. The rider remains in contact with both inner thighs as well as the seat. This makes up the three points of contact. In certain disciplines, you will be required to stay in full seat position. This is used when riding with the motion of the horse, or when the seat has more bearing on how to influence the horse's movement.

Tara is riding Loops in a full seat otherwise known as 3 point position. She has all points in contact with the saddle, and is allowing Loops to canter beneath her.

The three point seat is your connecting seat and will help to keep contact with the horses back. It is also used later in training when asking a horse to lift the back to help with collection and to prepare the horse's body for proper frame in order to sustain self-carriage.

The half seat or two point

Half seat means exactly what it says; it's half of your seat. You will basically peel the tailbone away from the saddle (lift the back section of the diamond up) and ride with the front portion of the diamond, keeping the right and left sides in contact. This will free the horse's back, and allow the horse to carry the rider while it can exercise the muscles along the spine, and build the muscle tone in order to become stronger without the added weight of the rider.

When discussing two points of contact, it is important to remember that the rider must also include the upper calf contact as we discuss the leg as a whole unit. The right and left thigh will bear most of the weight, but the rider will feel contact along the insides of the entire leg. The third point of contact is the rider's seat. This will be absent from the saddle in two point position.

If the rider's stirrups are shorter, the distance between the rider's seat and saddle may be increased slightly with the thought in mind to keep the body surrounding the horse and to hover, so to speak, not necessarily to push up and away from the horse.

The two point position is the main seat for the english rider who jumps. In two point the rider can allow the horse its maximum jumping effort without interfering. This will be the seat the rider is in before, during, and after the jumping effort.

Tara's Test: Take a riding crop and stand on the ground. Put the riding crop in front of your hip flexors so it's parallel to the ground. Now fold over so you are holding the crop with your hip flexors and no hands. You will feel your seat slide back and your weight should remain balanced over your heels. You are now in jumping position known as two point position.

Light seat

This seat is halfway between a full, balanced seat and a two point position. In a light seat, you position the point at the front of your diamond so it's lightly touching the center of the saddle. This, then, allows the inner thighs to support more weight than they would in a full seat and you can use your thighs to help you balance and maintain correct body alignment. A rider can change from a "driving" seat in full contact to a two point position fluidly while jumping a course of fences. Keeping the seat away from the horse's back will allow the horse to move forward naturally, round its back, and maximize the jumping effort in addition, to allowing the horse to move more easily, a light seat will help the rider balance and stay with the horse in each phase of jumping- the take off, the effort, and the landing.

A light seat is also used when schooling a young horse because it frees up the back muscles and allows the horse room to lift the back up under the rider's weight. In disciplines that require quick responses from the horse and rider, such as barrel racing or eventing, the light seat is a great asset to your riding skills. It allows the rider to lift their body weight, and lets the horse roll forward beneath the rider so the rider will not fall behind the horse's motion. A rider behind a horse's motion could cause the horse to lose their balance in high speed work.

Location and alignment of the pelvis

The alignment of the pelvis is guaranteed to be mentioned more than once in a person's riding career and you will learn how to vary the degree of tip and tuck that is vital to great balance for your seat and riding position.

The anatomy of the pelvis is made up of several bones that help give shape to the lower back and the hip area. These bony structures create a shape that resembles a round bowl. Let's call this the "the pelvic bowl". It holds the organs located in the lower abdomen.

When you "tip" the pelvis, the top part of the pelvis comes forward, while the bottom part goes back. This usually forms a soft arch in the lower spine. Imagine the pelvic bowl, but instead of the regular organs the bowl holds miso soup. When the instruction is given to "tip" the pelvis forward, the goal is to keep the legs steady and tilt the bowl as if the rider were going to pour the soup in front of them. The "tip" seat is what is used along with leg aids to signal to the horse to move forward.

On the contrary, "tucking" is the counterpart of tipping. To tuck the rider will find a slight round in the lower spine. The bottom section of the pelvis comes forward, while the top part goes backward. Try to keep the soup safely in the bowl without spilling a drop. This is the stopping seat aid.

In between tip and tuck will be the neutral seat which is the seat that signals to the horse to keep the current motion and rhythm or lack of forward movement. It is the seat that says everything is correct.

How to locate the seat bones

Most riders probably have an idea where the seat bones lie, but practicing the following exercises will help locate the exact spot where the seat bones are. You need to learn how to feel each seat bone in order to become extremely effective with them. You may be surprised how it feels when you begin to use them with pin point precision. You will begin to understand why your horse hollows its back and shies away from them if you are overusing the seat bones, or why your horse tends to ignore them because they are not even close to where you thought they were. On the other hand, you will begin to realize that when used correctly, how the horse can pivot around a fixed seat bone, or learn to lift and raise the back to elevate into the rider's seat.

EXERCISES TO LOCATE THE SEAT BONES

Legs over the pommel

Have a friend hold your horse or if you think your horse will stand quietly, perform this exercise at a halt. Bring both of your legs up and over the pommel of the saddle. Slide your bottom forward until you are in the deepest indent in the middle of the saddle and your rear end is not touching the cantle. You will begin to feel two protrusions touching the saddle's seat. They feel like knuckles. If you do not feel them, then tilt forward with your upper body a few degrees or tilt back until you can feel the seat

bones digging into the saddle. Welcome to the world of feeling your ride. This is the key to making a big communication difference with your horse.

Slowly lower your legs until they are resting in neutral position along your horse's sides. Test to see if you can still feel the seat bones. Do they feel even? Does one feel more prominent? How much did you have to lean forward or back in order to feel them both?

You can practice by lifting each thigh without stirrups, one at a time, until you feel the seat bone take hold and become apparent. Familiarize yourself with the feeling. Practice each day. Start your ride off by finding your seat bones. If you feel as though you have lost that connection, stop and reorganize. It will make a world of difference if you pay careful attention to this small detail.

Hands under your seat bone

Do this at a standstill on a trustworthy horse that will let you use both hands to experience this feel. You can begin to get familiar with your seat bones by laying your hands out flat as if you were holding a tray. You will be sitting on your palms.

Caitie is sitting on her palms as Tara helps her to maintain a neutral spine and a level foot position. She is learning to find her seat bones.

Take both hands and position them under each seat bone until you can feel the protrusion that feels like two knuckles digging into the palms of each hand. Those are your seat bones. Again ask yourself the previous questions and become familiar with the feeling. This is what your horse feels. They may have a saddle and a saddle pad separating this feeling, but they can still feel the weight shift. How you move each seat bone makes a vast difference in the feeling of your ride.

Learning to sit on the "sit bones"

A rider can spend countless hours trying to figure out the exact degree in which to sit down on the horse. But what does "sitting on the sit bones" mean?

As part of the pelvis, the sit bones or seat bones refer to the ischium bones in your pelvis. They create two bony protrusions on the underside of your seat. Because this area is notably fleshy, these protrusions can be difficult to feel. Ideally, when we sit up straight we balance on them. Our poor posture can lead to significant curvature of the lower back and we redistribute weight to other areas. The rider needs to sit up straight, pull back the flesh from the underside of the seat, tip the pelvis forward pouring the soup in front of you, and try to connect the protrusions to the saddle seat letting it support you.

The Connection and Plug to Communicate

Checklist for Proper Alignment of the Seat

✓ Flashlights shine through the middle of the horse's belly.
✓ Engage a compass seat, north, south, east, west.
✓ Seat bones resemble the bottom of a rocking chair.
✓ Limbo under the limbo stick.
✓ Bicycle tire and two training wheels.
✓ Plastic underwear remains level upon the horse's back.
✓ Soup bowl is upright not spilling soup forward or backward out of the bowl.
✓ The soup ladle resembles the spine of the rider.
✓ Your belt stays level and even.
✓ Hold the hula hoop.
✓ Let go of the quarter.

Riding Realities

Common Errors and Enigmas

Ever have the feeling that you are not connected in any way to your horse? You feel as though you temporarily lost the communication button? As you ride you feel as though your seat is never in the same place twice and you don't understand why sometimes you are leaning too far forward, and other times you are leaning too far back. You have tried everything from lengthening your stirrups to riding without them, all in hopes that you will find that connection to help you stop feeling like you are polishing the saddle with your behind. Let's look at some common faults that may be familiar.

Familiar Faults

Fault 1

The "hollow backed rider" is the rider who allows the pelvis to roll forward in the saddle, often sitting more toward the crotch. The bottom of the pelvis resembles the bottom of a rocking chair, and often this area will roll to the front for balance. This leaves the seat bones pointing back behind the rest of the body in an attempt to keep the legs under the rider. This may help with connection of the thighs, but it will not help with the connection of the seat. The hip angle will close too much, making it difficult to sustain position. The lower back will also suffer and the constant concussion from the horse's movement can create a lot of lower back issues and pain later on. The rider should keep a neutral spine alignment instead, and align the pelvis in the center.

Tara's lower back is hollow, taking on the shape of a bad banana. This is not only uncomfortable for the rider, but also unstable. It will force the rider to lock the hips. Feeling the horse's back will be almost impossible.

Fault 2

The "round backed rider" gives the illusion of the opposite effect in the saddle. This is a pelvic rotation in the opposite direction of fault 1, often with the tailbone tucking under, and the front edge of the pelvis lifting up toward the belly button. The lower leg of the rider tends to swing forward, causing the rider to brace through the lower back in an effort to hold the body in place. The midsection will lose its tone and holding power. The result will be a feeling of heaviness through the horse's back, creating a withdrawal of the muscles from the rider's seat. This will hollow the horse's back and cause more of a trap for the rider to sit in. You will feel like a sack of potatoes to your horse, and your heavy seat will tend to hollow out the horse's back causing the head to raise and the horse to come above the bit.

Tara's lower back is now overly rounded. She will have to compensate for this loss of balance by moving her lower leg forward if the horse were walking. This leaves the rider as a very heavy burden for the horse to carry.

Fault 3

Despite all our best efforts to relax our backside, often riders will resort to clenching the muscles of the behind together in order to try and trigger other muscles to develop holding power while riding. This always results in an opposing effect as this acts like a clothespin, popping the rider up and out of the saddle. This will lift the seat bones causing a disconnection with the horse's back. It is important to have equal amounts of tone, along with a slight relaxation through the gluteus muscles. Once the rider becomes aware of how to fire those muscles, it is useful to be able to make the seat bones prominent when the rider is in need of steering mechanisms. Allow yourself to spread across the saddle and remain centered.

Fault 4

If you do not line up with the horse's spine and maintain a steady contact with each seat bone, then you will sit crooked with more weight on one seat bone than the other. A "tilting seat" will result from one seat bone being weighted too much. Symmetry in riding is a must. All of us have a dominant side as do our horses. We must do our best to strengthen each side of our body equally and allow both seat knuckles to straddle the horse's spine and carry our weight equally. This will allow the rider to keep in balance with the horse during turns or a change of direction and to guide the horse in a straight line.

Fault 5

A "sliding seat" gives the illusion of the rider polishing the saddle seat. They move about with a stable leg, but the seat is never in the same place twice. Often this is hard for the rider when learning how to canter. The seat floats between a rocking position of either too far forward or too far back. A still seat will be the end goal for this type of rider, but often finding the perfect spot to rest the pelvis becomes the challenge. The answer often lies in the position of the hips and the thighs. Let's look at how to improve the seat.

Now envision your picture perfect pieces for the improved ride

Imagery examination:

The connection and plug to communicate

Further Explanation

There are many different ways we can sit in the saddle. The key is to be effective while sitting. The horse must feel both seat bones of the rider as they will be used to communicate the rider's instructions. Finding the correct position can be tricky, but with practice the rider will become accustomed to this specific spot, which I refer to as the "home seat". Once secure, the rider can build on this and evolve into other balanced positions to help the horse advance in training.

Essential Details of each Imagery

Flashlights shine through the middle of the horse's belly

This analogy is borrowed from one of my favorite authors Mary Wanless. This imagery helps the rider understand how to position the pelvis. There are so many different ways we can sit in the saddle. The key is to be effective while you are sitting. The basic seat that the rider will revert back to at a moment's notice or what is neutral in terms of how you will use it to ride any discipline is what I call your "home" seat. The home seat is the seat from which everything else stems. Once this seat is mastered, a rider can adjust the balance point and never skip a beat keeping the rhythm of the horse's stride. The full seat is the base to build from. It will evolve into other balanced positions to help the horse advance in training. The horse must feel both seat bones from the rider's weight in the saddle. It's the riders comfort and the communication device. Finding the correct position can be tricky to feel, but with practice the rider will become accustomed to this specific spot.

Once the rider is bearing weight equally on each seat bone, think of shedding more light on this subject. Imagine flashlights positioned under each seat bone. When you turn them on, where would their circles of light show up? Would they be pointing toward the horse's front legs? Back legs? Or

would they point straight down right through the middle of his belly making two beams of light between all four feet, shedding light in a perfectly balanced round circle on the ground?

Once the lights are positioned correctly down through the horse's belly how does the image appear on the ground? Are the spotlights evenly round as they shine on the ground? Does one spotlight have a big beam of light hitting the ground while the other is a smaller beam of light? These are also important questions to ask yourself in terms of how evenly you are placing weight on both seat bones. In the beginning stages, it is not uncommon for a rider to bear more weight on one side over the other. Be sure your lights are even as they touch the ground and are pointing directly through the midsection of the horse. This is the constant check that the rider can make to insure that the position of the seat is stable.

Tara has positioned the flash light beneath the area of where her seat bones are located. The direction is pointing down through the horse's belly.

Compass seat: north, south, east, west

The seat may be one of the most important aids that a rider has, and yet, it is most often the least utilized. It is responsible in helping aid in directional control for the horse's body. It is in direct contact with the horse's back, which makes it difficult for the horse not to be affected by it. No matter how the rider sits, a horse will always be aware of it. Unfortunately, many riders are not aware of what the seat is doing, let alone using it actively as an aid to help to communicate with the horse and establish control of the horse.

The seat affects the horse's steering and straightness as well as its speed and balance. For the moment imagine your seat is a compass. This is your directional control communication center. A camper will rely on their compass to point them in the correct direction. The seat must be used in the same way. If the rider thinks of the four parts of the diamond as discussed previously then the pubic bone is the north section of the compass. This is used to help tell the horse to move forward and also as a reference spot to maintain the light seat or two point position. The southern point of the compass is the tailbone. This piece is used to slow down, or speed control section of the seat. It is often used when the rider needs to encourage the horse to move on, or get behind the motion for a split second to rev the engine, before coming back to the balance point. To the left is the west point of the compass and to the right is the east point of the compass. Both the west and east sections are held accountable for directional control (turning aids). A rider must learn to evenly distribute weight first to all four sections of the compass. It is then that variations in balance and changes can be made to ask the horse for different speeds or for turns or directional speed control.

It is useful for the rider to practice securing this circle of points on the compass and becoming aware of which sections are weak and which sections are more dominant. Almost every rider will show obvious signs of more weight on the west or east side of the compass. Strive to create even weight on both the sit bones and your west and east points of the compass. The north and south sections must meet somewhere in the middle. It is a very fine line between too far forward and too far back. Experiment until you can feel your four compass points.

Seat bones to resemble the bottom of a rocking chair

Once again we are going to imagine the pelvis as a bowl. The bottom section of the bowl is round just as the base of a rocking chair would be. To get a feel of how this will affect your riding, sit in a rocking chair with your feet off the ground. Sit toward the edge of the seat, and keep your spine straight so the sit bones are evident.

The bottom of the pelvis (the section of the body that we use primarily as our floor when we sit in the saddle) is what we are going to focus on. If you sit forward in the rocking chair and put your weight toward the front of the chair, you are going to be rocked forward. This will cause the chair to be balancing weight on the front legs, similar to how a rider would position too much weight on the horse's forehand. This can sometimes speed up the horse without your intention of doing so or cause a loss of balance for the horse.

If you tip your weight backward causing the rocking chair to shift onto the back section of the rocker legs, the rider will be bearing most of the weight on the tailbone. This can cause a horse to hollow out the back muscles, or draw them away and down from the rider's seat.

Look for the point in between forward and back where the balance point is perfect and the bottom of the rocker is level. You are teetering right in between, much like a seesaw that is suspended in mid air due to equal amounts of weight on both sides.

Once the balance point is reached, the rider is closer to feeling the internal balance needed to be above the horse's center of gravity while riding.

Even when you are sitting in the two point position or the half seat, you will still be centered over the middle of the horse's back. You do not want to sit toward the horse's loins or up over the withers with the majority of your upper body. The difference between the distance of forward, backward, or neutral is a few inches. Try to experiment to find the spot that becomes comfortable.

Limbo under the limbo stick

The pelvis is a tricky section to the human body when riding. It is very easy to close the hip angle too much or to stiffen the surrounding muscles. It is a natural reaction for any rider to resort to a fetal position when they become nervous. However, bringing the upper body forward too much causes a problem when riding. We must train our muscles to go against what is natural and open up our hip joints and elongate the upper body. In order to achieve this, try the following exercise.

Imagine being able to cut your body in two at your belt line and detaching your upper body. Your instructor then places a limbo stick on the pommel of your saddle and asks you to limbo under it. You would need top open your hip joint slightly and in doing so your thighs would point more toward the ground. This is the correct angle for riding. However, do not be tempted to lean back excessively. Keep your upper body stacked on top of your hips. Also, be sure not to slip back too far onto the pockets of your jeans. Opening your hip joints is a small correction.

Sherrie is practicing opening her hip joints while Tara holds the stick. Once her hip joints are open she will keep that position, and bring her upper body forward to a vertical position once again.

Bicycle tire and two training wheels

As we explore more of the body as it relates to riding, there is also confusion about asymmetry in the body. Often a rider will drop the hip and collapse through the ribcage. This will cause the opposing side of the seat to lift slightly and allow an "opening" where the horse will feel a possible escape. Even with the riders best efforts to try to turn with the inside seat bone down, the outside seat bone will give way and the horse will begin to slide in the opposite direction. The rider must think of keeping both seat bones air tight to the saddle with a seal much like that of a bicycle with training wheels.

Visualize that your seat area and pelvic region has transformed into the back of a child's bicycle. This bicycle has two training wheels to aid the child with his/her balance. The training wheels represent your seat bones-one on the left and one on the right. The split of your derriere is now the bicycle tire when cueing the horse to turn. Keep both training wheels on the ground. Do not allow the wheels to lift up, as this will cause your seat to tilt. The bicycle tire stays lined up directly above the horse's spine. Keep the direction of the tire steering along with the spine at all times during the ride. As the horse turns or changes direction, the rider must follow the horse's backbone. When riding a straight line, keep the training wheels down and in place to help support the balance of the bicycle tire.

Often a rider thinks more of how to connect with the saddle by trying to still the seat. This is often misunderstood, and the rider will push against the saddle or try to sit too deep by sitting too heavily along the horse's back. This will often cause the horse to hollow its back away from the rider's seat and brings the opposite effect of what the desired response is. If the rider were riding bareback, think of the long back bone of the horse's spine. The rider would never want to exert extra pressure onto the area that is prominent as it would cause the horse discomfort. This holds true for any saddle that is sitting on the horse's back.

As you learn to ride better, you will discover your hips play a big role in shock absorption. The rider needs to imagine sitting on a bouncing balloon filled with air and how would this change the way the legs and seat bones connect. The balloon is soft, elastic, and has a 'give' to it. The balloon will move your seat. It has rhythm to it, and a gentleness that is different than sitting on the hard seat of the saddle. Pretend the saddle is not present and you are wrapping your thighs and seat around this balloon, paying careful attention not to squeeze through the balloon, or as that will cause the balloon to burst. A gentle hugging sensation is the feeling that you want the seat and upper thighs to emulate.

This will help riders who tend to be too heavy with their seat bones. You don't want to ram your seat bones into the horses back as this will hollow out the horse's back so it resembles a hammock. Your goal should be that you are sitting on a teacup that is upside down in its saucer waiting to be flipped over. This will resemble the start of collection with your horse. The balloon will keep the open roundness of the inner thigh and calf. This in turn keeps the contact area of the seat and thigh in connection with the horse's body, but does not allow the rider to heavily take over by excessively gripping or squeezing.

The foot will slip out of the stirrup if the rider is sitting too heavily on the seat bones. It's important that the rider does not just stand in the stirrup to fix it, but, rather, fixes the issue from the seat bone area. Too much weight on one seat bone will begin to close the hip and cause the rider to lighten weight in each stirrup.

Plastic underwear

Okay-I apologize for being direct, but this analogy has always helped riders position the pelvis and also to laugh and giggle, which helps to relax the rider. This eases tension when trying to control all the different parts of the body. Simply put, this imagery is funny, but will really help the rider to position the seat bones in the correct direction by moving the pelvic floor.

Imagine wearing underwear that is made of a hard plastic, similar to Tupperware. Imagine your underwear is placed on top of the horse and you fill it to the top with water. The water needs to remain in the underwear. In other words you cannot tip your pelvis forward in any direction. Hold the water within your underwear and do not spill a drop. Yes, it's a funny thought, but it works!

Keep a good sense of humor while you ride; it helps to prevent tension. You will be smiling with all four cheeks (if you know what I mean).

This exercise helps riders who use the stomach and back to move with the horse too much. You need to let that go and move with softness, elasticity, and timing. It also helps to extinguish the driving seat that has too much action and pushes from the rider's midsection and body. Sit still, let the horse do the moving. The rest of our body moves enough. Keep a nice stillness and solitude about your riding. Your horse will thank you.

Soup bowl

Once the neutral position is established using the plastic underwear scenario, it is important to shift gears and learn how to influence the horse's feet through the position of the pelvis. While neutral position and finding your "home" seat, as I refer to it, is very important, it is also necessary to influence the speed control, as well as the lifting seat so the rider can be intricate and consistent with how to ask for a change of speed each time. Envision your pelvis as a soup bowl now. This soup bowl is filled to the rim with soup. When requesting any forward movement from the horse, the soup bowl must slightly shift forward to gently pour the soup in the direction of the rider's two feet. The soup must not pour out quickly, or for too long, but just enough to trickle out the edge of the bowl, over the rider's belly button. This is what I refer to as your "tip" seat. This will encourage the horse to move forward at any gait or at any given moment. This is even useful during the posting trot if a horse needs to move forward more swiftly or with more energy.

Once the horse is going forward, there is a different seat that we will refer to as the "tuck" seat that will signal to the horse to slow the feet down or to rebalance the movement. Position the pelvis so the soup is sitting in the bowl without spilling a drop in any direction. The pelvis floor must remain beneath the rider and lie relaxed along the horse's spine. At no time during a ride should the rider tip the pelvis backward spilling any soup out of the back edge of the bowl. The tuck seat will signal the horse to transition downward, or while moving in a gait, the rider can tuck the seat and the horse will perform a half halt in response to the quick action of the differing seats of tip to go forward and tuck to rebalance. The tuck seat is also a way to slow down the trot and can be incorporated into the posting trot.

Do not allow the body to lean back at any point during your ride. The entire body must remain on vertical. The body may sometimes come in front of vertical, but never should it go behind vertical to lean backward or to pull on the reins.

Soup ladle

The spine is a direct connection to the seat. It is almost easier to think of the spine remaining attached to the seat in order to allow both pieces to interact with the horse in harmony and not to break apart the movement within the rider's body.

The soup bowl must now turn into a soup ladle. The seat and pelvis are the scoop to the ladle and the rider's spine is now the handle. When the rider is switching from a neutral seat to a tip or tuck seat, the soup ladle or spine must follow in that movement.

It is a hard concept for riders to allow the back to follow without bending that ladle. Think of keeping the ladle lined up from the tailbone to the nape of the neck. At no given point can the rider give way by leaning back, or bending through the ladle. Often a rider will break, or bend in the middle back or the lower back. When that option is removed, the rider will bring the top section of the back behind vertical or peel back with the shoulders. Keep strong as a unit. Leave the soup bowl intact first, then be sure that the ladle is in position as well. This is a tremendous calling for the abdominal wall and the back muscles to work together in order to sustain power so the arms do not have to do all the pulling against a strong horse who is powering through the bridle. This is the first step toward influencing the motion of the feet and gaining control of the speed and balance.

Belt stays level and even

Proper alignment and balance with the midsection of the body is a key ingredient of maintenance and stability as the horse moves the rider about in each gait. The center of the rider's body is, essentially, where a belt would be if the rider were wearing one. This is the imaginary seal between the upper portion of the body, and the lower portion of the body. It is a visual point of reference for the rider to think about as the connection takes place between the upper and lower extremities. If the rider folds over the belt line with the upper body rolling forward, or if the rider's spine spills over the rear of the belt, then the body

will need to play catch up in order to keep the alignment without losing the seat bones along the saddle as the horse is moving.

This is unnerving to some riders as they bounce about in the saddle and resort to gripping with the knees or thighs. The secret lies in the midsection of the body and how the rider uses the core muscles of the stomach and the lower back to maintain position. Keep the belt level and even, and do not allow the front of the buckle to drop down toward the seat of the saddle or the back of the belt to tilt back toward the cantle of the saddle. Keep it level and even from left to right so neither side is dipping down.

Hold the hula hoop

You could also practice holding the hula hoop. This is similar to the exercise above, but a hula hoop covers more of a circle than a belt. Picture you are holding the hula hoop with both hands by your waist. The hula hoop should not tilt forward, backward left, or right. This will help to keep your midsection stable and free from tilting or wobbling in unnecessary directions. The pelvis must remain in a fixed position (the "home" position). It will stray from this position every so often when you are asking for something different, but for the most part, it needs to remain still, but not rigid.

It also helps riders who hold a lot of tension in their back to think of using the hula hoop. Instead of the back staying stiff as a board, think of the mobility and relaxation the back will have to move with the hula hoop. The gentle circular motion is NOT what you want to emulate. Instead keep a deep softness within your body all along your back-from your lower back to the middle section, all the way to the top between your shoulder blades.

Tara's belt remains level and even. Strive for this position while riding. This is your "home seat".

Let go of the quarter (coin)

For the sake of remaining polite we are going to refer to the backside as your buns. When repositioning the body, it is not uncommon for the rider to clench their buns together, creating tension in that area. The tension will cause the rider to "pop up" out of the saddle and will make the rider become stiff and rigid. If a rider tightens the muscles it would be as if the rider were holding onto a quarter between their buns. The thighs, knees, and in some cases the ankle joint, will grip or tense up. Think of letting that go. There should no longer be any tension there and the backside should feel as though it's completely relaxed with your buttocks and seat bones making contact with the correct parts of the horse's back. Think in your mind, just to be funny, and give yourself a little laugh, keep the coin slot free.

Important

The seat is a highly tuned receptor that is very useful in riding. When changing disciplines or learning new skills you will be forced to change and adapt to new feelings on the horse's back. Practice good skills, and alignment to allow yourself to advance to higher levels of riding. It is useful to keep a journal of your new feelings. Continue to educate yourself and watch top level riders. Notice how they change their bodies or balance to better align themselves with their horses at a moment's notice. That is a sign of a great rider-one who is always striving for perfection within a ride to be better for their horse.

Coordination and strengthening exercises

Do a split

I use this as a warm up exercise for riders to help make the hip joints more mobile. It is easy to close the hip sockets and to lean forward in the saddle or allow your knees to ride up so the feet have less contact with the stirrups. During the split exercise you are going to remove the feet from the stirrups, then gradually let one leg move forward while the other leg moves backwards. In the beginning this may be a difficult exercise, but as you practice, you will notice that you are able to move your legs a little farther forward each time. As the right leg is forward, the left leg should be back. You are going to hold that position for a few seconds, then switch legs, and put your left leg forward and your right leg back. Think of your legs as a pair of scissors. The scissors are opened as far as they can go, and we have positioned the scissors on your horses back.

As you progress with this exercise you will be able to stretch your legs even farther forward which will increase the flexibility through the hip joints.

TIP

Keep a mental note of this exercise because this will be your steering as we progress into side-to-side balance and your turning aids. It is a key exercise to better your seat bones and allows the rider to feel how the seat works in order to make the horse turn right or left. It is far more effective once you do not allow your seat bones to slide off the side of the saddle and collapse in the ribcage. For upper level work you will even need to stabilize one seat bone over the other so the horse can pivot around it, and make smaller and smaller turns and circles.

Frog exercise

The frog exercise is one of the more difficult exercises. If you need to start on the ground and sit in a chair to get the feel of the exercise, do so, but be sure to keep your hip flexors and your thighs stretching at all times. This will keep the muscles from freezing.

While sitting on your horse ask the horse to walk forward. You are going to position your legs to look like a frog. Bring both thighs out and away from the saddle. Push your thighs back until you feel as though you are making a diamond shape. Your thighs will point out and away from the horse's sides as far as your muscle stretch will allow. Both back sections of your lower calves will rest along the horse's sides directly above each foot. You are going to turn both feet directly out to the side to their full extent. The right toe will be pointing toward three o'clock and the left toe will be pointing toward nine o'clock. Both knees will do the same. You will feel the platform of your seat rest upon the saddle. Stay in balance with your seat. Keep your upper body over top of your hips. Your feet, knees and hips should be stacked one over top the other. Strive to stretch as far as you can and hold this position for a few steps.

Once you can hold the position, then begin to pulse your thighs backwards in tiny movements. You will feel the back of the gluteus muscles begin to work. Just below your buttocks you may experience a small burning sensation. This is the seat working hard. These muscles need to remain relaxed while you ride. Begin by working in reps of 10 and then increase the amount of reps.

Once you are good at this exercise, you can begin to trot in this position. It will also teach your lower leg to hold with the correct section instead of gripping in the upper portion of the calf. This is very useful when jumping or performing any other activity where you need to feel the use of your lower calf.

It will also help with recognizing which muscle to trigger in the back of the thigh when you need to pull the back of the thigh down in order to deepen the seat. This muscle strength is key to major riding issues that may occur later in training.

Floor walking exercise

This exercise can be done in the comfort of your home after a long day of riding. One of the best ways to feel the seat bones hard at work is to sit on a carpeted floor. Extend your legs forward. Sit with your back straight. Put your hands on top of your head and think of your seat bones as tiny legs. You are going to walk forward on your seat bones. Strive to use one seat bone at a time. Try not to contract the muscle too tightly. Instead, relax the muscles that surround the seat bones. These will strengthen your muscles, and allow you to trigger one seat bone at a time. This will give you an idea of how to keep your seat bones evenly weighted while using one at a time.

Putting Pieces & Position into Practice

Using the seat as the steering wheel

When learning how to distinguish the placement of the seat bones, riding in straight lines is far easier at first. Traveling in a direct line will promote better body balance. Once this is established you can then start to work on the balance of the seat and upper body when turning and changing direction.

It is helpful to think of carrying a passenger on your shoulders. If that person were to lean forward or backward, you would need to immediately step underneath their weight in order to balance yourself. Likewise, if they were to lean to the left or to the right you would also follow their direction to sustain your balance. Your horse is no different. They must keep getting underneath a rider's center of balance in order to maintain their own. This is why it becomes so important to develop good skills to stay centered over top of the horse as you ride.

We expect our horses to keep a round circle or to perform better transitions while riding. This cannot be possible for the horse until we, as the rider, take responsibility for our own balance.

Let's look at how we can become better balanced for optimum performance of turning and aids.

Steering with the three prong plug

The "three prong plug" is comprised of the right seat bone, the left bone, and either the front or the back of the pelvis. When moving forward on the horse, the rider will rock slightly onto the front of the pelvis, and the two seat bones. If you are maneuvering to the left then you will begin to add slight weight to the left seat bone and the pelvis. It is important, however, that you do not lose the right seat bone which is a common mistake. Do not collapse throughout the ribcage or tilt your upper body toward the inside of the direction you are turning.

Envision a teeter totter that is placed across the midline of the saddle. The ends reach past the stirrups to the right and left. You are sitting in the middle of that teeter totter. You are trying to keep the weight from rocking past the point of extensive weight so that the end of the teeter totter would touch the ground on the left. If the left side of the teeter totter begins to fall toward the ground then the right seat bone is losing contact with the saddle, causing the rider to drop the left shoulder. The majority of their bodyweight will fall to the left, and the horse will follow suit by dropping their left shoulder and performing a turn out of balance. The horse's feet will lose the rhythm, and they will begin to take faster steps to keep their balance. Our goal is always rhythmic footfall and even balance.

The same would hold true when traveling to the right. The rider's hip will actually do more of the steering than the torso. Oftentimes riders will swivel with their upper body creating a twist in their seat and throughout their upper framework. The connection will be lost because the seat bones are not advancing. You are still in essence telling the horse to travel a straight line with the seat, while the upper body has twisted and asked for the horse to turn. This becomes a conflicting signal to the horse, and the horse will choose to follow one aid over the other. The aid they choose to follow may not necessarily be what you are looking for.

I think in terms of a never rotating past the degree of eleven o'clock when traveling left and one o'clock when traveling right.

It is helpful when making any turn or change of direction to think of shining your lights. If you are turning use your first aids which are your eyes. They will look towards one o'clock if you are performing a right turn and eleven o'clock if performing a left turn. Both shoulders have a flashlight which will light the way of the intended path of travel. The shoulder lights must remain level and even. If one light appears to be crooked, then the rider is leaning in that direction.

TIP

Uneven shoulders is a tell tale sign that you are not holding the reins with even tension on both sides of the horse's mouth. Keep your shoulder lights steady and even in a turn.

The third section of light would be the belly button, which I often refer to as the third eye. If you had a laser beam projecting from the belly button, it would shine in the direction of travel below the rider's shoulder flashlights. It will not extend any further than one o'clock or eleven o'clock. Too far will cause the rider to twist their torso, and lose contact with the seat bones. You can also apply too much rein pressure, in some situations, causing the horse to swing the hindquarters to the opposite direction of travel and lose the rhythm of the footfall.

The fourth set of lights and perhaps the most overlooked, but the most important, are the hips. If you envision high beam lights that shine brightly, they will project a steady stream of light at approximately the neck level of the horse. Those headlights will help to aid in the turns and keep the seat bones level.

When this happens correctly, you will finish the turn with gentle ease because the hands and legs will be in a position to influence the horse's body without you turning into a human pretzel trying to figure out how to use what hand and leg aids. Just concentrate on your eyes, shoulders, belly button, and hips making each turn, and not extending past the point of 11:00 for a left turn and 1:00 for a right turn. You will feel as though you have gained power steering, essentially. This will help to develop an 'invisible' turn.

Transitions to speed up and slow down using the three prong plug

When using your seat bones to speed up or slow down in a transition it is often exaggerated by most riders. The truth of the matter is that it is a very small movement within the body to shift the weight from pelvis to neutral, then neutral to tailbone. I speak of the tailbone as if you are sitting on it, but in all reality you are not actually going to be sitting on your tailbone. You understand that the direction of the tailbone is, instead, what I want you to grasp.

In any upward transition whether it be halt to walk, or walk to trot, or even trot to canter, you must think of shifting into gear with the seat bones first. This is what I call your pre-cue.

You will follow the seat cue with leg to establish forward movement, but if you use your seat bones in a way that your horse can feel, you will first allow the horse the chance to move forward. This also is true for stopping or any downward transition from canter to trot, or trot to walk, walk to halt.

Keeping a steady seat is key to obtaining those smooth transitions that look as though the rider never added any rein pressure. Gaining control of your three prong plug will help you to visualize exactly how much pressure needs to be added with each seat bone in order to gain control of the horse's feet.

To slow the horse's feet down, think of using the left seat bone and right seat bones together to keep the balance on the teeter totter. You can think of down shifting as if you are tilting a chair backward so the front of the legs lift off the ground slightly. Your upper body must remain in balance. Your shoulders will stay stacked over top of your hips.

The angle of the pelvis in a downward transition is sometimes overdone by riders. Think of attaching a cat tail to your tailbone. Take that cat tail and pull it between your legs in an upward direction. Doing this would shift your pelvis ever so gently into the position needed to stay in balance with a horse in a downward transition.

To speed the horse's feet up, you are going to think of the opposite, and roll forward onto your pelvis while leaving your two seat bones level and even on the teeter totter once again. Do not allow the upper body to collapse forward. It must remain open and stacked above your hips. Your hip joints must remain open.

We will talk in great detail about the hips and upper body in later chapters. Just keep in mind how the diamond works.

Puzzle Piece #7
Stomach & Back

Postural Balance

Checklist for proper Alignment of Stomach and Back

- ✓ Locating and engaging the core.
- ✓ Belly button as a source of water.
- ✓ Green laser beam light shining out of your belly button.
- ✓ Wrap your midsection in saran wrap.
- ✓ Push the bottom rib towards the hip.
- ✓ Swallow the beach ball.
- ✓ Keep the torso in a tube.
- ✓ Bungee cords attached to the front and the back.
- ✓ Breathe through the spine and blow out the birthday candles.
- ✓ Ribs and the blinds
- ✓ Breathing with strength

Stomach and Back

The primary function of the core and the back while riding are to help stabilize the upper body and act as the foundation for weight distribution. They contribute to a strong, well aligned pelvis, and allow the rider's hips, low back muscles, and hamstrings to work in conjunction with one another to move with the motion of the horse. The abdominal muscles help to flex and rotate the spine, as well as to provide support for the lower back. These are two functions that are of primary importance for balance and support while riding.

The lower abdominals take on the huge role of maintaining correct pelvic alignment so that the weight is balanced correctly on each seat bone. This allows the rider to use the seat effectively. To build the core takes a long time and needs to be done, essentially, from the inside out. An off-horse exercise regimen is a daily routine for most upper level equestrians and if a rider ever wants to develop their skill, strong abdominal muscles are a must.

The rider's back also plays a huge role as the back can absorb a lot of the concussion from the horse, whether the rider is sitting in correct alignment or not. This can cause problems if the rider is not taught to strengthen the back and the abdominal muscles equally. A bracing back will often halt the movement of the hips. This is good when asking for a half halt or a stop. However, if the rider wishes to keep moving, but the horse keeps breaking the gait, then the rider must look for the cause. It may be that the abdominals or the back is not strong enough to support the rider and more work must be done in these areas to insure that the rider is in top shape. It is then that the aids can be clearer.

Riding Realities

Common Errors and Enigmas

Although the stomach and back are opposing muscle groups, while riding they need to be thought of as a unit. Core strength is key to good balance and is the link between the upper body and legs. When referring to the upper body, this is the entire front of the body from the hip to the first rib directly under shoulder girdle in the front of the body and from the tailbone to under the armpits down the back of the body. It is, in a sense, the biggest section all together that needs to be in good working order while riding

If the rider tips too far forward or too far back with this section, a domino effect may result with the loss of other body parts not maintaining proper balance and alignment. The stomach and back are, essentially, the glue that holds the body together when all else fails during riding. It is easy for the rider to collapse in the midsection of the back or the stomach area. Let's discuss in more detail how some flaws enable this to happen.

Familiar Faults

Fault 1

There is a common misconception associated with riding, and that is to keep the tummy sucked in. While the rider needs to keep the contractions of the stomach muscles strong by pulling the belly in, doing this will often round the rider's shoulders, as well. The result will be a round-backed rider who will lose their seat if they are not careful, and their lower leg will swing forward. In reality, your core muscles must be stable, but the back muscles must offer a similar resistance in order to sustain stability. The rider's shoulders remain over the hips and the core area becomes equally strong from back to front and front to back.

Fault 2

On the contrary, other riders go to the extreme of becoming hollow-backed which means that the belly button has come in front of the hips and pubic bone. The lower back remains rigid and tight, and the rider gives the illusion of sitting up tall and elegant, but in reality, they have become locked, and tend to rock forward onto the pubic bone too much. The lower back will resemble a hammock, or a banana shape. Over time, the concussion of the horse's movement can injure the rider's back if careful attention is not paid to this section of the rider's body. The hollow-backed rider will tend to pull the shoulders back too much. This will only create more tension between the shoulder blades and become hard for the rider to keep a gentle contact with the reins. Once again, the rider must display equal amounts of tummy hold and back hold.

Fault 3

Some riders have the alignment of the lower body all worked out but the upper body will sneak forward, especially at the canter when the rider rocks excessively with the upper body in order to keep the illusion of being soft with the horse. The shoulders begin to fall ahead of the sternum or the rider allows the sternum to fall forward in front of the belly button. This will gradually begin to peel away the section of the seat that is supposed to be in contact with the saddle. A midsection break in the body such as this one will split the body in two. While the lower portion remains stable and steady, the upper portion will fall forward causing the shoulders to slump and the back of the body to become weak. The rider's seat will lift because of the lack of stabilization between the top and bottom portions of the body.

Fault 4

Some riders will go to the other extreme-leaning back too much with the upper half of the shoulder girdle. This is common in attempts to fix the sitting trot, or with canter work. The shoulders have fallen behind the tailbone. Even if the rider has not become hollow-backed, they still will lose the seat bones and begin to lightly brush upon the saddle. It will cause the rider to be behind the motion of the horse's feet, and in turn, the horse will slip out forward underneath them. The rider will then have to resort to heavily using their hands if the horse has not already dropped the front of their body. This forces the rider to become the fifth leg by allowing the horse to lean excessively on the hands in order to help balance. Leaning back is often performed by riders who are extending the paces as well or asking for the horse to open the stride. When asking the horse for an extended gait, the rider will tend to lean back too far with the upper portion of the body. To deter the body from doing this, pretend we had placed marbles on your shoulders. It is important to keep these marbles in place. If the marbles would  tend to roll off backwards, then you know you have fallen into this trap a time or two.

Tara is really leaning back to show how the lower leg swings forward, and the pull on the reins for balance becomes evident. She would land on her rump if the horse were not beneath her anymore.

Fault 5

In retrospect, there are also problems with the outer rims, meaning the side to side portions of our bodies. The ribcage is a common problem with riders who tend to lean to one side or collapse throughout the ribcage. This creates uneven weight in the seat bones and the rider's hip will slip out instead of becoming a strong barrier to help keep the horse upright. Curling the ribs or contorting the midsection to help the horse change directions will always lead to bigger problems with the seat and with leg cues. It will become hard for the horse to decipher what you are asking if you allow your midsection to collapse to the left or to the right. Keep the ribcage stacked one rib at a time. The rotation to turn the body comes from the center of our core.

Picture Perfect Pieces

Now envision your picture perfect pieces for the improved ride

Imagery examination:

The core as the nucleus

Further Explanation

The core, or central part of the body, is the nucleus of our riding position. It includes the stomach, chest, shoulders and the three sections of the back. It is important to keep the front section of the body and the back section of the body in the correct alignment.

The midsection of our core meshes the top half of our sternum and lateral muscles to the lower section which includes the area from the belly button just before where our hips and gluteals begin. The core will help absorb some of the shock and helps the rider to move in motion and develop proper timing with the horse. It is also responsible for holding the rider in position during transitions up and down. Often a rider will use the upper back to push the horse forward, or hold the front of the body to slow the horse down. Once control is established in the core area, the rider may then surrender the hands instead of resorting to leaning on the horse's mouth for balance. This will create better balance throughout the entire ride.

Essential Details of each Imagery

Locating and engaging the core

Engaging the abdominals is the basis for the beginning stages of how the rider begins to strengthen the body in order to withstand the push and pull generated by the horse while in motion. To feel how the core engages, first pull up the pelvic floor of the lower region of the body. It is the same feeling as how one would hold off urination. The area just above the pubic bone is the area to focus on. Draw the tummy in, at the same time gently blow out through tight lips that are slightly closed. Concentrate on the tummy, and drawing it in. This is the contraction of the transverse abdominals. The rider must strengthen these muscles in order to maintain stability from moment to moment during different phases of the ride.

Belly button as a source of water

Stabilization and placement of the core is hard to reproduce in a manner that is repetitive and productive for balance. When on the horse, a rider's body is stabilized to a considerable degree by the transverse abdominals. That is the deepest layer of muscle, and it is found around the entire midsection. It is useful to think of the belly button as remaining stable, and aiming toward an imaginary target while riding. This reminds the rider to keep upright and toned.

Let's imagine that the belly button is now a source of water. By this I mean, pay careful attention to the positioning of the midsection. If the belly button was replaced with a sprinkler like the kind used to water the garden, it would gently trickle out, and land at or about the horse's withers. The flow would not be very powerful.

Let's move to a water source with a little more "oomph" and think of a garden hose. The flow of the water would be more powerful and more accurate, but the force would still not be enough to hold the front of the body against a horse that is pushing back against you.

If the rider is leaning slightly forward, picture where that water would start to flow. It would land somewhere in front of the horse's two front feet. If the rider is leaning back too far, it would go right over the horse's head in a spouting motion. Neither of these directions is accurate for what we are looking for with our horses. Instead, sit so the water hose pressure would flow directly between the horse's ears.

To generate maximum power and control, let's now picture a fire hose. The fire hose can generate a lot of pressure when the water is flowing out. Aim the hose towards the horse's poll, and keep the direction steady. This will help guide the midsection in the correct direction without collapsing or dropping the upper body. By achieving the power of the fire hose, the rider can then target the tummy as a shield against the horse's pull forward and push back. The rider will be able to stabilize the body, and lessen the force generated by the hands and arms.

Green laser beam of light

The proper angle of the midsection is important to help balance the body. A collapsing midsection can lead to an abundance of other issues while riding, such as collapsing shoulders and ribcage, which lead to a trickle-down effect with the hands and arms holding and adding unnecessary pulling pressure to the reins.

For better directional control, it is useful for the rider to think of another analogy. A green laser beam of light that is radiating from the belly button is an excellent visual. This light is a thin, streamlined green light which points in the direction that you wish to travel. The light must beam straight out and direct; you don't want it to shine down toward the ground or up over the horse's head. Keep the light steady so it doesn't bounce, similar to car lights. If you are driving a car and hit a bump in the road, the lights would bounce, but never move off the intended path of travel. The same should be true for this imaginary green laser beam.

As we discussed before, the green laser beam light becomes a key part of turning left and right. It is the third aid used when asking for a change of direction. Learn to use it when necessary to keep the upper body connected to the midsection.

Wrap your midsection in saran wrap

It is important to be able to keep your midsection still and steady while riding. The best way to accomplish this is to strengthen the core muscles. The rider must think of inflating the midsection inside the body. This is a very strange and new concept to most riders in the beginning stages of exploring. Once you master it, however, the change within yourself and your horse will be amazing.

The secret to a strong core is to expand within and allow your insides to leak through the ribs from the front to the back portions, as well as the side to side portions. Think of wrapping your middle in saran wrap from below the chest, to the top of the hips. The saran wrap is tight and very neatly overlapping the middle. Think of this saran wrap keeping the body from collapsing through the sides. It will hold the alignment.

Abdominal strength is built from the inside out. It will expand into the lower back region as the rider learns how to control the contraction, and the breathing.

In order to trigger the proper muscles, imagine that you were trying to remove this saran wrap without using your hands. You must use your inner core muscles to break free, and expand your insides enough with muscle strength to break through the plastic. This is how you are going to use your muscles from the inside out. This will help to stabilize the midsection and keep the rider from being juggled or wobbly from the horse's momentum as it changes gaits.

You will almost feel as though an inner tube is around your mid-section and you're slowly inflating it with air. Your insides will push against each rib. Once this core control is gained of the upper, middle, and lower parts of the stomach, you are on your way to developing strong core strength.

A rider who has a strong core will, in turn, protect the back muscles, and vice versa. It is difficult to work on a specific muscle group and keep the muscles in top working condition for the full ride. By working in small cycles, the muscles will strengthen, allowing the body a longer duration of time to keep them contracted and operating correctly for a stronger ride.

Bottom rib towards the hip

A common catch phrase used by riding instructors is to sit tall and keep the appearance of an elegant silhouette. Straighten throughout the body, stretch through the torso, and brace the back. I believe that the rider must think in the opposite direction. When a rider is taught to sit tall they sometimes make the mistake of stretching the body away from the saddle. This will, in turn, cause the rider to lose the connection with the horse's back.

In order to balance the body through the midsection, the rider must think of standing taller, but in turn, making the midsection smaller. Tighten the abs, as if someone was tickling you, and you are contracting those muscles in order to shy away from the sensation.

Think of becoming smaller without slouching in the saddle. The body needs to align correctly, but by bringing the last rib down towards the hip. The inner muscles will feel as though they are an accordion, and will begin to strengthen as they pile on top of each other. Don't wrinkle the midsection by bending over.

This will make a greater connection with the horse's back and use the seat to influence the horse's movement. This also helps with being able to push the stomach muscles out against a resistance. This will make you strong and stable.

Riders must target and train the core muscles to improve balance and performance while riding. It is important to attain good posture in everyday life as well.

Swallow the beach ball

While this analogy sounds silly, it is very helpful to imagine. The lower abdomen and lower back are hard sections of the body to target and manage muscle tone and strength. Imagine swallowing a deflated beach ball. Eventually, it will come to rest on the pelvic floor. Now, imagine the feeling as it is inflated to it normal size.

As you inhale the lower abdomen will expand. When the full breath is reached, the rider must hold the ball in place using the abs and lower back as you inhale in order to be ready to exhale once again. The breathing pattern of the rider will keep the ball inflated as you inhale. This feeling must remain that the roundness of the beach ball as it sits on your pelvic floor until it is something that comes naturally. This power is used when you need to anchor the seat and teach the horse to seek contact on the bridle. The muscles of the backside will help to anchor the body, especially in downward transitions, when the core becomes the power source and begins to equalize the tone from the hands and arms. This is when the rider is truly on the way to good posture, alignment, and balance.

Another way to think about this is to picture a plug that holds the beach ball in place on the pelvic floor. The midsection of your body will act as the "plug" and by keeping the ball low allows the body to fill out and expand against the ribcage. The concept of stabilizing inside the rider's body can be rather confusing and difficult to master, but it is a huge piece of the puzzle. Once achieved, the rider will be much more powerful to act against the forces that the horse will generate. You will find that you will not need as much rein pressure if the pre-cue is through the body first.

Torso in a tube

Once the midsection is stable and the muscle tone can support the ribcage, belly and back, the rider can learn how to turn the midsection as a unit. This is similar to the feeling of being trapped inside a tube. There must be no collapsing sensation in the ribcage to the left or to the right side as a rider turns with the horse in the direction of travel.

Asymmetries are a huge downfall to some riders, as they never fully become aware of how to maneuver their body in order to sustain proper balance and to help the horse align and keep proper balance as well. The upright incline from the under the rider's armpit muscles to the top of the pelvis must be involved in turning, or changing direction. Once the rider can feel the sensation of remaining inside a tube that holds the body tightly upright, the hips can begin to initiate the turn. This is similar to shifting the hips as if the rider were doing a split. The horse will feel the change in balance of the seat and the torso much more so than if the rider was not inside the tube, and twisting the torso so the ribcage would collapse. You will find that you will not need as much rein pressure if the pre cue is through the body first.

Bungee cords

As the horse is being ridden, it is difficult to gauge how much to move with the horse's motion, or how much to hold against the motion to stabilize the body. How much do you rock forward and back?

The abdominals and the back must act against one another in order to stabilize the body in movement. If the front section of the body shortens, and the back lengthens, or vice versa, the result could be too much give and not enough hold, or too much brace throughout the body which will act against the soft movement that ripples through the rider's body while riding.

> *Most problems that arise when sitting the trot are due to weak stomach muscles, or unbalanced core strength. Riders will grip with the knees and the thighs and bounce on the horse's back. Instead, they should work on becoming stronger through the core and learn to balance through the torso.*

Imagine that you have a bungee cord attached to the center of your collar bone at the front. The other end is attached between the horse's ears. There is also a bungee cord in the back. This bungee cord is attached at the back of the neck, and extends behind the body to the horse's tail. The bungee cords must remain even and exhibit even tension as you ride.

If the rider is stretching either bungee cord an adjustment will need to be made in order to help the body balance between the cords and keep the tension even, with the flow of the forward and backward push from the horse's body.

This will help the rider learn how to move along with the horse's motion and not disturb the natural movement while keeping the body in the center.

Tara's Test: Try to sing the ABC's or recite a nursery rhyme while you are riding. It is important that once you learn how to engage your core, you also learn how to control your breathing. Singing or talking will help you get past this tough transition in your riding.

Breathe through the spine and blow out the birthday candles

So many times while riding, the lower back will begin to stiffen. The rider will struggle with the muscles and letting go of that ring of tension in order to sustain elasticity through the body.

To help you release that tension, go back in time to your last birthday celebration with cake. You are going to repeat that moment when a wish was made and the candles were blown out on the cake.

Breathe from the bottom of your back way down at your tailbone and lift up through your shoulder blades, inhaling deeply. As you exhale think of blowing out all the candles on your cake. The breath will be deep and come from your diaphragm. This will soften the lower back muscles and release some tension in the lower back region. This action needs to be repeated as you are riding. It will deepen the seat and allow the seat bones to settle along the horse's back.

This is also useful when moving along with the horse's motion. The gentle rocking motion will keep the rider's back in a swinging motion.

Think of Cyclops the old myth of the one-eyed man. The belly button becomes that eye. Think of the belly button pointing in the direction of travel while traveling straight, making turns or changing direction. Keep the belly button lined up, and use it effectively to maintain an erect position. This will keep the body from collapsing through the ribcage.

One day a student of mine was watching me ride one of my personal horses. All of a sudden she stopped me and said, "Imagine while you are riding that you have a piece of string or a long piece of dental floss. Attach it from the back of your pony tail to back of your pants along your belt loop." I pondered what she said for a moment, and began to imagine the dental floss. Suddenly I felt my head become stable, but lightweight. Sometimes in riding, you just need another set of eyes to help you figure out a puzzle.

I rode off with this amazing feeling of lightness throughout the back of my body. For all the trainers and fellow instructors who are reading this book, you will sympathize along with me when I say that the trainer has a way of looking down at the horse constantly to check what the horse is doing, or feeling, where the ears are, the eyes are, the neck position, and head position etc. Once I opened up the front of my body by thinking about the back of it, my horse immediately responded by becoming lighter on the forehand. It was one of those amazing moments for me. Not because I had changed my body and helped my horse, but because my student was able to look at my body and find the piece to the puzzle that was missing. There are no greater moments for a teacher than to realize the moment you have taught someone to learn and change what they have always done. Under my student's watchful eye, she helped me to attain one of the most beautiful rides I have ever had on my personal horse. What a wonderful moment!

The ribs as blinds

Collapsing through the ribcage from the underline of the arm pit to the top of the outer portion of the hip joint is a common error while riding. It is important to keep the sidelines, as I refer to them, open, so each rib has an equal amount of cushion between each bone. A horse will often follow suit with the weight shift of the rider. If the rider sticks the ribs together by bending sideways so the shoulder gets closer to the hip, then the horse will respond by making that side of the body concave. The result will be the desire of the rider to turn in the direction of their body bend, but the horse will be forced in the opposite direction to keep their balance on all four feet.

Picture the ribs as window blinds like you would see in a window to block the sunlight. These blinds must remain open, with the same amount of separation between each slat. Don't close the blinds and block out the sunlight from shining through. Keep the ribs separated with equal space between each bone, so that the outer rims of both sides of the body remain even. This will help with changes of direction, serpentines, and circles. If the rider thinks of the horse's ribcage as remaining upright and in balance, then the ribcage of the rider will remain upright and in balance, as well.

Breathing while strengthening the abdominals and back

Often when the abdominals or back muscles contract, especially down in the lower region, it becomes hard to breathe and hold the contraction at the same time. Riders are forced to let go of the contraction and breathe, or, contract and hold their breath. It takes quite a long time to be able to turn the strength of the abdominals and back on and off. I think of it as a volume switch which can be turned up to be louder or stronger in this sense. Or it can be turned down if the horse can hear the rider with the current level of strength displayed.

I often teach a three stage breathing regimen to riders so they learn to hold a contraction or make the tummy muscles strong, and then, breathe long with it so the muscles stay toned at the same time.

Stage 1: Blowing bubbles

To contract the tummy muscles, think of doing a sit up. You have reached the top of the rise and you now feel the contraction, this is what you hold. Once the abs are strong, then think of using a wand to dip into bubbles. You are going to gently think of blowing the bubbles through the wand in a steady stream. This is stage one. Do this until you can keep the muscle tone. When you lose it, begin again.

Tara is gently blowing the bubbles through the wand with a steady, light flow of air. The stream of bubbles are floating forward much like how you would like your breath of air as you exhale,

Stage 2: Blow up a bubble of bubble gum

Contract the tummy once again, but this time think of blowing a bubble with a big wad of chewing gum. The lower abs will still contract and you may feel a deeper sensation below the belly button. Test how far you can blow up the bubble without losing the tummy contraction. When you lose it, begin again.

Caitie is gently blowing a bubble with chewing gum. She is focusing on keeping the air flow steady enough not to break the gum's bubble. The exhale is slightly more powerful than the bubbles through the wand.

Stage 3: Blow up the balloon

To deepen the breath and to make it more powerful, you can practice with a balloon. Hold the balloon between your teeth and use your tongue to block the opening. Do not allow any air to escape until you are ready to blow a big deep breath into the balloon to fully inflate it. This breath must come from the depths of your lungs, using your abdominals to push it out. The more you can fill the balloon with one deep breath the more you are on your way to discovering the secrets to what the great riders do within their abs and diaphragm.

Tara is breathing deeply into the lower section of her abdominals. The section of the abs where her hand is resting is the area that is a huge piece to the riding puzzle.

Once you gain control of your abdominals, you can begin to turn the volume up or down by controlling the muscles within the confines of your midsection.

Coordination and Strengthening Exercises

There are many exercises that can be used to strengthen a rider's back and stomach. A strong core and back will always promote better posture for your everyday life. To keep an independent seat, and a steady hand, you must always be conscious of how strong and toned your mid-section is. Gain control of not only your muscle tone, but your breathing, as well. Once you learn to control your muscles, the next challenge will be to breathe and to hold the muscle tone and strength while riding. Practice in small increments; the learning process happens in stages.

Finding the lower back muscle

It is often hard for the rider to keep the lower back muscles strong while maintaining a neutral spine. The following position will help the hollow-backed rider to fill out the lower back and plump up the muscles there in order to use the mid-section effectively.

Lie on the floor, flat on your back with your knees bent, and feet flat on the floor. Place your hand on your abdomen directly below the belly button. Think of pushing your lower back into the floor by bringing the belly button through to the spine. You will feel your lower back touch the floor. This is the position you are striving for, and the feeling needed in order to use the lower back to help bring the seat closer to the saddle. It will also aid in slowing the horse's feet down and allowing the rider to learn how to manipulate the muscle tone and contractions within the body. (It is then that the rider can turn on the tone, and turn it off like a light switch in order to activate the muscle for more power while riding.) With plenty of practice, the rider will find that he or she can turn the tone on and off like a light switch in order to activate the muscle for more power when riding.

You can also place a book on your abdomen and practice lifting and lowering the book using your breathing, and your muscle tone inside your stomach. Practice this for reps of 10. You will feel the difference in your riding by paying careful attention to this tip.

Pant like a dog breathing

Once you have mastered how to contract your abdominal muscles and toned the inside of your body, it is important to be able to breathe as well. My student who is a vocal coach helped me with this exercise. She uses a dog panting analogy to help her students strengthen their abdominals to hold a vocal note.

Think of a dog on a very hot day and picture how they pant. Do a series of short panting breaths, but only in groups of five or six. Relax the abdominals and do it again. It is important to take a break in between the series of breaths so you do not become light-headed. Put your hand below your navel and feel how this strengthens your abdominals. This muscle must protrude when riding in order to help the body stay in alignment, and fight against the horses push-back at the rider's body. The abdominal wall will keep the rider steady and strong.

Blow up the balloon

Another exercise to help strengthen the abdominals, and allow the rider to feel what pieces of the lower stomach to use, is blowing up a balloon. The prior talk about breathing addressed the balloon. It is important, however, to put this into practice so the rider can understand how to use the deep inner core muscles.

Practice with a real balloon. Take a deep breath in and begin to blow up the balloon while leaving your hand below your belly button to feel the strength you suddenly gain throughout your abdominals. Blow up the balloon to the very last moment when you run out of breath. You will feel your lower abdomen sink lower. This is the anchor that holds your seat in place. When your horse is hard to stop or is pulling through the bridle, instead of going straight to your hands and pulling on the reins for strength, first blow up the balloon to anchor your body. This will free up the hands so they can direct the horse, instead of pulling on the mouth and shortening the horse's neck.

Wear a waist trimmer belt

A waist trimmer belt can be found in your local store in the exercise department. It is extremely useful to wear while you are riding. It helps you to push the abdominals and back muscles against resistance. Most riders will do the opposite and pull their muscles inward or just keep them relaxed and flaccid.

If you wear the waist trimmer belt, you will become more aware of keeping the lower portion of the body in check while you ride an upward or downward transition. Keep everything below the belt anchored and everything above the belt directly above it.

Tara is wearing the waist trimmer belt as a reminder to keep her abs pushing out. The feeling of keeping the abs toned is helpful once the belt is in place. It gives the rider something to push against.

Upper back against a wall

Now we are going to examine the upper back muscles and their role in helping to become more effective in upward transitions. It is important to use the back for the extra push forward when the horse is beginning to slow the feet. Strengthening this section of the back is hard to do while riding, so you will need to do this exercise on the ground. Stand with your back against the wall. Allow your lower back, middle back, and especially the upper back from shoulder to shoulder, to press against the wall. Picture the area of your back especially between the shoulder blades expanding as if you were wearing wings, and you were extending the wings out past your shoulders. Push back

against the wall as you are doing this. This feeling of pushing backward against a resistance, but not actually leaning backward is the feeling you need to emulate while on your horse. This will help greatly when you can harness this power to ask your horse to move forward while being able to use the front portion of the stomach, as well.

Puzzle Piece #8

Shoulders
Upper Arms

Imagery
Essentials

Equalizers and Balance Beams

Checklist for Proper Alignment of the Shoulders and Upper Arms

- ✓ Up, back, and down with the shoulders.
- ✓ Carry two full buckets of water,
- ✓ Activate the arm pit muscle.
- ✓ Keep a Pencil arm.
- ✓ Water faucet in the shoulder.
- ✓ Keep the barbell in the elbow.
- ✓ Marbles balanced on the shoulders so they don't roll off.
- ✓ Shoulder girdle to remain over the ribcage.

Riding Realities

Common Errors and Enigmas

When the shoulders of the rider are aligned correctly they hold a lot of power. They can help to balance the rest of the arm and also serve as a brake that can be connected to the midsection if the horse becomes strong in the rider's hands. The shoulders can be the tipping point for the rider. If the rider allows the shoulder to move either too far forward or too far back, the rest of the upper body will slowly begin to follow. This will result in other issues that can become major alignment flaws.

The triceps and bicep muscles of the upper arm also play a big role in stabilizing the power used by the rider's hands. The upper body tends to be the weakest part of the rider; so many riders will resort to pulling with the bicep muscles and flexing the upper arm to add a giant pull to the horse's mouth. This will always result in a harder pull from the horse. The rider needs to learn how to use the tricep muscle instead, and sink down through the upper arm.

As you read through this book, know that you are taking gigantic steps to becoming a balanced rider who is taking the utmost care to give up overusing the hands. The new communication between you and your horse will reach places you never dreamed possible. You have opened new doors, and will feel a different feeling on your horse when the magic happens. Good luck in your journey.

Familiar Faults

Fault 1

Many riders experience issues with the shoulders. If the rider allows the shoulder girdle to collapse, the chest will lower. This will round the upper portion of the rider's back, causing the shoulder blades to spread apart. It is the same scenario as letting the collar bone come in front of the sternum. The upper chest will fold over and drop down closer to the sternum instead of lifting slightly. The key to the fix is bringing the shoulders back above the ribcage and above the hips without hollowing the lower back.

Tara has rolled her shoulders beyond the point of her sternum. The front section of her armpit is now closed.

Fault 2

Another fault a rider may exhibit is rolling the shoulders back too far behind the ribcage which pinches the shoulder blades together. This forms a ring of tension in the upper portion of the body and a hollowing of the middle and lower back. Another result of rolling the shoulders too far back may be stiffening of the forearms, which can cause the rider's hands to rise, putting unnecessary pressure on the horse's mouth. The overall effect is likely to be a 'fork seat', which is when the pubic bone drives down into the saddle like the prongs of a fork.

Fault 3

The "fly away" shoulder is sometimes a direct result of a rider trying to sit tall. Sometimes a rider misinterprets being elegant with stretching the body. The rider will stretch the top portion of the body away from the hip and seat which elongates the rider's midsection and causes a lack of stability when the horse moves. The core section will not be solid enough to handle any surprise movements the horse may present. A rider will often get left behind in the movement or thrown forward toward the horse's neck.

Fault 4

Often a rider will lock their elbows or ride with one elbow or shoulder lower than the other, all of which results in the ribcage collapsing. The key is to keep the shoulders, elbows and wrists level and even.

Caitie has collapsed through her ribcage on her right. This results in a dropping shoulder and also and an uneven elbow line. It's a chain reaction.

Fault 5

The bicep muscle is sometimes overused by riders. If the rider uses the "Popeye arm" to ride (which means flexing the bicep muscle that he wore his spinach tattoo on) then the rider is using strength to slow the horse down or to rebalance the horse instead of a solid connection and body balance to counteract the weight of the horse. In emergency situations, the rider may need to engage these muscles. When asking the horse to become responsive to the bit, the tricep muscle is the section of the arm that needs to be activated, not the bicep.

Picture Perfect Pieces

Now envision your picture perfect pieces for the improved ride

Imagery examination:

Stabilizers for steadiness

Further Explanation

The shoulders and upper back, including the scapula, help with stabilizing the upper portion of the body, especially with the forward and backward motion presented by the horse. However, the rider needs to be aware that opening the shoulders too far can cause the midsection of the back to lock which prevents the rider from using the core as the nucleus of their strength. Conversely, riders who round their shoulders too much will not be able to use their abdomen as a means of stopping power to improve downward transitions. Nor will they be able to easily perform a half halt to help rock the horse back onto the two hind feet.

The upper arms, which include the tricep muscles that run along the back of the arm and the bicep muscles which are along the front part of the upper arm, play a key role in the connection that is made with the horse and the bit.

Essential Details of each Imagery

Up, back, and down shoulders

Incorrect posture in our daily lives takes a toll on our bodies. Our back and shoulders pay the price. This has a way of carrying over into our riding, especially for those of us who train horses every day and are constantly looking down to see what the horse is doing.

Be very mindful the next time you sit on your horse. Take a deep breath and bring your shoulders up toward your ears. Hold that for a brief second, and then slowly begin to roll the shoulders back to open the chest. You should feel your shoulders align over your hips. Allow your shoulders to gently drop down to allow the tension, stress, and all your problems to rush out of your elbows and hands. Repeat this exercise until you feel your body relieved of all tension. You will find that your elbows come down and align themselves over your hips, making them ready for the deep bouncing motion needed in order to keep the bit still in the horse's mouth for better communication and connection.

Carry two full buckets of water

How many times are riders told to sit tall and elegant? Sitting tall and elegant is certainly something that is desired when riding, but it can also be taken too far; to the point where the rider can be raising the shoulders up too high and pulling the ribcage and seat away from the saddle. This, in turn, will hollow the back of the rider causing too much tension.

While keeping the image of the shoulders going up, back and down, from that position let the shoulders rest over the elbows. Do not let one shoulder drop lower than the other or tilt backward or forward. Keep your shoulders square, as if you were holding up a jump rail across your shoulders behind your neck keeping it level and even. This will help keep the top portion of your body level.

Now think about carrying a water bucket in each hand as Tara is doing in this picture. The water buckets are filled to the top with water and the rider must imagine not spilling or allowing any of the water to splash out above the rim of the bucket.

To remind your body to weight your elbows, place your fingertips on top of your shoulders and apply a slight amount of pressure. This will also remind you to drop your shoulder blades. As the pointy section of the scapula drops down toward the middle of the back this will open up the chest cavity to a greater degree and allow the elegance of sitting tall to shine through.

If a rider is nervous or scared while riding, the natural reaction is to lean forward, grip with the knees, and grab onto the horse's neck. Rider stability is lost. The rider becomes even tenser and the spiral continues. When nervous or scared, instead of rounding the shoulders and starting the downward spiral, try relaxing the shoulders and pulling the chest open.

Activate the arm pit muscle

Perhaps one of the most eye-opening riddles I have solved is how to eliminate the fly away shoulder or the rider who has the shoulder or arms that flap like a chicken. This often happens when a rider allows the arms or shoulders to float forward. This is necessary at certain stages of riding, but a rider must learn how to activate the underarm muscle to hold the shoulder cap down and prevent too much lift in the upper shoulder girdle.

Caitie has her thumb under her armpit on the tendon that is activated, while Tara is placing her hand under her elbow to give her a feel to push into. This sensation is the main key to lowering the shoulders.

A good test and a way to feel exactly which muscle is activating, is to relax the arms. Take the opposite hand and place the thumb under the armpit in the hollow section. Press up into the belly of the armpit until you feel the muscle cord. Keep the thumb under the armpit and drop the shoulder. A muscle will pop out against the thumb. This is the muscle you need to activate in order to hold the shoulders steady and still and to keep the forearms relaxed.

Practice this exercise to activate this sensation. It will help riders who tend to round the shoulders and collapse in the chest. Keep activating this muscle until you can tighten it without using your thumbs. It will also bring the shoulder blades closer together along the back and stabilize the upper body during movement on the horse.

A locked elbow will cause stiffness through the other joints of the arm, as well as tensing the muscles. Allow your elbows to be floppy, in a sense. They will bounce along with the horse's stride as if you had a ball underneath each elbow and you were gently dribbling it.

It is helpful to place two sponges under each armpit. Hold the sponge with the back section of the muscle under your arm so that the sponge is squished toward the back by your muscle. This will help the rider to pay extra attention that the correct section of the upper arm is activated.

Pencil arm

A person's body build may be of importance when considering alignment of the upper arm. A short-armed rider will have a problem extending the arm forward and may run the risk of the elbow leaving the side. A long-armed rider will have the opposite problem and have a tough time keeping the elbow in a fixed area without pulling backward.

The "pencil arm" in theory, will help the rider to find the correct position of the upper arm in relation to the rest of the body. The elbows of the rider tend to draw backward if the rider tries to pull too much. We are going to think about doing just that, however, and "draw" with the elbows. Your arm will represent the pencil and your shoulder is the eraser. The point of your elbow is the tip of the pencil. It has the sharpest point possible to draw very distinct lines. Keep the pencil, or in this case the upper arm, completely straight up and down. When the rider feels it is necessary to pull on the reins, instead, press the pencil point down. The forearms will rise slightly. This is the power in your triceps to initiate a stop or a momentary balance check for the horse.

This analogy can also be very helpful as your horse is in motion. Think of the tip of the pencil doodling a line underneath. The line is straight, even though it goes forward and backward. This allows the rider to follow the motion of the horse and the head nod that the horse will create in the walk and canter. There is no head nod at the trot. A head bobble in the trot usually indicates a lame horse. The rider must create the movement within the elbows or the elbows will lock and the bit will move about in the horse's mouth instead.

If you imagine your pencil staying upright at all times with the eraser being your shoulder, and your upper arms being the bulk of the pencil, you will be able to correct your arm position if you feel as though you are beginning to pull with your upper arm muscles.

173

Water faucet in the shoulder

As a rider, it is difficult to let go of the whole arm as a unit. Riders have a tendency to tense through the whole arm and in turn, add too much pressure to the reins causing the horses to tense through the jaw.

Think, instead, of a hole in the top of each shoulder. There is a faucet attached that constantly supplies a water flow. The water will run through the entire arm, and out of the hands through the tips of each of the ten fingers.

When we tense throughout our arms we interrupt this water flow. The water will go from a full steady stream to a trickle or stop all together. It is important that both arms allow the water to flow through evenly. Otherwise, the horse will always feel tension through one rein, and the result will be crookedness or head tilt which is one ear being lower than the other. This will always result in the horses becoming heavier in our hands and increasing our need to pull more, thus, closing the water flow altogether.

Marbles on the shoulder

Stability with each shoulder is a must while riding. The flow of tension will follow along the line of the arm and into the fingers unless the rider is aware of how the shoulders are balanced. An elastic, steady motion is necessary to keep the upper body aligned over the hips.

An imagery essential that helps the rider to keep the shoulders square is the image of a marble on top of each shoulder. These marbles must stay still and in place as the horse travels, as well as when the rider turns the body for changes of direction or transitions. If the shoulders drop forward or the collarbone begins to collapse along with your upper chest, the marbles will roll off the shoulders and land on the horse or in front of their feet. The same holds true if the rider leans too far back with both shoulders. This is mostly an issue when learning how to stop properly or perform a downward transition when the horse is heavy or unbalanced in the bridle. The rider tends to lean back in hopes of using the upper body for strength and in turn compounds the problem as the horse will then brace against the rider's hands and use them for balance. Balanced marbles will help to prevent this problem.

When riding through a turn it is common for the rider to drop the inside shoulder lower than the outside one. If you think again of the two marbles you must make the turn with your shoulders level and soft to keep the marble on a flatter surface area of your shoulders.

It will help the rider to think of creating a small indent in the shoulder that the marble can rest in. Sometimes riders will lift the shoulders up and tense the muscles too much. This will result in fly-away shoulders-a common problem for riders who try to stretch up and away with their upper body. Keep the shoulders relaxed yet still. As the horse moves in all three gaits, keep the marbles steady and in place.

The shoulders are positioned directly over the ribcage. Often riders will allow the shoulders to fall forward and curl over the ribcage. For a woman the area we are referring to is the area just below where your bra line ends in the front of the body. If the rider leans too far back, it would be over the bra strap in the back of the body. Keep the shoulders overtop of the ribcage. Your shoulder girdle is the entire area of your shoulders and your upper ribcage. Keep it all elevated and upright. This will help greatly when trying to align the front of the body with your pubic bone, belly button, sternum and collar bone. Your collarbone will sit correctly once the shoulder girdle moves over the ribcage.

Coordination and Strengthening Exercises

Scarecrow arms

The scarecrow arms are a fantastic way to build up the shoulder muscles and the deltoids. Your shoulders are always the stabilizing muscles for the rest of the arm. If you think of a scarecrow, they lift the arms up and keep both upper arms horizontal to the ground. The forearm will hang down

from the elbow and the shoulder will be in line with the elbow. In some cases, with contact where you will need to get in touch with the corners of the horse's mouth, you will need to use your arms in this fashion.

Scarecrow arms are not the permanent position for the arms, but this does help the rider to form a barrier with the reins and establish the first steps toward feeling contact with the bit. In this picture Tara has formed a slight polite contact with Mouse that extends from her elbow to the bit.

Off the horse you can use an exercise band and loop it through a fence post so you are holding both ends of the band, one in each hand. The bands are a great tool because not only do they add a little resistance to build muscle strength, they also have the elastic feel of giving back that a weight does not have. The rider can learn to slowly give back to the horse, so to speak, and not just let the band snap back as they would if they would just drop the rein. You are learning to set the horse down as you release the exercise band.

Windmill circles

It is helpful to keep the shoulders stretched. By rotating the shoulders around in full circles it will help to keep the muscles loose. Often in riding the shoulder joint takes a lot of stress from the movement. It is a big demand to call on our body to keep the shoulders down and activated. Windmill circles forward and then backward will help the rider to also become coordinated.

Puzzle Piece #9

Forearms & Wrists

Imagery Essentials

Elastic Cords for Feel

Checklist for Proper Alignment of Forearms and Wrists

- ✓ Keep the barbell in the elbow.
- ✓ Balance the china plates on each forearm.
- ✓ Breast stroke through the water with your forearms.
- ✓ Hold the whip across the wrists.
- ✓ Push the watch bands out.
- ✓ Hold the ice cream cones.
- ✓ Figure "8" with the exercise band.
- ✓ Hold the ski poles upright.

Forearms & Wrists

The forearms are the link to the hands and are comprised of the ulna and radius bones. If the rider stiffens the forearms, the result will immediately transmit to the fingertips and create tension within the horse's jaw. If you were to fill the forearms with some sort of substance, what would you choose? Would it be feathers, gum, putty, mud, or concrete? Think about this the next time you ride. The consistency should match that of sifting sand. Sometimes the sand is wet but other times when the situation calls for it, the sand suddenly dries, and can sift around in each forearm, giving it a lighter feeling. The forearms must convey intensity at times, but also transfer to a cloud-like feeling at times.

Often the wrists are involved with pulling on the reins and adding additional unwanted pressure to the horse, which will always result in the shortening of the horse's neck.

When riding, it is important to keep the wrists directly in front of the elbow and at the same height as the elbow. This eliminates any bending or twisting with each wrist.

The elbows are also an important piece to the puzzle. The elbows must become like shock absorbers to handle the elasticity to the horse's mouth. It must follow the horse's movement at walk and canter. You should feel as though you have sinkers on each elbow to aid in lifting the horse up, but a steadiness to keep the horse consistent.

Riding Realities

Common Errors and Enigmas

The rider's forearms and wrists are responsible for an immense amount of communication with the horse. They become the lifeline to generate information from your body to the horse's mouth. If that lifeline is blocked or forced, the outcome will be far less than what the rider had hoped for. There will be a communication breakdown. A stiffened forearm or wrist will result in a stiffened jaw and poll. The elastic feel of contact will diminish and the softness in the ride will be compromised.

Always strive for a neutral wrist. Although the rider may feel as though their wrists are soft and gentle, due to the fact that the wrist can move in many directions, they may also have bent or dropped one or both wrists. This will add backward pressure to the horse's mouth. Remember, also, that a jammed wrist will always result in stiffness through other parts of your arm.

A horse's mouth should be treasured, and as riders, we must preserve the natural softness in order to establish a trusting relationship with each horse we ride.

Familiar Faults

Fault 1

The "Piano Hand" is a common flaw that occurs when riders flip the palm of the hand downward so that the top section of the forearm is facing upward. In this position, it's tough to use the arms in a good stable position to add any slowing power to the horse without adding tension to the reins, which transmits to the horse's mouth. In some cases, a rider will use this position thinking that it is creating a light feel that follows the contact of the horse's mouth. In most normal cases after the fine tuning work is done, a rider will need to hold the forearms so the forearms are facing out and the thumb is the highest point.

Fault 2

"Broken wrists", or what I call "dog paw wrists", are when the rider turns the insides of the wrists in towards the horse's withers. The knuckles of each hand begin to draw closer to one another toward the center line of the horse. In some cases this may feel softer to the rider, but the reality is that it transmits a dragging feeling to the horse and creates a feeling of added tension that the horse will brace against. The result will never be softness. A stable wrist position is the home base for the rider's wrist and is needed for al communication between the horse and rider.

Tara is demonstrating both faults in this picture. The right hand is stuffed into the withers, and also pushing against the horse's neck. The left hand is broken outward causing a disconnect in the flow of energy to the horse's mouth from her elbow and forearm.

Fault 3

Riders often feel the need to position the wrists to where they feel comfortable and also to leave some slack in the reins to create a light feeling to the horse. When the moment arises where the rider must take up contact and communicate with the horse, often the wrists will bend in different directions instead of taking up some of the rein contact.

Another direction in which the rider can contort the wrists is to bring the two wrists toward each other, which forms a "v" shape from the wrists to the hands. This will also result in a pulling pressure felt by the horse. This makes the the reins come in too close to the horse's withers and communication is lost due to loss of contact with the bit.

Fault 4

The elbow is the joint between the upper and lower arm. Turning the elbows out to the side can cause the rest of the forearm to brace which may limit the rider's ability to achieve the softness possible if the elbows were kept next to the rider's midsection and directly above the hips. The elbows should be mobile and transmit the energy to the horse's mouth.

Fault 5

"Chicken wings" are when the rider's elbows extend out to the side and move in a flapping motion while the horse is moving. Often, this is done to keep the hands still, but it becomes ineffective. If the rider needs to generate extra pushing power to move the horse forward, it should always come from the seat, a strong core, and the lower leg asking the horse to change the leg speed.

Picture Perfect Pieces

Now envision your picture perfect pieces for the improved ride

Imagery examination:

Creating and keeping the connection

Further Explanation

Let's take a look at how the forearms and the wrists can become the main connectors to start the communication before we reach the hands. Keep in mind the elbows play a big role in the connection also. Using these methods will help the rider use tone and stabilization to circulate the contact, instead of pure strength to hold the horse in place.

A firm, steady wrist allows for information to transfer from the rider's seat to the rein through the horse's mouth, and vice versa. The wrist and forearm become the life-line between the horse and rider. The rider must learn how to keep the communication flowing as opposed to interrupting that flow.

Essential Details of each Imagery

Keep the barbell in the elbow

Two common misconceptions related to using the hands effectively is that a rider keeps the arms straight or feeds the horse more of the reins. The first issue will create tension and possibly cause the joints to lock. The forearms will become stiff and the rider will appear to be riding with two sticks rather than two flexible elbow joints that move and bounce gently to keep with the rhythm of the horse's stride.

The rider may open the elbow joint too far instead of keeping a soft, slightly cushioned bend in it.

To help keep your elbow positioned correctly, think of a 5 pound barbell that is resting in the crook of the elbow joint. Balance the weight of the dumbbell and keep the shoulders down. The barbell will go in a downward motion each time the horse takes a step, as the weight of it brings the arm down.

This will increase the awareness of keeping the elbows balanced and even. It will also keep the elbows weighted when asking for a stop. If you allow the elbow to open too much, you risk losing the connection with the horse.

Caitie is holding the dumbbell in her elbow to gain the feeling of a sense of heaviness through the bottom of her forearm. This "L" shape should remain while riding.

Balanced china plates along the forearm

Perhaps you have seen the lovely expensive china that your ancestors have passed down through generations in your family. Keep in mind how beautiful, and expensive that chinaware is. Imagine that you have placed one of those lovely plates on each of your forearms. You are handling those plates with the utmost care and precision. Your elbows must remain bent and moveable because if the forearm would lock, the result would be the plate bouncing about and eventually bumping off the arm and shattering.

To save the plates a balanced arm and flexible elbows are a must. The shoulders should remain pliable and the concussion of the horse's movement should flow gently through the arms and into the fingertips. The tension will evaporate and the rigid feeling will disappear from the arms and upper body. If the elbows stiffen, the result will be tension through the reins, which will signal to the horse to stop forward movement. You will essentially be putting on the brakes while touching the accelerator.

Tara is balancing Frisbees along her forearm to create a good arm position.

Another common mistake is to let the forearms extend too much and become straight. If you allow the elbows to open too much, the china plates will slide forward and hit your horse in the withers. Try hard to maintain the line from elbow to wrist, while remaining soft and mobile and following the horse's movement. It is sometimes hard for riders to imagine lifting the forearms to this level, but it is necessary to promote a good connection with the horse and also a solid feel throughout the arm. And by the way, if you decide to try this exercise, I suggest using Frisbees instead of your heirloom china.

Breast stroke through the water

It's a beautiful hot summer day and its lap time in the pool. The stroke of choice is the breast stroke. Instead of extending the fingertips and slicing through the water, think of making a fist with each hand. Keep the thumb up. Punch forward through the water, then push the water away from the body with the wrists slightly leading. This is similar to the feeling when asking the horse to slow down, stop, or step into bit contact.

The elbows should never come behind the body or past the waist. It is important that the hold does not resemble that of pull starting a lawn mower. This will position the elbows behind the body and pulling will result in unwanted pressure on the horse's mouth.

This analogy will help the rider to keep the muscles of opposition pushing outward instead of becoming so relaxed they are droopy and ineffective. It is much the same for a dancer who holds the frame with their partner; there are no noodle arms involved, nor is there pushing the dance partner across the floor. There is a unity and synergy between the partners. This is what the rider should strive for in riding with contact and the bit.

Wrists

The wrists can be a very tricky part of the rider's body. We rarely pay attention to such a small piece of the puzzle, but the wrist contains the softness and the connection to the horse's mouth.

The wrist is a very small joint which has delicate tissues packed into a small area. These tissues include ligaments that knit the wrist bones together as well as tendons that connect the forearm muscles to fingers and help give fingers their remarkable dexterity.

Riders can use the wrist in a variety of ways to actually add unnecessary pressure. Used incorrectly the wrists can add a pulling pressure. In some instances, the horse will also add unwanted pressure by pulling away from the rider. This sets the rider up for a pulling match, and the horse will almost always win because they are five times our size, with strength that is tremendous compared to ours.

A locked joint will be like a kink in a garden hose. It does not allow the softness to flow from the forearm to the fingertips. Turning the wrists in different directions takes away from the power and overall balance of the rider.

Essential Details for each Imagery

Whip across the wrists

In riding today we always hear that the thumb should be the highest point, and this is absolutely true. You will never see an upper level dressage rider with their thumbs turned inward or outward. That would break the connection with the horse that they so desperately need to perform all their maneuvers.

Tara is holding and balancing a piece of bamboo across her wrists in order to keep the arms and hands in a good balanced position.

In order to teach and train yourself to ride with the wrist in the correct position, a dressage whip or riding crop is needed. First, have a helper place the whip across the wrists while holding the reins. (Use caution, and be sure you have introduced the whip to your horse first) You will lose the whip often in the beginning as it will fall off the wrists. The helper can retrieve it for you and place it on the wrists again.

Once the whip is positioned, it is time to practice holding the whip steady and balanced while the horse is moving. The forearms must move with the horse at a walk. Don't lose the whip.

This exercise is also useful to identify if one wrist drops lower than the other, or if one wrist begins to turn or drop by tilting the knuckles.

Practice walking, trotting and cantering with the whip balanced and steady. Your horse will thank you for your softness, dexterity and ability to move along with its motion at any gait. Your riding will improve, as will your joints.

Push the watch bands out

Often riders will lock the wrist joints inward, but it can be done outward. In fact there are many distorted directions in which the rider can position the wrist in reference to the hand, the forearm, or elbow.

Put on two watches making sure the face of each one is pointing outward. Once the wrists are in position, gently push them out toward the watch faces. This allows the forearms to soften and the fingertips to feel the contact with the bit. It is much like making a fist in order to punch through something. If you were to divert the wrist by bending it inward or outward, the power behind the punch would be less. It would also injure the wrist once the fist makes contact with the object. Keep the wrist in a good solid position while riding.

When riding a turn use your watch band to lead the horse forward with the opening rein. Your soft wrist will be taking the lead as you open your forearm like you are opening a door.

Hold the ice cream cones

A simple technique to position the hands in the correct direction and to be sure the wrists are relaxed and ready to align is to think of holding an ice cream cone in each hand while riding. Do not allow the ice cream cones to touch one another by turning the wrists inward. Do not let the bottoms crush by turning the wrist outward. Do not lose the scoop of ice cream by allowing the wrists to fall forward. The ice cream cones must remain level while

holding them steady in each hand. This keeps the position of the wrist effective as the wrist is responsible for the fine motor activities of the fingers and thumbs.

You can also think of holding a goblet of wine or a very fancy wine glass. Either way you will position your hands to hold the reins effectively with the reins stemming out of the circle created by your thumb and your first finger.

Figure 8 with the exercise bands

One of my most amazing discoveries to help riders keep their hands still and their wrists from breaking in different directions is by using an exercise band, otherwise known as a thera band. It is wise to use one with the least resistance first. In the beginning, this exercise can be tough on the deltoid muscles of the upper arm. Be sure to ease into it.

Form a figure 8 with the band and place it around both wrists while you are holding the reins. Keep the elbows bent and the wrists pushing out against the bands. Stretch the band to the point where tension is felt throughout. Keep the shoulders low and even. This exercise will be difficult at first until muscle strength is developed to hold the tone throughout the arms. If an intense burning sensation in the outer shoulder is felt, do this exercise in shorts bursts until strength is developed to avoid injury.

This helps the rider feel how to use the hands in the most effective way. It also helps the rider to refrain from crossing over the horse's withers when steering. The rider will learn how to use the outside rein effectively, and at the same time, use the opposing muscle groups on the outside of the arm to become toned, which will give the rider's arms stability.

This is also great for riders who tend to hold their hands too close to the horse's withers. In some cases when teaching a horse to seek contact with the bit, you will need to widen your hands in order to gain a better contact, instead of drawing your hands backward with the reins.

If you are a rider who has learned to see-saw with your hands, which is using one rein at a time to force the horse's head down from a high position, this exercise will help greatly to fix your bad habit. You will not be able to see-saw and keep the contact with the horse if you are wearing the exercise band.

Hold the ski poles

Stabilization of the forearm is critical to advancement once the stomach and back have taken control of the midsection. The rider can, then, surrender the hands to the horse in order to start to maintain a constant communication and contact with the horse.

A skier uses the hands and forearms to hold a ski pole in each hand. Use the thought of those ski poles to help capture the feeling of floating with the forearms. Lift the ski poles a few inches off the ground, but keep them straight-perpendicular to the ground and on either side of the horse's shoulder. As the horse moves, whether in a straight line or changing direction, the ski poles must stay by the horse's shoulder or a few inches in front of the shoulder.

If your horse begins to lean on the front two legs when traveling, then the rider must think of gently lifting the ski poles. This will help to rebalance a horse who is heavy on the forehand. The forearms will remain in a straight line from elbow to wrist, so the rider could balance a tray upon the forearms in this position.

Experiment with two dressage whips as well. Be sure to keep the thumb placed on top of each whip and the tip of the whip perpendicular to the ground. This helps simulate what it feels like to hold the ski poles.

Tara is holding two dressage whips one in each hand. The tip of each whip is pointing back toward Satuii's hip.

Coordination and Strengthening Exercises

Take a moment to do some of the exercises below to help establish some coordination and some strength through your arms.

Weights on the elbows

If you have two ankle weights that velcro, it can be useful to put them on the elbows so you can recognize the feeling of riding with a grounded feeling in your forearm. Do not exceed a few pounds. If you use ankle weights, you will be able to ride effectively without the bulk or restriction of movement in the arms. The rider can feel the deep anchor resemblance that will be needed to sustain a halt or a horse that is heavily pulling through the bit.

When you remove the weights, the arms will memorize the feeling and the rider will become used to weighting the elbows when needed while riding, instead of leaning back with the upper body to compensate.

If you really like to challenge yourself, then add a set of wrist weights, as well. Keep the line of the elbow weights and the wrist weights at the same height.

Wrap the elbows by your sides

This activity will be especially helpful for riders who tend to let their elbows "fly away". First take some time to introduce your horse to an Ace bandage. Let it touch him and wave it about just in case it should unwind when you are doing the exercise. When your horse is used to the bandage have someone help you wrap the bandage around your lower mid-section. Your elbows should be by your ribcage and the bandage should be wrapped over your elbows with light pressure. It should be secured by tucking the end through the bandage. DO NOT wrap the bandage too tight and DO NOT secure it by knotting. You should be able to move your elbows, stretch the bandage, or free yourself easily if the need arises.

Practice this in small increments until you can generate enough thinking power to maintain your elbows softly in their home position.

Cupped hands

To help keep your wrists relaxed, try this exercise. Hold your hands so the palms are facing upward. Keep the fingers together and cup your hands slightly, as if you are holding a little water in each hand. Slowly rotate your wrists upward so that your knuckles are facing up and then rotate your whole hand so that it is in regular riding position with the thumb the highest point.

This is the softness required in the wrists as you ride. If you allow the fingers to be stiff and keep them rigid and straight, then you will find that the wrists bend inward slightly. This is a mistake made by most riders. Although soft wrists are a hard concept, it is a huge part of riding and very important to what the horse will feel in terms of connection to the bit.

Magic fly away arms

This exercise is really fun, and it can help the rider obtain a floating feeling in their arms once they practice it a few times. This exercise can be done anywhere there is a door. Stand in the middle of a doorway. Position your arms by your sides. Turn your palms toward your thighs. Take your wrists and push the outer portion against the doorway on both sides at the same time. Use some muscle power as you do this. You are going to hold this for a count of thirty. Keep pushing with the same strength as when you began. Keep your wrists in position.

After you count to thirty step out from the doorway. Allow your arms to float where they please. You will feel the sensation of your shoulders lifting as if they were magically being pulled upward. This is the feeling I want you to capture- the sensation of the floating arm, with no resistance. Quickly, try to put your arms into an on-horse position as if you were holding the reins. Memorize this feeling because this is the essence of relaxation through tone. This is the end result and what you are striving for constantly with your horse. The resistance in your forearms should be gone.

Puzzle Piece #10

Imagery Essentials

Hands & Fingers

The Instruments for Perfection

Checklist for Proper Alignment of the Hands and Fingers

- ✓ Hold the chopsticks under the thumbs.
- ✓ Hold a grape, plum, or grapefruit.
- ✓ Push the wheelbarrow.
- ✓ Hold the cap on the toothpaste tube,
- ✓ Pads of the finger touching the palms.
- ✓ Hold the reins where your hands join your fingertips.
- ✓ Weight to the heel of the hand.
- ✓ Chicken bones on the outside of the hands relaxed.
- ✓ Hold the reins like a firm handshake.

Hands

Perhaps the most difficult part of the body to master is the hands. There are all kinds of hand positions used while riding. A rider can use a giving hand, a holding hand, a pulling hand, a passive hand, and a invisible hand. Perhaps, the most important of all the hand movements is the "educated" hand. The hands seek out education while teaching the horse and also learn to balance the forward motion with the backward motion, as well as, sideways and up and down motion.

You will struggle with your hands over the course of your riding career, but what I can tell you is that your hands are the key means of communication with your horse because they affect the most important parts of the horse. Use your hands wisely and you will gain your horse's trust and willingness to follow your lead, knowing there will always be a reward for a job well done. This is the foundation of all good riding.

Riding Realities

Common Errors and Enigmas

The hands lead and control the conversation between the horse and the rider. Unfortunately, most riders don't take the time necessary to educate the rest of the body so that the hands are not used to balance themselves. Work on correcting the faults discussed below so that you can clearly communicate with your horse and avoid overuse of the hands and fingers.

Familiar Faults

Fault 1

"Stuffing the hands" is the term used to describe when a rider turns their hands toward the horse's neck and holds them very close to the withers. To an onlooker, it will appear as if the rider's hands are nonexistent. Instead, the hands should remain at home base, floating above the horse's withers. They may move a few inches forward or backward at anytime, and slightly right or left if making a turn.

Fault 2

Open fingers are used by riders when they are trying to be light, or generate less pressure. If the fingers open too much, the horse will take advantage and pull the reins through the rider's hands. Often times, riding with the fingers open is referred to as using "tea cup pressure" which is when the rider can use the index finger and thumb to show how light a horse is to contact. However, riding like this all the time will allow the horse to take advantage of the situation. Use all ten fingers to grasp the reins. Keep a steady light contact. This way, if the horse decides to pull down against pressure, the rider will not lose rein contact and release the horse for misbehaving.

Fault 3

Clenching fingers is a definite fault that will cause tension through the horse's jaw. This happens when a rider closes the fingers too tightly against the palms. This, in turn, leads to stiffness in the wrists and forearms. It is good for a rider to learn how to keep the fingers a little loose so that the horse can free up the jaw. It's important to avoid having the horse lock or stiffen the mouth against pressure on the bit due to fingers that squeeze.

Fault 4

One more fault that will cause tension throughout the rider's wrists and arms is when the back of the hand is held stiffly. Check your hands periodically. If you can see your bones and/or tendons clearly, you are stiffening against the pressure. The back of your hands should remain soft and relaxed.

Using your fingers correctly as you ride is truly an art, and the first step to better hands is better fingers. Keep the pressure of your fingers firm, as in a solid handshake. Practice the following exercises to help you develop and maintain just the right amount of pressure.

Essential Details of each Imagery

Hold the chopsticks

Think of holding a chopstick under each thumb to help you refrain from squeezing too tightly. This will also help you keep your thumbs aligned with your fists. Be sure the chopsticks are lying flat and level. Do not allow either end of the chopstick to drop down. Maintain softness and flexibility in all of your fingers. Your grip should be firm, but not so hard that it would break the chopstick. If you notice your thumbnail appears white, you are gripping too hard. Keeping your fingernail pink is a good way to determine the correct amount of pressure.

Which one, grape, plum or grapefruit

When a rider uses too much tension on the reins, the result can be greater resistance throughout the horse's body. The hold on the reins and the placement of the reins should match that of holding a plum.

The rider who imagines they are holding a grape is probably closing the fingers too much, and creating a death grip on the reins. If you are holding a grapefruit, you are allowing the horse to pull the excess tension through the fingers. This allows the horse to receive a release of pressure whenever they see fit to do so. This will almost always result in inconsistent contact with the bit.

Become accustomed to holding your hands as if you are holding a plum. Allow the hands to be ready to receive the reins and feed the reins out to the horse as need be. There is no written rule regarding how to ride with feel. You will eventually figure out what you need. Ride to feel what is correct.

As you hold your reins, think of how a great composer such as Mozart allowed his fingers to flow across the keys, creating beautiful rhythmic tones. If you feel as though when you let go of the reins, your fingers are going to break in half, then you are, more than likely, using your fingers as an outlet to squeeze and over-controlling your horse's motion. Every once in a while, release your fingers and think of playing the piano. It will help to remind you to stay as soft as possible and to release the tension throughout your arms, wrists and elbows.

Push the wheelbarrow

If you own a horse or have ever been around one, then you definitely know how to push a wheelbarrow. When teaching a horse to receive the contact, the upper body position used to push a wheelbarrow will prove helpful. It is very important to follow the horse's movement at each gait, allowing the hands to gently float forward without losing the correct elbow, wrist, or shoulder positions.

This picture is showing how you can temporarily hold the reins as though you are pushing a wheel barrow. It will help to teach the rider how to feel the softness with the horse. Do not ride like this always, just use it in times when you feel like you need to feel contact with the horse.

The key to maintaining this forward movement is to imagine pushing the wheelbarrow. There will never be any backward pressure unless you need to stop (halt the horse) or rebalance the load (the horse). Only in these two instances should your hands pull back. Never shorten your horse's neck or close his gullet (the area where the throat and neck meet).

When you need to turn your horse, remember to pull gently on the inside rein so the turn is gradual. Going back to the idea of the wheelbarrow, do not dump the contents by picking up one side (rein) more than the other.

Find a "home" or neutral spot to work from with the hands while riding. There are times when you can't be 100% correct with every part of the body because the horse is learning, as well. A good rider will adjust to help the horse, then, go back to working on lightness and correctness. I use the frisbee analogy to help the rider find the place to "go home to" so to speak. This area is where your hands will be working the majority of the time. If you took a Frisbee and placed it over the horse's withers, your hands should straddle the frisbee. Your hands will be allowed to float in the areas on either side, in front, and behind the frisbee. Whenever you make a correction you are going to go "home" to the Frisbee as quickly and as gently as possible, so the horse learns that the cues originate from that spot.

Hold the cap on the toothpaste tube

The idea of holding the horse without shortening the neck by pulling back is a hard concept for riders to grasp. It seems contradictory to what a rider thinks would work. A horse will automatically engage in a tug of war when a rider exerts a force backwards. This means that in the beginning stages of riding, before a rider has developed the proper muscle to hold the body in a stable place, the rider will be forced to use a pulling motion to slow down the horse. As time goes by, the horse learns to brace against a rider's hand, and the cycle begins. The idea is to break that cycle and offer the horse a passive resistance instead, so they learn to trust the rider's hands.

Let's imagine for a moment that the horse is now a giant tube of toothpaste. The bit and the mouth represent the cap of the toothpaste tube and the tail will represent the end of the tube. The job of the rider is not to create any wrinkles in the tube by adding too much pressure with the bit, and pulling in a backward fashion to make all the toothpaste burst out the back of the tube. Think instead of the hands gently holding the cap on the toothpaste as the legs and seat will try to push the contents to the front of the tube.

As you begin to send the toothpaste to the front toward the cap, the hands must allow the tube to lengthen so the contents do not explode out of the front of the tube. This is what collection and building a proper frame is all about.

By no means are you looking to ever pull the toothpaste from the front of the tube to the back. This will create a false bend through the horse's neck and cause the horse to lose all the energy you generate out the back of the body. There will be nothing left to recycle and the collection process will deaden. In some extreme cases, you will cause unwanted behaviors in your horse. You must always gently hold the cap on, but never create backward wrinkles in the tube.

Most of us have made finger prints at sometime. Imagine you still have ink on your fingertips. Touch your fingertips to your palms so that you make a soft imprint with each finger. Your thumb should rest on top as the highest point.

When a rider starts to make a tight fist as if they are going to punch someone, they usually end up clenching their fingers and creating pressure. Often, a rider who is trying to be soft through the arms or elbows will do just that. They send the tension somewhere else. Strive to remind yourself of this image. Just be careful to not allow the reins to slip through your fingers.

Hold the reins where your fingers join your hands

A good rule to follow is to hold the reins in your hands across where your four fingers join your palms. Often a rider will hold the reins clenched in their fingertips so the entire finger is what is holding onto the rein. Instead, let the rein slide farther back in your hand and softly caress the rein, always with the thumb as the highest point. This will enable the rider to always have a home spot to go to when using the reins.

Weight in the heel of your hand

While holding the rein, it is important to pay attention to which part of the hand is weight-bearing. If you were to make a fist and pound on a tabletop, you would be putting the majority of weight into the heel of the hand.

When you are holding the reins think of that tabletop still underneath your fists. Think of pressing down into the table with each hand while holding the reins. This will help when you need a little extra power if the horse generates a bigger push forward than you wish to pull back against.

Sherrie is placing the weight of her fist into Tara's hand. The bottom portion of the hand is almost flat as if it were resting on a table.

"Chicken bones" on the outside of the hands relaxed

Along the outer portion of each hand lie thin bones that attach to the fingers. If the fingers are extended, these bones become more prominent under the skin. When all five fingers are spread apart and the fingertips are raised upward at the same time, the "chicken bones" appear. Make it a goal to never expose those chicken bones while riding.

If you begin to see these tiny bones exposing themselves through the surface of your hand, you may be tensing the knuckles. Think, instead, of taking the knuckles forward slightly and pushing the outer part of the hand into cotton or a very soft substance. That will help eliminate the tension that follows in the rest of the forearm.

Hold the reins like a firm handshake

The question of how much pressure you need in order to make contact with the horse's mouth is always a big mystery. It should be inviting for the horse, but may also be assertive, cushioning when needed to help the horse understand when they are right or wrong.

When introducing yourself to a stranger the next time, pay attention to how they shake your hand. Chances are, if they ride horses you will be able to tell how they use their hands when they are riding. If they shake your hand firmly, and keep hanging on once you are uncomfortably trying to get free, they probably hold onto the reins and miss the opportunity to release the pressure at the right time for the horse to catch on. If they squeeze your fingers off and your hands begin to turn white for a moment, they most likely use lots of pressure to ask a horse to execute a maneuver. If the handshake is hardly a handshake, they would probably allow the horse to get away with every little thing and they would be very inconsistent on a horse.

What we are looking for is a handshake that is firm and inviting. You don't feel as though you have to pull back to get away and you don't feel as though there is hardly a connection. It is a gentle, warming grasp that invites you to shake hands again. That is what you would like to have with your horse.

Coordination and Strengthening Exercises

Grasp the tennis ball

To coordinate and strengthen your hands, take a tennis ball, and while you are watching TV or relaxing, practice squeezing the ball and letting it go. Do this with both hands until you can squeeze the ball lightly and gradually, and *slowly* let it go. This will help your coordination while holding the reins. The light contact will help you to feel the slow, gradual release. This is how we can learn to hold rein pressure.

Piano fingers

Pretend that you are now a musician and place your palms down on your legs. Tap each finger separately from your pinky to your thumb as if you were impatiently waiting for something. Start by doing this, one hand at a time, and then, do both hands together. This sounds simple but the ultimate results will be amazing. As you advance in your riding, you will realize that your horse is so soft that you only need the manipulation of two finger pressure to influence its movement. Strive to get there.

Pass the rope

It must be second nature to shorten or lengthen the reins without losing contact. To achieve this goal, start by using a cotton lead rope. Hold the rope as if you were holding the reins. Let your hands get softer and softer, allowing the rope to slide through your hands, but never let it go. Although this will probably be difficult at first, continue to practice shortening and lengthening the rope without looking at it. As your coordination improves, so will your speed and efficiency. Transfer this concept to the use of your reins once mounted.

Popsicle sticks and vet wrap

If a rider is having difficulty breaking the wrists in different directions, there is a sure proof way to keep the wrists lined up with the forearms. Grab two Popsicle sticks and some vet wrap, strap one stick to the inside of each wrist and wrap some vet wrap around the stick to secure it. This will make a gentle reminder to keep the wrists in a line while riding.

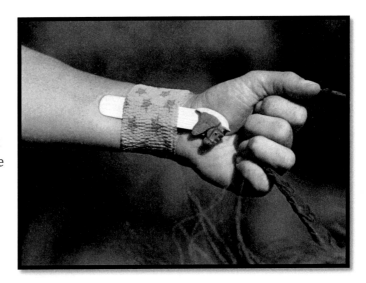

The Braking System

Let's look at rein aids

How to effectively use your rein aids to develop a stop cue with your horse

The rein aids are used to signal a horse to slow the feet down or to stop the feet completely. They can also be used as a half halt, which will rebalance the horse in preparation for more advanced work. The horse must be thinking 'forward' in order to use the rein aids or else the braking system will not work. The horse's feet must first be active before you can harness that energy and improve the rate at which the feet move. Both reins used in unison signal the horse to slow the feet down. If the horse does not stop off of two reins, then a one rein stop will need to be issued. The horse carries the engine in the hindquarters, so if the rider can displace the hindquarters the engine will not be able to work at full throttle. The straight line of power from the horse's nose to the tail will be disconnected and the surge of full power will be lost and redirected.

What are the most important components of the stop?

We are going to start out with the lightest possible cue to ask the horse to slow the feet. Keep in mind if you are asking for a stop, that means that all four feet must stop moving. It is important that you do not hold the horse in the stop position by keeping a mild pressure on the reins. This would be the same scenario as shaking up a two liter bottle of soda and removing the cap. The fizz would explode. The same scenario is true when the rider holds all the energy and bottles it up with no place for it to escape. The result will be a rearing horse or a horse that is extremely confused between a whoa cue and a go cue.

Do not be the horse's fifth leg or the kickstand. Instead, give the horse the option to move the feet if it wishes. Then, go ahead and go through the four phases of cues once again. The four phases will be detailed on the next page.

Teaching a horse to stop is very similar to teaching a horse to go. Be very clear about the series of cues used. Otherwise, the horse will begin to confuse the stop cue with the rider pulling on the reins. The horse will begin to pull through any pressure exhibited by the bit if they feel like they can lean on that pressure and drop the front of the forehand creating more pull through the reins.

We talked about numerous ways to use the body in order to not pull on the reins using strictly the biceps and arms. You will be using the core muscles, the back muscles, and the seat to help with the process of teaching a "whoa."

Putting Pieces & Position into Practice

What are the four phases of the stop cue?

Follow this system using four different cues which increase in intensity for the stop. If you focus on a specific spot on the horse, then the stop becomes easier to obtain. Most riders will try to stop the whole horse which is more difficult. A horse outweighs us by a thousand pounds or more. Don't use muscle to stop the entire horse. Instead, think of stopping the poll, then the withers, and then the horse's belly button-which you can imagine is the chest. After the three phases of thinking of those specific body parts, if the horse is still in forward mode, the rider must move the horse's hip. This shuts down the engine which is the propulsive driving force that comes from the rear. By realigning the horse, the stop can happen.

Phase 1 The lightest cue

During phase one, the rider will pick up both reins and shorten them until contact with the horse's mouth can be felt evenly on both sides. This is the meeting phase of the contact. You meet the horse, they feel you and you feel them. Focus on the horse's poll or look at the crown piece of its bridle on the top of the horse's head. If the horse had a vase that was balanced on this section of the head, the horse should keep it upright. You do not want the horse to chase the vase. In other words, if the horse is heavy on the forehand or feels like they are falling forward in your hands, then the vase needs to be rebalanced.

Take the slack out of both reins long enough to say the word "stop". Be very careful that you do not draw back on the reins so harshly that the neck becomes shorter. By doing so, the throat or gullet begins to close up, causing the horse to bring the chin toward the chest. This will cause the horse to slip behind vertical, which means that the angle of the throat latch under the chin will begin to decrease, and the rider will lose the brakes all together, because the horse can escape bit contact completely. There is a moment when the chin comes toward the chest that the horse feels a release of pressure. The more the rider pulls, the further into the chest the nose will wander, giving a release for the horse. Keep a long neck position, with the horse relaxing the top line muscles. The ears of the horse should be level with the withers.

Phase 2

If the horse ignores when the rider picks up the reins to ask for the stop during the lightest phase, then the rider must, immediately, move onto phase two which is to spread the hands slightly wider without pulling any harder on the reins. Change the focus to the horse's withers. Make sure the hands straddle the imaginary frisbee on the horse's withers and the reins are short enough so when the rider applies pressure, they do not come toward the rider's mid-section. If the elbows are extending behind the rider's ribcage, then the rider needs to shorten the reins so they will not be tempted to pull.

When the rider focuses on the withers, it puts his/her body and seat in a position to signal to the horse to slow down. Keep the hands soft, and keep weight low in the elbows and triceps as opposed to the weight in the biceps which will cause too much resistance and spiral into unwanted pulling from the horse. Keep the wrists in good alignment and do not allow the pinky to drop below the line of the wrist. If you allow your pinky to drop, the horse will feel drag along the rein and be tempted to brace against it. Lightness will occur when the horse and rider have a very positive and comforting contact. That is when true connection can take place and the horse can learn to follow the connection to a loose rein.

Phase 3

The horse should have made an attempt to significantly slow the feet when the rider adds pressure and thinking of the horse's shoulders or area of the wither slowing down. If the horse has not stopped, the horse may be unbalanced on the forehand. This will make the horse harder to stop because the horse will feel as though it's tipped forward. To understand how this feels to the horse, do the following experiment. Stand up and place your hands on a table palms down and fingers spread. Lean down and bear weight onto both hands with as much weight as possible through the third finger on each hand. You can begin to feel how the weight through your whole arm and wrist is heavy and your arms have stiffened. It is hard for you to lift your palms from the table. It will cause a tipping forward sensation, which is quite similar to what a horse feels if it is unbalanced on the forehand. It becomes hard for the horse to lift the front legs as well.

Focus now on the horse's chest, and pretend that the horse has a belly button. In most cases, when a horse does not stop, the rider lowers the hands in an attempt to pull downward. This causes the horse to draw the head forward and upward in an attempt to pull through the bit, or brace against it. Instead of the downward action, you should focus on the horse's chest and imagine the horse has a belly button. Think of slightly lifting the hands as if lifting the belly button up to rebalance the horse and set it back on its hocks. It helps, immensely, to think of the horse's ears staying level with the horse's withers. The rider needs to elevate the two front feet so the stop is effective. The area that the rider is really focusing on is the thoracic sling of the horse. These muscles are difficult to get to and need ample time to develop enough to hold the horse in position. The horse will then be able to use the hind end properly for a good, balanced stop. Sometimes, the horse will need the rider's hands for balance at first, but will slowly begin to ease off the crutch of the reins and bit as they begin to balance better.

Phase 4 The Reinforcement

If, after trying all of the above, the horse is still trying to pull through two reins, the time has come to take that option away. Use one rein to *make* the stop happen. By the time you reach phase four, drop one rein and take the slack out of the rein that you are still holding. Draw the rein toward your belly button, which will be in the direction behind the horse's withers in a diagonal line. A rein aid used in this direction will always signal to the horse to move the hip when the pressure is behind the withers. If you do not bring the rein toward the belly button, but, instead, move it more toward your hip, the horse will just turn in circles and the cue will be useless.

Look for the horse to stop the front foot that is on the same side as the rein you picked up. The hip of the horse will travel in the opposite direction approximately two steps. You must release the rein when this happens and give the slack in the rein back to the horse so the reins are lying on the horse's neck. If the horse begins to move after you release all rein pressure, then, immediately, pick up one rein and ask the horse to move the hip over once again. Repeat this until the horse stops completely.

The one rein stop is used to "make" a stop happen. Here, in the teaching stage, Tara is using her opposite hand to touch the hip of the horse. This will activate the correct seat bone, and change the angle of her hip to make it easier for Phantom to feel it.

Praise the horse for stopping, and begin to add leg cues to ask the horse to walk forward. When you want to stop again, begin with the lightest cue to ask for the stop.

It is important to only go to this phase if the previous three phases have not connected with the horse. This is, indeed, a way to make a stop happen, but by no means should it be the constant means to stop the feet. This phase is often used at higher speeds when the horse begins to pull through the hand abruptly. Eventually, the horse will figure out that the motion of stopping the forward movement, adjusting the feet, and beginning to adjust the balance is harder than trying to re adjust the balance off of two reins that are asking for a holding pressure to rebalance.

Sequence to set hand pressure

When using the hands and upper body to signal a halt, follow this sequence. It will help to keep the body honest before getting frustrated and pulling with both hands and arms. When adding any pieces to the sequence, use the piece before it in conjunction. The pressure will build and the horse will learn to halt off of the first cue, which is the easiest to administer and keep the rest of the body still. Your upper body must work as a pulley system and must stay soft, comforting, and elastic.

Shoulders

When asking for a halt, start with the shoulders. Do not allow the shoulder blades to pinch together through the back. Keep the lower back relaxed. Keep a firm hold of the reins with all ten fingers and keep the wrist, tension-free. Be very careful not to lean back with the entire upper body. Open the collar bone in the front, making it wider. Keep the elbows by your side or you will be cueing too early with too much force. The cues must raise in intensity, so the horse understands that it must walk into the comfort of the rider's hands and body and keep a gentle connection with the bit.

Triceps

The triceps are the second part of the sequence. Most times in a halt, a rider will use the bicep muscles only and just use strength to slow the horse down. This takes away our advantage of using our body to align ourselves so we become more immoveable for the horse to pull against. After the shoulder is put to work to hold, if the horse has not slowed down or come a stop, add in the triceps by thinking of having a nut that you need to crack in the crook of your elbow. Use the tricep muscle the same as you would to do a reverse push up. The elbows will begin to sink lower if you think of the tip of the elbow being the point of a pencil and you are breaking the point off by pushing downward. You will notice, if it is done correctly, that your hands will slightly elevate. This is the beginning of lifting your horse off the forehand without pulling backward.

Forearms

The next cue in the sequence is to use the forearms. Do not draw the forearms back, however. Instead, think of pushing through resistance as if you had a stretchy band that you were trying to pull apart. Imagine pushing against water or thick mud. Keep the elbows close to your sides; do not allow them to fly away. Spread the hands over the horse's withers. Use the shoulders and triceps, allow your elbows to sink and open your forearms.

This will work on the corners of the horse's mouth and alleviate a pull toward the rider's body. The horse will learn to stay on contact. After a few practice runs you will not need to spread the forearms apart so widely, and will be able to work closer and closer toward the end position of directly beside the horse's withers.

Hands

The hands are the tail end of the sequence. Up until now, you should have had the soft pads of your fingers touching your palms. Now, you are going to close your fingers into a fist and hold the reins until the horse stops. We save the hands for last because by now, your body is a force to be reckoned with. The horse will find it extremely hard to pull against you.

Instead of just thinking of your hands next time you ride, you now have three other pre-cues that can keep your hands soft and trustworthy. The horse must learn to trust your hand. We do not want to abuse that trust. Keep a firm connection, but once again, the horse must feel like they can always walk into the comfort of the rider's hands.

TIP

The seat and core must also be mentioned as the seat is used to signal all downward transitions and the core is used to become the sturdy, strong glue that holds all the sections together so the rider is not solely dependent on the use of the hands.

What is a half halt?

We hear the term "half halt" a lot in the equine world, but what exactly does it mean? A half halt is actually a rebalancing of the horse. It is a momentary check to tell the horse to lift the front end and lower the haunches. It is not a request for a change of pace or a change of direction. A half halt is a very disciplined use of the body and of the aids of the seat, hands, and legs. The intensity of each aid will vary from horse to horse. You must have the utmost timing and skill to administer a meaningful half halt. A half halt is not, in fact, a half "haul" on the horse. Instead, you are using your body in balance with your legs touching gently to signal a go forward cue as the rein aid comes along and asks the belly button to lift and the withers to rock backward.

Your body will be a big part of this half halt. First, focus on your seat-making sure you are connected with the horse. This means you are not rocking forward onto the pubic bone. You are lifting your pubic bone toward your belly button. Your thighs are in contact at the three sections we discussed earlier, and the lower calf is touching just below the knee. Sink deep in the elbows, keeping the wrists and fingers gentle until you feel the horse lift with its body. You will need to practice this a lot in the beginning. The horse will also be learning too. During the course of most rides a rider may use a series of hundreds of half halts. They are "quick and sweet" to get in and get out. They do not linger or the horse will do the opposite, sometimes and try to run through it. Practice and feel the weight shift. It's not a huge movement, so it is hard to feel sometimes. A half halt, however, is a way to ride from one movement to another, and also a means to control the pace, direction, feel in the hand and to constantly keep the balance of the horse equal between its front half and back half.

Important

Always use your cues for a halt or a half halt in a "hold-give-hold-give" fashion. Don't just sit in idle and wait for your horse to figure out what the pressure means. You are always trying to break resistance and not give the horse anything to brace against.

Puzzle Piece #11

Head & Eyes

Imagery Essentials

The Vision of your Success

Checklist for Proper Alignment of the Head and Eyes

✓ Keep the witch chin aligned above the chest.
✓ Keep your earrings level and even.
✓ Wear a neck brace.
✓ Smile as you ride.
✓ The head is a helium balloon about to float away.
✓ Wear the sunglasses with tape.

Head

The rider's head and eyes are the last primary key to the riding puzzle. I often will tell my riders that this is the final piece to fall into place. When I began riding seriously many years ago, I remember that many of my instructors constantly told me to keep my eyes up. I needed to look where I was going, so my horse would be able to determine what direction was expected. I felt the need to study the horse's ears, the poll, the neck. I would constantly look at that section of the horse in hopes to see it change, or to see if I could offer assistance in any way. This would cause my body to fall forward, at times. It wasn't until later in my riding career that I could feel the horse in my hands, through my seat, and control them through my legs. This changed my riding for the better. My word of advice for each rider is, no matter what stage you are currently riding at, pay careful attention to where the weight of your head falls. Be sure to lift your eyes and level your head while you ride.

Riding Realities

Common Errors and Enigmas

Many riders don't consider the fact that the human head is quite substantial in weight. If a rider looks down, they may add as much as ten pounds to the rider to topple forward or possibly overweight the horse's forehand and should be avoided. Instead, the head should be kept level.

Once the rider's body is in correct alignment, the rider's seat, hips, legs and upper body will change position slightly if the rider just looks in a different direction.

The horse will learn to respond to the subtle changes in the rider's body and these soft aids will be all but invisible to onlookers.

Familiar Faults

Fault 1

The "jutting chin" as it is often called, is when the rider sticks the chin out beyond the upper body. It looks as though the rider is purposely stiff in the upper body and the neck is stretched in a very forward position. This will throw a rider off balance slightly. It will also increase the tension in the rider's upper back. The chin should remain above the sternum so the cervical vertebrae of the rider's neck align and keep the muscles relaxed.

Fault 2

"Head tilt" is a common error among many riders. If you feel as though one ear is closer to the shoulder, then you are suffering from head tilt. Unfortunately, this can ripple through the body quickly, and cause a collapse in structure throughout the hips or ribcage. It will also push weight to the outside seat bone and the horse will begin to bulge through a turn meaning that they will feel as though they are pushing through the shoulder. When making a turn or change of direction, always keep the ears level.

Fault 3

As a trainer, I tend to look down at my horses to see what they are thinking as I am riding. This is one of the biggest errors made by any rider. If you look down for a prolonged period of time you will begin to round the shoulders and drop and collapse through the front of the chest. It is a very bad habit to develop, especially, if you are going to jump. Any time you are about to jump an obstacle, keep your eyes up and look beyond where you want to be. This is true when you are riding, as well. Keep your eyes looking ahead forward where you want to be. I promise the horse will be underneath you.

Fault 4

The "head bob" is a common mistake seen with riders who are attempting to sit the trot and use too much of the midsection to move along with the horse. The head will often bounce, giving the rider the look of a head that is loose and a chin that lowers and lifts in the trot, especially. While the neck should absorb some of the movement, allow the horse's movement to ripple through the spine and into the seat as well.

Picture Perfect Pieces

Now envision your picture perfect pieces for the improved ride

Imagery examination:

The Vision for Success

Further Explanation

The eyes create the vision tunnel. All the pieces of riding, such as straight lines, circles, and insisting on forward movement, stem from the eyes being the guide to help the horse know where the rider intends to go. The head of the rider helps to establish direction, as well. Both the head and the eyes help the horse to keep moving on a line of travel that is confidently drawn by the rider's mind.

Essential Details of each Imagery

Witch chin above the chest

To help find and maintain a level head set, imagine that it is Halloween and you are dressed up as a witch-mask and all. The mask you are wearing has the elongated chin that most of us associate with a witch. The tip of this long chin needs to be positioned behind the center of the chest, just above the sternum. To help you obtain this position, pull your shoulders back to realign the upper body and put your spine in neutral position. The tension between the shoulder blades will feel as though it has melted away and the tip of the chin should rest gently above the chest plate of the rider. This should help keep the rider's head level and reduce the chances of the rider looking downward.

Think of the days when women would go to school to learn proper etiquette. They would learn to walk with a book balanced on their head to learn better posture. As you ride, think of this again. This will help, immensely, with the rest of your body by keeping it level and balanced. You can also think of the exercise where you imagined marbles on both shoulders.

Keep your earrings level and even

Keeping our ears level is one aspect of our body that is often overlooked. Just as a horse needs to keep its ears level and even to avoid tilting its head and dropping weight into one shoulder more than the other, so must a rider keep his/her ears level.

It may help a rider to keep level ears by imagining large rhinestone studs in their ears. The earrings need to be kept level to shine to their brightest. Do not allow the head to tilt. Not only will this affect the shine of the earrings, it will also cause crookedness in the horse's body because the rider is, unknowingly, cueing the horse to move in a different direction.

Wear a neck brace

The idea of wearing a neck brace while riding will help to keep the neck in a stable position. Often, riders will allow the neck to move about too much or to lock in place and become stiff. When beginning to rotate the neck to make a turn, keep the neck parallel to the shoulders. Envision the neck brace under your chin and the back of your head as well as below your ears. You should not be able to alter your neck position because the neck brace would block you from dropping the front of the neck, or allowing our head to fall backward too much. Keep the neck laterally and longitudinally balanced in the neck brace.

Smile while riding

While riding should bring you joy and make you happy to be with your equine partner, smiling while you ride has another benefit, as well.

A smile will relax your facial muscles and help relieve stress. If you are smiling, it is difficult to lock your jaw. A locked jaw should be avoided at all costs because a locked jaw leads to tension in your neck making it harder to turn your head and use your eyes effectively. If your jaw is locked, there's a good chance that your horse is locking its jaw as well, creating tension on the bit.

A key point to enjoying your riding is to smile even you are frustrated. The tension will disappear for a few moments and your horse will thank you!

Head is a helium balloon about to float away

If you feel as though your head is an anchor that always feels as though it's a heavy burden, it's time to change your thinking.

Instead, think of your head as a helium balloon. Imagine the lightness and the feeling of it floating away from the shoulders. The gentle feeling throughout the upper body will help to break down any tension there.

The head needs to float as you gently find your center and allow the head to rest upon your shoulders. You will also discover that the tension in the jaw has disappeared, and you will become stress free in the neck area. Let this carry on through the spine all the way down to the waist. The light, airy feeling will emanate through your body.

Keep in mind that your eyes are very powerful while riding. You will not only see what lies directly in front of you, but also what is in your peripheral vision. You will use your eyes to sense when to turn or when to lock onto a distance before a jump. You can use your eyes to gaze off in front of you, or to signal for a turn. Your eyes are very important as you learn to ride. Use them wisely, and judge accordingly.

Sunglasses with tape

You may feel and look rather silly, but this is a fool-proof way to keep you from looking down. Your line of vision will be blocked, taking away the subconscious thought that there is a constant need to keep looking down.

Take a pair of old sunglasses and some duct tape. Place the duct tape across the bottom half of the lenses on both sides. Wear these glasses as you ride at a walk first. Begin to turn and change direction. You will not be able to look down while riding, and your head and ears will remain level.

Glancing down constantly at the horse's neck is a habit that many riders fall into. English riders look to see if they are on the correct diagonal while posting. Many riders look down to check to see if they are on the correct lead. When the eyes remain level it keeps the upper body more elevated. The sunglasses will help you to form good habits and your eyes and head will pre-cue the path of travel so the horse has an idea of what direction to travel to.

Coordination and strengthening exercises

Wear a bell in your hair

By wearing a small bell in your hair, you be able to hear if you make any unnecessary movement with your head and neck. You can purchase a small jingle bell and tie it to your ponytail or if your hair is short just go ahead and attach it to the back of your helmet. You want the noise from the bell to be rhythmic as you trot and canter. It will help you realize if your head has a mind of its own.

Focal points

While this exercise sounds very simple, I am amazed at how I must point out to keep at least four focal points while riding. You can pick anything to look at just make sure one point is at 12:00, one point at 3:00, 6:00 and 9:00. This will help the eliminate tunnel vision, which is staring at one spot. This is extremely important when jumping. You must never look down as you are jumping. Instead, pick a point at 12:00 in front of you and keep your intention of getting there. If you are learning to jump, do not turn while in the air. Your focal point will change to 3:00 or 9:00 and you will not land where you want to land.

The Steering System

Let's take a look at your turning aids

How to use the hands to help steer

We have already talked about how to use the thighs as a steering wheel for the horse's ribcage. We've also talked about using the lower leg to teach the horse to move away from the leg laterally. Now, we are going to add in other useful aids to make the turning cues even more sensitive.

We are now going to add power steering to the list of additions to the horse's training. The horse will learn to follow the motion of the rider with the magnetic seat that was discussed previously. The hands are the reinforcement to make the turn happen and to teach the horse to take the turn with fluidness and direction.

Hips

The first step in turning is the use of the hips. The hips must remain open, as in the image of the head lights on high beam. They direct the turn. The light remains even and steady, not bumpy or crooked. The lighted path will be in full view if you imagine these streams of light as if you are in the car and driving around a curve. Do not allow the light to become less bright or streamlined by closing the hip joint or bringing the torso closer to the thighs. Even in two point position, the rider will still keep a relatively open hip joint, except during the jumping effort. As the horse becomes more seasoned, the need for the constant open hip joint may not need to be so apparent.

Seat

The seat, as we have discussed, has many jobs. It's the connection between the upper body and the lower body. The seat goes hand in hand with the hips. The seat will also need to be in the position needed to ask the horse to control the leg speed or to aid in the turn. It is a useful bit of information to store in your data memory that most often the shoulders will fall past the width of the hips in a turn. What I mean is-if the rider uses too much shoulder and leans to the inside, then the seat bone on the opposite side of the turn will lift. This allows the horse to leak out through the aids, instead of following the aids of the seat. Keep the shoulders and hips stacked on top of each other in a turn.

Belly button

The belly button is, in fact, the third eye. Think of the green laser beam light keeping a steady stream in the middle of the two high beams that the hips generate. Do not allow these lights to drop. Keep them lifted. If the rider leans too far forward, the light of the belly button will begin to shine down in front of the horse's two front feet. Keep the light steering the horse and generating power from the inner core. If the rider has flopped forward, then the resistance is lost against the horse's power to push back at you. The hip will fold and the degeneration of the front to back balance will begin.

Shoulders

The shoulders must also have two flashlights attached to the front of them with the stream of light illuminating the intended direction. Do not allow one flashlight to drop lower than the other. Be sure the flashlights are above the hips. This is the common terminology heard when talking about keeping the shoulders stacked on top of the hips. Do not twist at the torso so the shoulders are going one direction, and the hips are traveling in another. This will confuse the horse, and twist the body so the momentum of the horse will move in an unwanted direction. The rider will have to resort to the hands to correct what the body signaled to the horse.

Eyes

The eyes must always be up and looking in the direction you are traveling. Never, should the eyes drop down. They must be fully functioning so the rider can make a quick plan for where to go next. By looking down, you will automatically weight the horse's two front feet. The horse will feel like a table top that is about to topple over forward. Your body will become like the tablecloth that is being pulled out from underneath the dishes and your hands will need to take over to save the body's balance point. Don't fall into this trap. Eyes up!

Hands

The hands are now staying between all the lights of the hips and shoulders. If two additional flashlights were hooked to the top of each hand, they would also shed light on the path. The hands will surely deviate from the path every so often if the horse needs help in order to go in a specific direction, or hasn't quite developed all the body control needed to make sharper turns or an even circle, the rider is there to assist with one of the following rein aids.

If you are experiencing difficulty with your hands and adding the rein aids, then take your index finger while holding the reins and point it like you are holding a fake gun. Point that gun to where you are aiming to go. This will help you trigger the aids you will need to use in your body to make the turn work, and to know how you can improve.

What are the different types of rein aids?

Direct rein

The direct rein, also known as the opening rein, is used when applying the brakes, as well as when asking the horse to turn right or left. However, the rider must remember to use a holding pressure rather than pulling too much with the reins as that might cause the horse to lean against the pull. Also, the rider's elbows should not be drawn back behind their ribcage as this signals the horse to back up. This easy, elementary rein aid can be used at any time to re-teach the basics as the horse moves up the ladder of training.

Indirect rein

The indirect rein, also known as the bearing rein or neck rein, is used to signal the horse to move away from it. Although the rein is applied toward the horse's body, it is never a good idea to leave the rein along the horse's neck for a prolonged period of time. If the rein is held against the horse's body, it will give the horse something to lean on, which you don't want to allow. The rein is simply there as a signal, not a pulling option. The rider must use other parts of her body to communicate with the horse to move its body.

Rein of opposition

This rein is used for one rein stops or when moving the horse's hips. It is a rein aid that is used in a diagonal line behind the horse's withers.

Indirect rein of opposition

This is the rein aid used in a diagonal line in front of the horse's withers. This will move the opposite shoulder as in lateral work, or when asking the horse for a slight bend inside.

What is contact?

Contact is, essentially, when a horse feels like he moves or is traveling into the hands. This is not to be confused with a horse that is leaning on the hands. The pressure that the horse submits to will be the same as a firm handshake. Essentially, you feel the horse, and the horse feels you.

The development of the rider is essential in order to establish and maintain contact with a horse. A rider with a strong midsection will not be pushed out of the way by a horse that is pushing back with the energy we generate, or pulling forward. The horse's back will find it necessary to support the hind legs and will start to lift and swing. The horse will begin to develop a strong top line from the tail to the ears. This will lead to self-carriage, which is, essentially, the horse holding itself up and becoming lighter in our hand and more comfortable to ride. As this happens, your horse will develop an even, steady tempo and will not need to be reminded to rebalance as often.

Contact on the bit happens when the horse is free from any energy blockages (stiffness) and any energy leaks (false bending), both of which lead to a place for the energy to escape. This is true with the rider's body, as well, and what we are striving so hard to correct.

When we are in balance, our horse is in balance. When we learn to make contact, our horse will learn to make contact. When we pull, our horse will pull, and when we release and set the horse down, so to speak, with the rein pressure, the horse will learn to stretch and reach forward into contact and the bit. This is our ultimate goal.

What does contact feel like?

When a horse is "on the bit" it will feel as though the horse is moving as one unit-not a lot of disconnected pieces. The horse will become more comfortable to sit on because the back is swinging and working properly. This, in turn, will be easier to ride because the hollow that we are used to sitting in will turn into a flat surface or a round ball. This will also raise the back behind the saddle because it is up and swinging, instead of dropped and tense. What you will also find is the horse has replaced his cement boots with a pair of ballet slippers. He will feel as though he could float anywhere at a moment's notice. It will feel as though the bit is a magnet in your hands and the horse is constantly being drawn forward to seek it.

Always remember if your arms are stiff, you will create a blockage which is an impaired connection with the horse. Your muscular contractions will lead to rigidness. This will always disturb the elasticity and your oneness with the horse.

How to use the last puzzle piece

I have talked at great length about how to use each piece of the body to develop your body and encourage strength and balance from the horse. Use these skills in your riding and training regimen. We are on the final chapter. I have split the last section into three portions. These three portions are an overview of how to use your planes of balance to effectively influence your horse's athletic ability, as well as your own. You can integrate these skills, and slowly, but surely, you can change the way you ride your horse now, and forever.

Keep in mind you will gain and lose pieces. It is all part of the learning process. The most important part is realizing the mistakes you make and the corrections used to improve your riding journey.

The top to bottom portion improvements will determine how and where the rider sits in the saddle to help lift the horse's back or lowers its body. It is your grace and beauty when someone watches you ride.

The front to back portion is the extra push to tell the horse to move forward or the resistance to slow the body down. This is your transition work: whoa and go.

The right to left portion is the side to side balance you have on a horse. It's how you utilize your body to keep the horse underneath you in a turn or change of direction.

You will be using all three portions of balance every time you ride your horse. They will work in unison and develop into the feel that every rider strives to reach. Let's take a closer look at each portion in our last piece of the riding puzzle. We are on our way to solving the riddles of riding.

Overview of the overall structure

The main pieces of the overall structure of our riding position can be used as a whole series of muscle responses in order to use the body in the most effective way. We have gone over each piece individually, and now we are going to focus on three main parts to trouble shoot and trigger the body to align properly for overall performance and balance for both ourselves and our horses. They are comprised of three main sections.

The first part to consider is the trunk, which includes the seat and the torso. This is our center of strength and balance. As we have already discussed, the seat is one of the main riding aids. The second section is the lower appendages, from the hips to your toes, including your legs. The third section would be your upper appendages from the shoulders to your fingers.

The three main sections can be trained to go in six different directions: up, down, forward, back, left, and right. The rider must learn how to use muscles of opposition in these sections to obtain overall balance, tone, technique, and form in order to allow the horse to function properly to the best of its ability.

Let's now learn how to use all our puzzle pieces to make a connection and steady contact to communicate with our horse.

Connection

A flawless riding position is what we all strive for. The horse moves and generates enough force that rattles us in the saddle. It bounces us about. Until we can learn to keep still in the saddle and develop a good seat that remains plugged in, the rider will always feel less confident and unable to communicate to the horse because all the aids will be moving up and down, instead of remaining steady and still. This creates the 'NO' static ride. We must always pick away at our position in order to develop a connection with the horse.

Our trunk is, in essence, our tree of life. We allow the roots to grow down and the branches to grow up. Our tree will be able to gently sway in the breeze, but will never topple over forward or backward, or even side to side. Our trunk is what we use to stop the horse, or ask the horse to move forward. It is a definite aid in turning and needs to be the most stable section of the body in order to allow the appendages to do their job with the most influence and least inconsistency. The trunk will also absorb the movement of the horse and allow it to ripple through the joints and muscles, receiving the information that the horse is channeling to us through our bodies.

Neutral spine

Neutral spine is the alignment that will put the body in the most effective riding position. Proper posture allows for the natural curves in the spine to happen. Rider position errors often stem from improper posture with the curves of the spine being forced or stiffened by the rider. A hollow-backed, or round-backed rider are prime examples. Once the rider has found neutral spine, the postural muscles will stabilize the balance and allow free, and soft mobility throughout the hip and shoulder joints. These are two major joints needed in order to ride in balance, and follow the movement generated by the horse into the seat and through the hands. This is sometimes called recycled energy from the horse-to the rider-and back to the horse.

Keep practicing to find your neutral spine in all areas of riding. Always remember to keep the seat bones pointing down, the normal curves of the spine, and the shoulders and ribcage balanced over the pelvis.

Body control

Effective riding requires the rider to have complete command of the legs and the arms. This can only happen when the rider surrenders the hands and legs and does not rely on either one, solely, for balance as the horse is moving. When a rider can stabilize the body and learn to fire the muscles that are needed in order to work in conjunction with the movement, and requests to the horse, then the rider will be able to free up the legs to ask the horse to move the feet forward or in a specific direction. The hands will then be free to communicate with the horse, and use the bit effectively to teach contact and control. The signals to the horse become much clearer and the conversation between horse and rider will change drastically.

Legs

Large, strong muscles connect the legs to the pelvis at the hip joint. The rider must become aware of these muscles and control must be developed in order for the rider to be able to move with the horse's body. When tightness or gripping occurs the muscles of the upper leg will block movement at the hip joint and result in a leak of energy, or a blockage of movement. If the rider uses the legs to grip for balance, it will be hard to give a clear aid to the horse. The leg should hang down in an outward rotation, which puts the posterior thigh against the saddle and the calf against the horse's ribcage.

Arms

The arms connect to the trunk at the shoulder joint. The shoulder houses many muscles that supply us with a great range of motion. These muscles can also disrupt posture. Excess stiffness in the shoulder at the front of the armpit can tend to pull the shoulders forward and the spine will deviate into a rounded posture. When this happens, trunk stability is lost and a chain reaction begins. If you tend to keep the shoulders back too far, this can lead to an arched spine. Let the arms hang straight down from the shoulder joint. The arms will feel as though they are part of the horse's bridle. This happens when you are centered and in good balance with the trunk and legs in a stable, suitable position.

Riding Aid Assembly #1

Imagery
Essentials

Trunk

The main root for the aids

Checklist for Proper Alignment of the Trunk

- ✓ Sit in the middle of the bullseye.
- ✓ Keep the marble under your seat.
- ✓ Keep your trunk in neutral spine.
- ✓ Shoulder pads over your poodle skirt.
- ✓ Keep your trunk in the slinky.

Riding Realities

Common Errors and Enigmas

One of the most puzzling areas of the body is, indeed, the trunk which houses all our power and "ready muscle". Often, we overuse or misuse this area and begin pushing with the seat or trying to do the work for the horse, instead of allowing the horse to roll underneath us. We use our seat, stomach and back in ways that block movement and stiffen joints. We begin to fight against the natural motion of the horse. Study the horse's movement and become a critic so you can understand the horse's body in all three gaits-walk, trot and canter. If you realize the placement of the horse's feet you will be able to use your body in a more correct way to influence the balance. A horse in the pasture has natural balance and it floats from one gait to another. Once we sit upon their back, the once fluid movement can turn form, grace, and beauty to short and choppy gaits. Help your horse and understand how the body moves, as well

Familiar Faults

Fault 1

Moving the body as one unit is a common error for riders. We have discussed how to separate the pieces of the body in great detail. Do not allow the arms and legs to attach themselves completely to the trunk and begin moving and pushing the horse forward. This would resemble a rider who is constantly doing the work for the horse, and tiring quickly, as the horse is slowing down in the stride instead of speeding up. A rider who uses a pushing seat or pushing midsection will fall into this trap. Plug into the horse's back and sit still. Signal to the horse to move forward with your two legs instead, and allow the horse's back to move beneath you. The horse should be encouraged to move forward from a still seat and trunk and the legs should be used separately to signal the horse to move forward into the rider's receiving hands.

Fault 2

As riders we are always more dominant on one side. If there is a noticeable twist in the trunk from side to side, or an over-bend through the ribcage of the rider, then the horse will begin to show signs of crookedness related to the rider's trunk and body position. They will follow our balance and our asymmetry issue. It is of utmost importance that the rider constantly picks away at their own position. Asymmetry issues in the trunk can greatly affect how the horse will turn, but will also really affect how the horse does not turn, due to a blockage in our own bodies.

Fault 3

Getting left behind in the motion is the same as putting banana peels under the horse's feet and then pulling all four peels forward and out from under the horse. The rider will get left behind the motion, and will need to catch up to the horse's motion. This way of riding will always cause confusion for the horse as the rider needs to stay above the balance point of the horse's body. It is best if the rider's trunk is sturdy so that it can withstand the sudden motion forward or backward from the horse. Make it a priority to feel when change is about to happen. Know when the horse is about to pick up speed by using your trunk to the best of your ability and staying balanced over the horse's center of gravity. When the horse feels like it is going to shoot forward, then the rider will be one second ahead and be able to correct the movement while staying in balance.

Fault 4

The same holds true for a horse that is lazy or not willing to move forward, or in certain steps of a movement the horse has paid more attention to the hand aids or rein aids to slow down than to the trunk, seat and leg to step up to the contact. Once the rider is in a position to hold the trunk stable, they will feel when leg needs to be added in order to ask the horse to stay in front of our leg aids by keeping substantial forward movement. The rider will then feel as though they do not constantly have to ask the horse to carry the bit or ride into their hands.

Now envision your picture perfect pieces for the improved ride

Imagery examination:

The mediating zone for the three sections of the body

Further Explanation

The trunk is the core stability and the zone that holds together the other two sections. If the trunk is not stable, the legs and arms will move too much and the result will be extra static with the communication to the horse. Balance will be jeopardized and the rider will be forced to balance by other means including the legs and hands. This is never the best way of communication with your horse. It will generate many bad behaviors or unwanted scenarios.

Essential Details of each Imagery

Sit in the middle of the bullseye

Confusion often arises regarding exactly where the rider should sit on the horse's back. Where does the seat form a nice seamless feel with the horses back during movement? To help locate the best spot, picture placing a bullseye under the rider's seat. The rider then needs to keep his seat bones on either side of the bullseye. This bullseye is what you are going to think about. When asking for forward movement or if the horse is asked to slow down, strive to aim the buttocks at the middle of the target. If the seat were to slip away from the target, then the rider is allowing the position to be influenced by the horse's strong force to pull them forward, or push them back. Hold the seat, and keep thinking of the target beneath the bum while riding through transitions or for turning purposes. This is the horse's center of gravity. Hold the center and the trunk over this target as you ride.

Keep the marble beneath the seat

Another visualization to use is the placement of a marble directly in the center of the bullseye. This marble must not roll around. Do not allow the pelvis to lift in a way that the marble would come loose and roll about on the saddle. The pelvis should resemble a suction cup over the marble.

This helps greatly with sitting the trot. If the rider were to stiffen the joints too much, the result would be that the rider pops up and away from the saddle. In most cases, the marble would be lost. By thinking of something as small as a marble, you are using specific visualization to really use the trunk to maintain stability and balance.

Keep the trunk in neutral spine

A neutral spine position will resemble that of three "C" curves. The first "C" curve will be at the cervical section of the neck which is just below the head. This "C" curve will be a small reverse "C". As you travel down the back a little ways you will reach the point of the rider's shoulders, and then travel down over the back of the ribcage until you reach the lower back. This whole section will have a slight curve in the normal direction of what a "C" curve will look like.

Farther down the lower back toward the sacrum, the reverse "C" curve will be apparent once again. This section of the back, in general, is the area that is most misused in riding. If this section becomes too stiff or too hollow, the rider will experience back pain and a lot of concussion from the horse's movement. This section of the rider's body must learn to relax and hold position. It should move with the horse's movement and will become like a door hinge when jumping. When a rider is in need of extra power, this section of the back can supply it by bringing the belly button toward the spine and filling out this area of the back. The rider will learn to turn it on and off as needed. As the rider excels and becomes stronger, the breathing pattern can be made stronger as well. This is known as breathing into your back, or diaphragmatic breathing. This will help to fill up the "C" curve so the back is more stable and able to combat the push and pull of the horse's movement. It also allows for soft static movement up and down like a rippling effect through the back.

Shoulder pads over the poodle skirt

Here is where we are going to combine the 50's girl with the football player. Think back to the rock and roll days of the poodle skirt. Pretend you are wearing the big hoop skirt upon your horse. Now, think of becoming a line backer and tacking yourself up in football shoulder pads.

In order to keep the trunk in good alignment, learn to keep the shoulder pads directly over the hoop of the poodle skirt. This will help keep the trunk stable from top to bottom. If the horse suddenly speeds up and the rider were to be left behind, then the world would get to see the rider's bloomers under that skirt. The rider would tip backward and the front of the skirt would lift up. A sudden slow down would also let everyone see the derriere, as the rider would fall forward leaving the seat to peel up and the trunk to fall toward the horse's withers or neck. Keep the hoop of the circle of the skirt down at all times with the trunk aligned.

Do not compromise your girlie ways. The shoulder pads must also, at times, feel as though they are weighted with heavy weights inside. They will help the shoulders sink to the hips. The most important aspect, though, is to keep them stacked one above the other.

Keep the trunk in a slinky

Visualize the amazing toy, the slinky. Understand why this is such an amazing image. If you were to hold both ends of the slinky so it resembled the shape of a rainbow that touches the ground on both sides, the ends remain stable, but the middle section moves about. It becomes like a chain reaction that can't be stopped once it is put into motion. This is the same scenario for the rider's body.

If the top half of the slinky, meaning the rider's head and the shoulders, and the bottom half of the slinky, meaning the rider's seat and pelvis, do not remain level, then the slinky begins to topple over or back, and the chain reaction begins. If the middle of the slinky is not brought close together, it becomes wobbly and moves about in all directions. This is what some rider's allow their midsection to do. Instead, keep the slinky rings close together.

If we were to slide a giant slinky over your head and have it encompass your body all the way down to your hips and let it rest on the saddle, your body should remain in the slinky. Think of those coils being bendable, but still managing to remain close together so the rider keeps bringing top to bottom. This imagery will help when your body begins to move too much with the horse's movement. You will have to focus on which section of the slinky you are losing stability and bring those coils closer together.

Core Alignment Exercises

The following exercises can be done as a series one right after the other. Ask a helper to hold your horse or perform and practice these exercises on the ground first.

Reach up and pray to the sky

In order to stretch the trunk and spread apart the ribs, you are going to reach up and pray to the sky. Ask a helper to hold your horse, or do this on the ground without your horse. By bringing your palms together, and stretching up over your head, you can feel your torso become longer. Do not arch the lower back, and try to keep all the coils of the slinky around your midsection stacked on top of each other. This will keep your ribcage aligned. Do this for a count of five. Then, immediately, go into the next exercise which is "airplane arms".

Airplane arms

The torso and the shoulders play a key role in the alignment of the trunk. By reaching out to the side with both arms and pretending they are airplane wings, the rider can feel the stretch all the way to the fingertips. It is important to keep the stretch and hold it for at least 5 seconds. The shoulders need to be level at all times. This can also help the rider who has an asymmetry issue. It will be more noticeable during this exercise. Once the rider has done this exercise, the next exercise is to keep this framework with airplane arms, and now rotate the torso to the left and center, then right and center.

Turn the torso left and right

From the airplane arms position the rider must practice how to rotate the torso to the left and right. The midsection must stay aligned, and the rider should rotate to the left so the trunk is facing to the left, with the right arm above the horse's head, and the left arm above the horse's rump. The rider can then rotate back to center and assume regular airplane arms position. Then rotate to the right, so the left arm is above the horse's head, and the right arm is above the rump. Do this in a series of rotations: left to center, then, right to center. Keep the shoulders level and even throughout the rotations.

Sleepwalking

Sleepwalkers usually walk with their arms stretched out in front of their body. Riders often drop the area of the chest where the sternum is located. To help correct this, you can pretend you are sleepwalking while sitting on your horse. Keep your shoulders level and allow your arms to reach straight out in front of you. Stretch your fingers also, so that the top portion of your body resembles a sleepwalker. Hold this stretch for at least five seconds. From this position you will move onto the "touching the tail" exercise.

Touching the tail

This twist of the torso will also help with the opening of the hip flexors. From the sleepwalking position, the rider will separate the arms and reach back and touch the horse's rump-almost reaching for the tail. The palm of the hand can slightly lean on the rump and feel the horse's muscle. Rotate back to the center and the original sleepwalking position. Switch to the right and repeat the sequence. It will also bring more weight to the seat bone on the side in which the rider is reaching.

Repeat this sequence as many times as necessary. It will help the rider to feel the need to stretch, turn, or rotate the midsection.

Appendages

The Legs

The legs are an extension of the trunk. They are attached at the hips, which are major shock absorbers for the rest of the body. (The legs of the rider have a main function of influencing the horse's movement.) They are the electric current to rev up the horse's engine and keep the power surging through the horse's feet. They are also what hold the rider down and in place. Gravity will always pull the rider downward. If the rider tries to fight against gravity and finds their body lifting instead of lowering, then the rider is trying to grip instead of allowing the joints of the hip and ankle to open and fall to the natural point where they will adjust and become molded to the saddle to ensure security.

Riding Aid Assembly #2

Imagery Essentials

Legs

The riding aid to balance the motion

Checklist for proper Alignment of the legs

- ✓ Wear the horse's hind legs.
- ✓ Sew the legs but don't break the seam.
- ✓ Ride between the electric shock walls.
- ✓ Keep the propellers on the knees pointing down.
- ✓ Keep the toe and knee slightly in front of the girth.

+

Riding Realities

Common Errors and Enigmas

The legs are, perhaps, one of the most important sections of the body because they can signal the horse to move forward. Many behavioral issues with horses stem from lack of forward movement. It is important that the rider can sit and ride a horse from a place of balance and ease. It is then that the legs can take on the job of training the horse to become more responsive. If a rider uses a lot of rein contact and not enough leg then they will in effect be riding a horse from front to back instead of the preferred back to front. It is the rider's legs that generate this surge.

Familiar Faults

Fault 1

The "nagging leg" is a leg aid that comes in contact with the horse's sides without the knowledge of the rider. If a rider is not stable or in complete control of the lower leg, then the leg will bump or wave upon the horse's sides, causing a swinging action that can be an annoyance to the horse. A stable still lower leg is key to instant performance from the rider's cue to move forward. Any rider who chooses to wear a spur should have complete control of the leg before wearing the spur. Otherwise, this particular leg position and fault will cause the rider to spur every stride. This is an even bigger annoyance to the horse and a major mistake for the rider.

Fault 2

A "gripping lower leg" is also a demon in disguise. If the rider tries to use force and muscle strength to hold the leg in position, the rider will become fatigued and the horse will become dull to the leg cue. A breathable touch is necessary, but the rider will need to learn to follow the horse with the leg. It is then that the rider will become knowledgeable about when to add a tiny vibration to a schooled horse in order to generate power to move forward or create impulsion, which is spring in the step.

Fault 3

A "pushing or bracing lower leg" will, more than likely, create no contact whatsoever. The horse will be confused as to whether he should move forward or slow down. The rider will lose their trunk stability and will begin to shift in a direction that is a driving seat. A driving seat will always signal the horse to move forward at a quicker rate of speed. The rider will not be able to keep the trunk stabilized and the result will be a hand-dominated option to slow the horse down.

Fault 4

The "floppy leg" is a leg that resembles a flimsy noodle. It is as if the leg just hangs limply in the stirrup. This occurs when a rider has gone overboard in relaxing the leg muscles. The grounding necessary to keep the rider's trunk stable and the legs around the horse have disappeared all-together. In some cases the rider who grips excessively must go in the other direction and learn to relax the legs first before learning to stabilize the legs. However, the rider should always think of form and function to keep the legs always striving to reach down and around the body of the horse. In later advanced work, the rider will learn to elevate the ribcage of the horse while keeping the integrity of the legs in check and balanced.

Fault 5

The "rising leg" is another result of position breakdown when it comes to the legs. Often, when the rider tries to hold with the thighs, the thighs will begin to rise and weight will lift out of the stirrups. It is important to develop all the muscles of the legs and thighs. If this is not addressed, the rider will end up with the quadriceps being more dominant than the hamstrings, or vice versa. Always go to your place of stability which is your pedestal in your stirrups, and build up from there.

Now envision your picture perfect pieces for the improved ride

Imagery examination:

The Power Surge

Further Explanation

The legs are the foundation of all good riding. Even when riding without stirrups, the rider must imagine having stirrups. Constantly work on strengthening the legs and refining the cues to make them almost invisible when asking for any forward or sideways movement. Generate power from within a horse's stride and within a movement.

Essential Details of each Imagery

Wear the hind legs

As silly as it sounds, imagine removing your own legs from where your hip attaches to your thigh. Now, take the horse's hind legs and fasten those in place of your legs. They must move in conjunction with the horse's two front feet and must have the same power, poise and grace that your horse has. They will follow wherever the two front feet lead them and will never skip a stride or go faster or slower than the horse's front feet.

This is a great exercise to learn to help the rider follow the movement of the horse. It helps with those riders who tend to raise the thighs up or leave the thighs loose. The legs will now have purpose and you will need to use them quietly, but with great strength to help the horse's stride and way of travel be the best it can be.

Sew the legs but don't break the seam

To get away from the gripping scenario, picture the world's best seamstress stopping by your arena and stitching your britches to the saddle. She began at the top where your thigh stems from your hip, and sewed all the way down to your mid-calf. She left the stitches rather loose, but all connected in a way that your legs could "breathe". As the horse moves, the loose stitching allows you to pull your legs away from the saddle slightly, just be sure not break any stitches.

The seam never gets to the breaking point, but it does slightly open as if you were putting pressure on it and trying to rip it. The sensation of the movable, breathable leg will take form with this imagery.

Even in moments of asking for forward movement with both legs, the rider should be able to use both legs, and never fully rip any stitching. This will help the action of the muscles of opposition start to take shape and to really start to develop staying power with the horse's back and ribcage.

Keep the stirrup leathers or stirrup fenders straight up and down. Do not allow for the leathers to extend too far forward or too far backward in a diagonal line. Always strive for a completely straight line. This will help the rider to have a checkpoint when positioning other parts of the body. The legs will sometimes get misplaced. If the stirrup leathers are straight down while riding, it eliminates some guess work.

Electric shock walls

The "electric shock walls" will help the rider who tends to leave the knee open, or the foot fanned out to the side. Imagine you are riding through an extremely narrow hallway. The walls extend high above you and your horse's head on both sides. You only have a few inches clearance as you ride through this narrow hallway. To make matters worse these walls are electrified, and if you accidently bump into those walls you will get a shock much like the shock we receive when we accidentally touch the electric fence.

This analogy will make the rider think of becoming narrower from side to side. This will, in turn, tidy up the leg position. Keep the legs snuggly touching, not just bouncing about nudging and pushing. Stay as still as can be and only add both legs when needed in order to go forward. When the situation arises to ask for more forward motion, make it count. Do not accidentally touch the electric shock walls when you do give a forward aid. Keep yourself close to the horse even in a turn or straight line. Remember this hallway does have corners and you must keep channeling your horse's energy through this tunnel.

Propellers point down

You are now going to envision having a propeller on each kneecap as you ride. They are (directly centered) on each knee. If the propeller is pointing down toward the ground it will, in a sense, be pulling you forward in that direction (down). Pretend as though the thigh is the airplane, and the direction of the thigh is going to go in a diagonal direction downward along with the propellers which are pulling the thigh that way.

This is the feeling of using the thighs to generate a pull forward, while the trunk anchors the rest of the body in hold position. This is an example of how the muscles of opposition will be working with one another to hold the body against the force that the horse thrusts. If the knees and propellers begin to point in a forward direction where they become more level with the ground, then the knee will lose contact, and the rider will begin to get too light in the stirrups. Your propellers must pull your thigh in a downward direction as you ride. Keep thinking of flying the airplane in a safe descent so it can eventually land safely and gently. While you are striving for this position, be sure that the feet are flat in the stirrups, and the weight is across the stirrup sealed down.

A good vision is to keep your toes and your knees slightly in front of the girth for balanced riding. This is not set in stone, however, and you may deviate from this occasionally in the jumping effort or in the effort to stop. However, for most riding on the flat, this is a good rule to follow to keep the knee directly over the toe. This will help to stabilize your leg.

Leg Alignment Exercises

Stirrup leathers straight down

A good way to check the alignment of the leg is to check to be sure that the stirrup leather or fenders are straight up and down. Whether the rider is sitting in an english, dressage, or western saddle, this is a good way to check alignment. The leathers or fenders should not stretch forward in a diagonal line, or backward in a diagonal line. In fact, the rider can align the seat and upper body around this easy self-check that can be performed just by peeking down at your legs. Check this periodically while riding. It takes a lot of the guesswork out of the way in which the body aligns over the feet.

The stirrup leather is hanging straight down, and should look the same with the rider's foot in the stirrup. The leg will move when asking for different responses from the horse, but use this position as your home base. Come back to this position to readjust or to tell the horse that their reaction to your cue to go forward is correct.

Hole of stirrup forward

Once the leathers are positioned straight up and down, the rider must take notice that the hole of the stirrup in which the foot lies is facing forward. This is the start position to align the feet, and to make sure that the lower leg and balance points of the sole of the foot can have a good starting point to balance from. It will also help with the symmetry of the left side and right side of our

bodies. If the rider had a flashlight on the front of the foot, it would be shining a beam of light towards 12:00 to light the way for the horse.

The foot in this picture is correct with the placement of the hole of the stirrup facing forward toward 12:00, however the bottom of the stirrup is on a slight diagonal. You can see that the inside edge of the stirrup is slightly dropped toward the horse. This will be the case most times while riding. Once the rider establishes a relaxed yet toned leg, the rider will then have all three leg alignment positions correct. You can feel a "breathable leg", or a very light leg cue once that is established.

Bottom of stirrup parallel to ground

The position of the bottom of the stirrup is equally important, as it will help the rider to establish how much pressure they are pushing onto the stirrup. The bottom of the iron for an english, or dressage saddle, or the bottom of the western stirrup, should always be parallel to the ground below it. The platform of the stirrup should not be a diagonal line with the ground beneath it. In beginning stages of riding, the rider will often be slightly off the parallel line while teaching other muscles. The goal, however, is to give all leg aids and hold balance with the stirrup irons parallel to the ground.

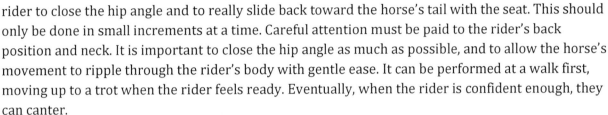

Jockey position

A fore-warning: this exercise is difficult. Jockey position is a reliable exercise to help stabilize the lower leg of the rider. It also helps the rider to close the hip angle and to really slide back toward the horse's tail with the seat. This should only be done in small increments at a time. Careful attention must be paid to the rider's back position and neck. It is important to close the hip angle as much as possible, and to allow the horse's movement to ripple through the rider's body with gentle ease. It can be performed at a walk first, moving up to a trot when the rider feels ready. Eventually, when the rider is confident enough, they can canter.

Tara is holding jockey position with a flat back and steady leg position. Notice how the stirrup leathers are straight down, the hole of the stirrup is facing forward, and the bottom of the stirrup is parallel to the ground. The connection with both reins is evident, and she is looking up and through Sydney's ears. If we were to pull Sydney out from beneath Tara quickly she would still land on her feet. This is the aim of this exercise. Remember to perform it in small increments.

Begin by shortening the stirrups as short as is comfortable for the rider. Then, the rider must fold over and move the chest toward the horse's neck. Keep a flat back. Do not hollow or arch the back. Try to keep the back relaxed and the legs buoyant. If needed, the rider may hold the mane until the balance is established. Work in short intervals at first. Practice this position for 2 minutes, then take a break. Build up until you can go for longer periods of time.

This exercise will greatly increase the contact area of the lower leg and will take the grip away with the inside thigh muscles. It also helps with jumping position and two point.

The Arms

The arms are the golden ticket to good riding. Riders spend years developing a good feel on a horse through elastic give and take. The arms allow for contact to happen, and for the horse to trust the hand and follow the bit that leads to gentle pressure. It is always a conversation with the hands to allow the horse to develop the body correctly and use the back muscles for ultimate control. The hands will follow movement and create softness through the horse's muscles. Never should the hands be used in an abusive manner or in a jerking, or frustrated state. The more anxious the horse the slower the hands need to be. They need to meet a horse and match the pressure it generates. Once the request is met the rider must melt away with the hands, never dropping a horse completely, but, instead, setting the horse down into contact.

The arms are separated from the rest of the body, and are an extension of the trunk. The shoulders are the joints that allow the release of contact and can initiate the stop or half halt. The hands and fingers play a huge role once a horse is schooled to a high level. They become an invisible aid for all riding skills and techniques.

Riding Aid Assembly #3

Imagery Essentials

Arms

The means to make a connection

Checklist for proper Alignment of the Arms

- ✓ The water hose must keep constant flow.
- ✓ Unlock the door.
- ✓ Roll the poll.
- ✓ Light bulb shines brightly.

Riding Realities

Common Errors and Enigmas

The arms can be one of the toughest parts of the body to master when riding a horse. It is only when the trunk is stable and our legs are beneath us, that we can then surrender our hands for balance and let them do the job they were intended to do, which is good communication with the horse. Unfortunately, there are many faults that can form from bad balance and mostly it will show up with the rider using the bit.

Familiar Faults

Fault 1

The "fixed hand" is a hand that is always set. There is little to no movement whatsoever. You will use this type of hand in the very beginning stages of a green horse's training, but as you progress you will need to develop a "following hand" that moves along with the horse's body, and encourages a quiet feel with the horse's mouth.

A fixed, or set hand, is sometimes used for young horses if the rider is not able to hold against pressure. By placing the hand against the saddle it creates a holding tension for the horse to learn to give to.

Fault 2

The "tug of war hand" is the hand that is always fighting when the horse begins to pull the hands forward. This hand pressure will always result in the horse being victorious, because the rider will not be able to "out pull" the horse. When a horse generates a pull forward because they are out of balance, then the rider must teach the horse to be in balance by using the body to rock the horse onto the hind end, instead of pulling with the front.

Fault 3

The "lifeless hand" is the hand that demands nothing from the horse. The rein contact is in a sense like a wet noodle. It droops and hangs with no connection at all. The horse will feel a loopy-tight, loopy-tight sensation, and be caught by surprise every time the rider picks up the rein, or needs it for balance. Riders often feel they are being light, but in a sense they are just throwing away any contact they could have.

Fault 4

The "bouncing hand" is a rein pressure that is always bumping and moving about. The rider uses the arms and the trunk as one unit. This will result in the rider's every move with the mid-section transferring directly to the bridle. The horse feels the bit bumping the teeth, and the connection is full of static.

Fault 5

A "rising hand" seems to have a mind of its own. When the rider feels like they have lost control with the trunk, they begin to try to nail the trunk down, but the hands begin to ride and fly away, mostly in an upward direction. When the trunk is stable, the hand can begin to come to home base, which is above the horse's withers or within two inches in front of, or behind this area.

Now envision your picture perfect pieces for the improved ride

Imagery examination:

The final touch to make the magic happen

Further Explanation

There is nothing better than to feel the magic that can happen when a horse feels like an elastic band in your hands. Pulling is non-existent, the balance is evident, and the "oneness" felt is like no other. Contact is one of the most sought after, but elusive finds in riding. Once a rider captures the feeling, it will become addictive. It is not forced, pulled, jiggled, seesawed, or abused. It strictly happens from good riding and good body balance.

Essential Details of each Imagery

The water hose must keep constant flow

Imagine a piece of regular garden hose taking the place of each of your arms. We have attached a piece of that hose from the shoulder on both arms. If water is not flowing through, it becomes very flimsy and soft. This is your following arm that must not disturb the horse's forward movement.

That is the softness that is maintained in the shoulders as the horse learns to follow the contact from the bit.

If the horse begins to lean or pull on that pressure, think of the water hose kinking for a moment as you sink into the elbows. This makes the water trickle through the reins, and to the bit. Once the horse is lifting and soft again, then imagine that you let the water run freely from the shoulders down the arms into the elbows, and allow it to keep flowing all the way through the wrists, and hands down to the horse's mouth where the water will then flow forward not back. This is the feeling of letting the horse move forward into an allowing contact, and freeing pressure.

Encourage the horse to seek the water that is flowing on either side of the bit. Use this imagery to allow the contact to happen in the arms, and hands. If the wrists bend and block the water, then the result will be spurting water in a different direction. Keep the flow constant, and correct the flow of water when the horse tried to pull each hose down and tries to aim the water in a direction any other way besides forward.

This view shows the connection from elbow to wrist. There is no break in the water hose meaning the reins all the way down to the bit where it lies in Phantom's mouth. It is even on both sides, and the water could keep flowing

You can also imagine that the two constant streams of water create a hallway. If the horse begins to bend too much with the head in one direction or the other, they will be sprayed in the face by the water flow. This is true for the shoulder leaking out, as well. Keep the horse's head and shoulders in between the two streams of water.

Unlock the door

Up until now we have made it a point to not bend or contort the wrists in any direction. As you advance and can keep the wrists very flexible, you will be ready to unlock the door.

Imagine holding a key in your hand, and looking to unlock a door. This will bring the pinky close to the horse and the thumb will rotate slightly over the top toward the outside. If you use your wrists and hands in this fashion, you will be able to ask the horse for a small bend through the neck.

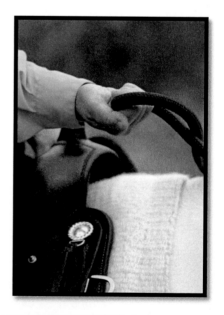

In some cases this is all you will need to change direction and initiate the bend to turn. It is also a great way to ask for slight flexion in the horse's neck. You will begin to see the muscles soften, and the jaw of the horse will peek out on the side where you unlocked the door. This takes some practice. If you feel as though you are losing ground more than gaining, go back to asking with the wrists gentle and soft. Once this is reestablished, return to this exercise.

In time, you will be able to keep your hands straddling the working area where the Frisbee lies and find you can give an almost invisible aid.

Roll the poll

As the horse and the connection become more intricate, the muscles of the horse's neck will soften even more. The poll area of the horse, which is right behind the ears, will begin to take on a great feeling of lateral flexion, (bending side to side). The rider can learn to use the fingers and hands in a very sophisticated manor. Rolling the poll is an ingredient that I have discovered really tweaks the use of the hands.

The rider is bringing the reins into her fingertips, but not allowing the fingers to open completely. This process takes some practice, but can be a great asset to your riding.

The rider is going to hold the rein and make a fist with the thumb on top. With the rein lying across the line of the fingers, the rider is going to roll the rein into the knuckles without completely opening the hand. This must be done with careful attention not to add any backward pressure to the rein or the horse's mouth. That accidental backward pressure will signal to the horse to close the throat latch or bring the chin toward the chest. This is not what we are looking for. Instead, we are looking for the corner of the horse's eye to be visible from the saddle.

The feeling is like rolling the rein to your fingertips. By doing this in a series of two or three, the horse will gently feel the massage of the rein, and begin to bend towards it.

Light bulb shines brightly

Let there be light! Think of having a light bulb under each arm. These light bulbs are screwed into the armpit, and the light is hanging down gently under each arm. Allow the shoulder to house this light. Do not be tempted to squeeze the upper arms into your side or you will break these light bulbs. Let the light bulb shine, and open the armpit area. If the light bulb has been on for quite awhile, it is sure to be hot to the touch. Do not burn the inner skin of the upper arm. Instead, keep the shoulders like a lampshade. They will drop down and cradle the light. The lampshade must also stay level. You cannot drop the shoulder forward or all the light will start to shine out backwards. Don't roll the shoulder back too far or the light will start to peak through the front. Keep the lampshade level and allow the light bulbs to shine down towards the ground.

This will help with the position of the upper arm and shoulder when extra power is needed. Learn to stabilize this area and keep the shoulders harnessed so they do not flop about. Most often a rider with the locked elbow syndrome will lock as a result of floppy shoulders. Instead, keep the shoulders strong, and allow the elbows to move gently with the horse's movement.

The Alignment Checklist

The alignment checklist is a great warm up before every ride. It will help to strengthen muscles, tone opposing muscle groups, and also perfect the balance of the rider. At first, the exercises may seem difficult, but as time goes on and the rider keeps practicing, these exercises become very simple, and easy to execute.

The phase one exercises will help to align and tone the lower leg, and also get the platform of the sole of the foot to bear weight equally. Begin these exercises slowly. Increase the duration of time allowed between the transitions from one step to the next.

Phase 1 exercises

1. **Stand up in the stirrups**
2. **Relevé onto the balls of the feet**
3. **Sink into the knee as much as the rider can allow**
4. **Backwards dive**
5. **Snow plow**

Stand up in the stirrups

This is step one in the phases of the exercises. The rider needs to stand all the way up in the stirrups so the legs are straight with a relatively soft knee. Keep the feet flat, and if the rider needs to hold onto the horn of the saddle, the cantle, or the horse's mane to remain in balance, it is okay to do so in the beginning. With more practice the rider will gain better balance and be able to stand on their own, without holding on with the hands.

Relevé onto the balls of the feet

From the standing position the rider can then raise up onto the balls of the feet in relevé position. Stretch the soles of the feet as much as possible, and keep the legs straight with a soft bend still in the knee. Hold this position for a count of three, and then proceed to the next step. Make sure that weight is equal across all five toes and the balls of each foot.

Sink into the knee

While in relevé position the rider must hold that contraction and not allow weight to fall into the heels. Slowly the rider will drop weight into the knee. The angle behind the knee will become more acute. The quads will lengthen down towards the ground. This step is usually the step that most riders can allow the knee to drop even more. Try to really allow the weight to fall into the knees. Once again, hold this position for a count of three before moving on.

Backwards dive

This part of the exercise can be tricky. Do not allow all weight to fall deep into the heels. The rider must control the lowering of the foot as if they were standing on a diving board getting ready to do a backwards dive. If the heels drop the diver would then be committed to doing the backwards dive, but if the diver remained in balance on the edge of the board with the weight distributed across the balls of the feet, they would, then, be able to remain in balance. The angle of the foot is in jeopardy here. The rider must only allow the heels to be level and weight across the stirrup evenly. Hold the foot level for a count of three.

Snow plow

The foot should now be level, and weight should be distributed across the stirrup evenly. Most riders will want to let the excess weight fall into the heels, but, instead, redistribute that weight to the outside as if you were wearing skis and your were crossing the front of the skis to stop. The back edge of the skis would move out to the side as if a snow plow were the way to stop. The rider's heels must push away from the horse's ribcage in order to activate the upper hip and outer leg muscles. Once again, the muscles of the inside of the leg will work in conjunction with the muscles of the outside leg in order to maintain a healthy hold and contact with the horse.

Complete this sequence of exercises in order numerous times. Start from the beginning and work toward being able to transition from one part to the next without losing balance. Keep proper body mechanics throughout. This sequence is usually one that I have riders warm up with for the first five minutes of a lesson. That will give the rider about ten to fifteen reps of the phase one exercises.

Phase 2 exercises

1. **Brake pedal**
2. **Neutral position**
3. **Hook**
4. **Heels push out**
5. **Stand up**
6. **Heels to gluteus**
7. **Sit down**
8. **Touch the right and left toe**
9. **Frog leg lifts**

Brake Pedal

In order to find the correct weight across the foot and to stretch the back side of the leg along the hamstring muscles and down the calf, perform the first part of phase 2 with an exercise called stepping on the brake pedal. You will never actually be in this position while riding at any point in time. It does, however, allow the rider to feel how much of the bottom sole of the foot is weight bearing. Press slightly on the stirrup platform, and stretch the whole leg out in front of the body. The rider should feel weight across the balls of each foot evenly. Be sure to correct the foot in the stirrup if it is crooked. Keep the line discussed with puzzle piece one, and the alignment of the foot. Hold this stretch until you feel the weight of the leg and foot relax into the stirrup iron.

Neutral position

After the first exercise, the rider will then position the leg into neutral position, or regular riding position. This is the spot that the rider must be fully aware of and must find quickly and easily. When giving cues or signals for other maneuvers, the rider may move the lower leg backward or forward. It is important that the rider be aware where the "home" position of the leg lies. Neutral position is the spot where the stirrup leather is vertical and the hole of the stirrup is facing forward toward 12:00 and the bottom of the stirrup is parallel with the ground. This is the position that the rider must always come back to.

Hook

After the rider has established the neutral position, it is then important to practice the "hook". The hook is the position of the rider's lower leg that will slide into the nook (as I call it) of the horse's belly. This leg position is often used in jumping on a flatter-sided horse, or when lifting a horse up in collected work at a later point in time. The hook is not a squeeze. It is a feather-light controlled touch with the lower leg. Imagine a hook on the heel of the boot. That hook is scooping into the ground and lifting up only an inch. It is a simple, small maneuver with the lower leg. The rider is not digging the heels down, or turning the toes out excessively. It is simply a feeling that will happen in riding that the rider must practice in order to know when it is happening and how to control getting back to neutral position.

Heels press out and away

From the hook position, with the feather light touch of the rider's lower calf on the horse, the rider will bring the heels out and away from the horse's sides. The rider must imagine wearing a very heavy weight on the ankle. Press that weight out and away from the horse, and hold it out with tone and elegance. Try to keep the leg in neutral position as much as possible. Really pay careful attention to the soles of the feet and the alignment of the lower leg. Be sure the leg has a sense of open space between you and the horse's side. This is the first step to developing a breathable leg.

Heels to Gluteals

The rider will now stand up again with soft knees and a stable lower back and trunk. At this point in time, if the rider needs to hold on to the horse or the saddle, do so in order to help with the balance of the body. Keep the feet in the stirrups and bring the heel up towards the gluteals or buttocks by bending the knee. Weight will need to drop into the outside stirrup that the rider is still standing on. By turning the inner thigh and knee toward the saddle, the rider is then able to bring the heel, toward the gluteals as if the rider were kicking their own backside. Lower that leg and repeat on the other side. Do not lift the leg high, at first, and keep the lower leg completely off the horse's side. This will help the slight turn of the hips, and allow the rider to take the thighs and lower leg off the horse. Most riders will say that it feels as if their knee is gripping. In all reality you are not gripping with the knee, but allowing the knee

to make contact with the saddle. It becomes a pivot point. Repeat this sequence four times. Do it two times on each side before moving onto the next exercise.

Reach down and touch the toes

After the rider has stood up and brought the heels to the gluteals on each side two times, sit in the saddle and begin the next exercise. Put both reins in your left hand. Take your right hand and reach in the direction of your right big toe. Fold over at the hips so the seat slides back toward the cantle of the saddle. Keep the eyes up-looking through the horse's ears, while keeping the back straight, not hollow or round. If you are riding in a western saddle, position your torso slightly to the right of the saddle horn. Switch sides by placing the reins in your right hand, and reaching down to touch the left foot with your left hand. Strive to keep the lower leg in position while touching the toes. It is easy to allow the leg to slide back slightly toward the horse's back legs. Do not allow this to happen. As you become more flexible, you will be able to reach further while holding the legs in position. Repeat

this two times on each side, giving you a total of four reps before moving onto the last exercise of phase 2.

Frog legs

The rider must now position the seat so the weight is not shifted toward the back edge of the diamond. In other words, there should be no shift toward the tailbone. It is easy to lean back with the upper body to cheat on this exercise, but the rider must hold the abdominals tight. The area below the belly button is going to be the target area for this particular exercise. It is also hard to keep the balls of the feet across the platform of the stirrup while lifting the whole leg. With practice you will be able to redistribute weight, and hold the stirrups. Remove the inside of the thigh and calf from the horse's side on the right side. Point the hip, knee, and foot slightly toward 1:00. Lift the whole leg as a unit, but only slightly as this exercise done too high in the beginning will result in hip cramps. Only go as far as your body will allow. Hold it for a count of two and switch sides. Lift the left leg with all your joints pointing

toward 1:00. Hold the horn or the saddle in the beginning to help stabilize the body. Repeat this two times on each side, for a total of four reps.

You have finished phase 2 of the exercises. Repeat this sequence numerous times in your warm up. When you are very good at phase 1 and phase 2, then combine them. Begin at phase 1 and continue right on through to phase 2.

These phases of exercises come from years of working with other trainers, taking pieces of what works, and putting the body into a cycle of allowing it to relax and reawaken the joints and alignment. I use this as a warm up for many of my students. It usually takes at least three lessons before they are aligned and balanced. Practice at a standstill first, then move to walking. Take your time with each exercise and develop better balance, tone, and strength.

Phase 3 exercises

This is the phase where we put form and function together. The rider will begin by standing all the way up in the stirrups while keeping a soft knee. Complete phase 1 exercises so the lower leg and foot are situated in neutral position. Slowly lower the seat toward the saddle in very small increments. The rider must control each muscle and allow the hold and strength to go through the leg. Just when the rider is about to make contact with the seat, immediately, raise the body and stand all the way back up to the balance point. The rider will never

fully sit in the saddle. These are called "tap downs". They force the rider to control the leg and slowly lower, instead of flopping into the saddle. Do reps of 10. Do not make full contact with the seat of the saddle. Keep a slight hover. After 10 reps, take a break, and sit in the saddle. Repeat this exercise numerous times until the rider can control the muscles.

Tara is in a slight hovering seat, or light seat. This is the instance just before her seat will touch the saddle. In this instance she will begin to straighten her legs and stand back up as in the picture below. Repeat this several times.

The Final Evolution

PUTTING ALL THE PIECES TOGETHER WITH PERFECT PRACTICE

What's next

We have now taken a close look at how most of your body parts will affect your horse's movement and how effective the training may be. Your body will be in a constant learning cycle. It is important to remember to not get frustrated. Top riders all over the world work on riding position every day for multiple hours to fine tune their skills. What is most important to remember is that a rider must keep filling the muscle memory bank with positive feedback.

When your riding comes down to the fundamental skills to get you through a new situation you must call on your muscles to just react. This comes from practice, practice, practice. I wish I could wave my magic "ride right" wand and all would be well, but unfortunately riding well, as I have said before, is an art. To be at the top of your game, you must communicate with your body so you can communicate with your horse. Always organize your learning into chunks that are attainable. You will further your skills more quickly without becoming frustrated and risking burn out or failure, within your thought process. You will gradually build to the point of muscle memory, and each step will become easier.

How to use the puzzle pieces

You have received a lot of information, and I am sure at this point your mind is whirling in mega-fast mode wondering how you could possibly be able to execute even a few of these exercises. You may have even practiced a few of these analogies. These imagery essentials have come from years of trial and error and a lot of hours in the saddle, making mistakes and correcting them. The main thing to remember is you are not alone. Let your muscles have a chance to imprint these new feelings. Practice daily, and remember you are improving your body for daily life as well.

Concentrate on each section, and try to improve your riding in the main areas first. Then, go back and try to readjust. You will gain great feelings and a huge smile will come across your face when you feel the accomplishments you have made.

Practice does not make perfect, but perfect practice will

I am a firm believer in that achievements are not only about skill, but practicing that skill. It is only then that you will reach limits and levels you never thought were possible. Keep practicing these skills. As I have said before some of these analogies may work for you, and some may not. As you are practicing, strive to really ride the journey. Enjoy yourself and find humor in your learning. That is when you will find the most amazing moments. Perfect practice does not stem from frustration or anger, it stems from a moment of enjoyment. Let your horse teach you and be proud of what you have accomplished. Even if you think it is small, I promise it will be big one day!

Form, function and technique

Form, function, and technique are the biggest accomplishments of any rider. Form is your daily activity on a horse and how you see your riding ability. Proper form is based on all the principles of how to use your body to influence the horse with balance and skill.

Function is how you react in a specific situation. Is your mind working along with your body to react to what the horse is thinking of doing? You should always be one step ahead formulating your next move with the use of the most invisible aids.

Technique is the balance of all that you have learned. It's what you fall back on. It's how you handle a specific situation. You will learn lots of techniques in your riding career but you will choose what works for both you and your horse.

Skill timing and balance are what will set you apart as a rider. Pay careful attention to detail with all that you do and take pride in knowing how hard you have worked to get there. Remember, knowledge is confidence, and confidence is a powerful tool.

Inspiring Riders.........

I hope at this point, you have become inspired and have begun to understand the true reason surrounding my thoughts as I wrote this book. I have had an interesting career thus far, and have met some wonderful people and riders who have truly shown me the meaning of hard work. Their horses are their partners with whom they share lots of time in order to become the best at what they do. They are a team and as such they continue to inspire generations with their performances and their wins.

By now, I hope you have learned and practiced a few new techniques to help your alignment, tone, and coordination on your horse. The final chapter is dedicated to those professionals who I have had the great opportunity to work with at one point or another, or who I have met along the way. They are top notch and ride at the top of their game every day.

I have chosen some of the best riders in this industry for you to study. Draw inspiration from their body position, their beauty and unity, and their connection with their horses.

It is important to note that different riding disciplines are represented. These professional riders and trainers are truly an inspiration to me. They spend countless hours in the saddle. They work on their riding each and every day. They fine tune their bodies and train their horses to the highest levels. They deserve to be called athletes and they deserve to be called professionals. Draw inspiration from what you see. Allow these pictures to absorb into your ride next time you are on your horse.

The horses are mirroring what their rider is doing. The connection is evident, along with the idea of trust and solidarity, with clear concise communication as the main goal.

My favorite saying is you never know where you may wind up with hard work and determination. You always ride with the ultimate goal of all top level riders. Ride as if you were training for the Olympics. Some of these riders have been alternates for previous Olympic games, and riders who aspire to make the next Olympic team. Others are riding their way toward elite titles and championships or out educating the public and bringing their ideas to life. No matter which rider strikes a cord deep within your soul and makes you realize that there is beauty and grace, heart and elegance, and above all the drive deep inside you to become just as good as these riders before you. Let that fuel your journey and go forward to reach toward and investigate how to become the best you can be.

These riders are true professionals, and they are always striving for better rides. Allow them to inspire you as well. That way you will pay attention to every minute detail, and always work toward the highest level.

Good luck in your journey, and as most of these riders have told me, it takes years of many rides, many mistakes, and many learning curves to become better at your skill.

Lindsay Jensen   Barrel Racing

Lindsay Jensen is running a set of barrels which requires great precision and control. To ride a top notch barrel pattern, the team of horse and rider must excel in correct overall body balance. Here Lindsay is displaying the beautiful balance throughout her body. She is allowing her horse to make the maximum effort to engage the hind end. Her hips and eyes are following through the turn to allow her horse to accelerate out of the turn.

Lindsay keeps a wonderful connection with the reins and rides along the outer perimeter of the horses outside ear. This allows her horses to run up to the bridle, and push hard around a barrel. Lindsay's left hand is opening the rein to guide Andi towards the exit spot of the barrel. This helps the horse to find the correct spacing to allow her to step forward with her left front leg and drive through with her inside hind leg for maximum power.

In this picture Lindsay and Andi have matching angles with their body balance. There is a soft connection and meshing rein from Lindsay's elbow to Andi's connection with the bit. The balance of her shoulders is following directly behind the horse's shoulder. You can see that the left hind foot is about to follow the path of where the front just left in the next stride.

Kim Walnes   Eventing

Kim Walnes is one of the most beautiful and talented riders of our time. She is pictured here riding the legendary Gray Goose. These two together were an amazing team. It is storybook ride for this hall of fame horse. Kim's position over this jump is stellar. She would land on her feet if Gray was not beneath her. He can make a huge effort over that rather large spread as she is in complete balance. Her connection with the bridle is elastic and soft, yet there to aid in case Gray needs her.

During the dressage phase again you can see the perfect lines from Gray's bit to Kim's elbow. It's a lovely connection between the two. You get the sense that they are floating with no resistance. They are displaying lovely and balanced lines with a flow of recycled energy in each stride.

This picture makes you want to gasp at the sheer power it displays. There is an unspoken trust and partnership apparent between these two. In order to have courage to jump an obstacle of this nature, proper body balance is a must. Kim and Gray are displaying the unique bond they both shared as they fly over this jump. It is the ultimate showcase of why these two were a remarkable team, always riding to greatness. Truly an inspiration.

Kate Gerhart   Jumping

Kate Gerhart always displays a magnificent balance and unity with her body. She has top notch equitation skills which come to life in her seamless jumping efforts. She has a beautiful release while keeping a balance of contact and connection with her horse so the maximum jumping effort can be reached. Her equitation has a very soft flow. If you look closely you can see all angles between horse and rider match. Her back, hips, and forearms match the horse's angles. Identical pattern.

Kate has a gorgeous line with her upper body. She has a flat back with a soft folding hip joint. When you look at the picture you get the sense that the horse has filled her up and grown into her. She is one of the best equitation riders in the jumping world. She always displays a solid lower leg which holds her stability as a secure pedestal for her to balance upon.

The elastic feel and flow in this picture is wonderful. You can see the lightness in the air as horse and rider take flight. Kate's foot position is something to be envied. The front of her ankle is not locked, and her heels are not pressed down excessively. She is grounded with the sole of her foot and the weight is distributed evenly. The contact with the bit is elastic and inviting. She has control of her balance so the horse can use the body to jump freely into Kate's hands. Magnificent shot.

Julio Mendoza   Dressage

Julio is always a beautiful rider to watch. He displays lovely lines throughout his body while his muscles remains toned and effective. He looks as though he is part of the horse in perfect balance directly in the center. The curves throughout the horses outline are wonderful. You can see that the weight has shifted to the hindquarters as Julio is riding upward to help the horse engage in preparation for a canter pirouette. There is no apparent stiffness or tension anywhere in his body, but the tone and body balance makes this movement possible.

Once again, Julio displays the amazing body balance needed to help the horse to use the core muscles. and lift through. The connection with the bit shows the direct contact from the weighted forearm to the bit. His wrist is in perfect form. As your eyes travel down his leg you can see that the stirrup leathers are vertical. Julio is also showing the hole of the stirrup is facing forward towards 12:00, and the bottom of the stirrup is parallel with the ground. It looks as though if this picture were to come to life, Julio would encourage a bouncy rhythm and a tone that would not only hold this together, but also encourage further impulsion. He is an amazing rider to watch. Always paying close attention to detail.

Jeff Wilson   Western Dressage

The beautiful elegance in this photo is wonderful to study. There is a graceful connection and a floating contact. Jeff's position is well balanced. He paints a picture of recycled energy throughout his body and into his hands. Jeff keeps such a lovely flow from his elbow to the bit. His morgan stallions are fantastic to watch.

Jeff has such a strong base of support through his leg position on his beautiful stallion Orion. It becomes a building block for the rest of his balance. You can see his lower leg and foot position are a solid pedestal. He holds a flat foot, with his stirrup leather vertical and the stirrup itself facing forward towards 12:00. It is the platform for his entire leg to be in excellent position. The overall look of this photo is complete balance.

Training is also about having fun and spending time with your horses. Jeff also teaches his Morgan stallion Valiant tricks. The sky is the limit with his fun, innovative horsemanship. He is paving the way for many who watch and adore his lovely horses.

In closing

One of my favorite statements that I mention to my students is:

The good riders settle for what they already know. The great riders never settle because they know they will never know it all!

Never stop learning, and reaching for new goals. I wish you luck as you find new ways to conquer your rides. We are so lucky to have so many wonderful trainers, and instructors out there that are willing to share what they know and have learned. Use your common sense to decipher what works best for both you and your horse.

Enjoy your riding journey, find the missing pieces to your riding puzzles, and as always, may all your puzzling aspects of riding and training... find a "pieceful solution".

All the best

Tara Jones

.

Special credits

Thank you to Jen Wenzel of Rein photography

(Cover photos, back cover, as well as main photos throughout the book)

Other photo credit to:

Emile Frede Photography

Stephen Weidler Photography

Sherrie Hilliard Photography

Cover design and back cover design by Susan Overton

Thank you to the riders who helped me to bring the imagery essentials to life.

Caitie Chovanes and Sherrie Hilliard

Many thanks as well to the inspiring riders who continue to be friends and mentors in this business.

Lindsay Jensen, Kim Walnes, Kate Gerhart, Julio Mendoza, and Jeff Wilson

Special thanks:

Dad, You are my biggest fan and supporter, and you are my hero. I thank you for being here to see me accomplish another dream. Your love and support has driven me to succeed, and to reach for higher levels. We will fight this battle together. I love you with all my heart.

Rock the Ride, Fight Cancer!

To those who could not be here to see this book reach its final chapter, I will always ride in your honor. Your name will always fly freely on the flag of heroes.

52506736R00144